Julie Coiro, Ph.D.

Jim Cummins, Ph.D.

Pat Cunningham, Ph.D.

Elfrieda Hiebert, Ph.D.

Pamela Mason, Ed.D.

Ernest Morrell, Ph.D.

P. David Pearson, Ph.D.

Frank Serafini, Ph.D.

Alfred Tatum, Ph.D.

Sharon Vaughn, Ph.D.

Judy Wallis, Ed.D.

Lee Wright, Ed.D.

UNIT 1 CONTENTS

Journeys

WEEK 1

READING WORKSHOP — Genre | Informational Text

Time Line: Immigration and Expansion in the United States

"The Path to Paper Son" and "Louie Share Kim, Paper Son" .... Informational Texts **19**
by Grant Din | by Barbara D. Krasner

Reading Comprehension • Analyze Main Ideas and Details

READING-WRITING BRIDGE **35**

Academic Vocabulary • Word Study: Suffixes *-ic*, *-ism*, *-ive* • **Read Like a Writer** • **Write for a Reader** • Spelling • Language and Conventions: Simple Sentences

WRITING WORKSHOP **41**

Immersion and Introduction

WEEK 2

READING WORKSHOP — Genre | Informational Text

Infographic: The Places Scientists Will Go!

from *Life on Earth—and Beyond* .... Informational Text **51**
by Pamela S. Turner

Reading Comprehension • Analyze Text Features

READING-WRITING BRIDGE **73**

Academic Vocabulary • Word Study: Greek Roots • **Read Like a Writer** • **Write for a Reader** • Spelling • Language and Conventions: Independent and Dependent Clauses

WRITING WORKSHOP **79**

Develop Elements

WEEK 3

READING WORKSHOP — Genre | Historical Fiction

Map: The Age of Exploration

from *Pedro's Journal* .... Historical Fiction **89**
by Pam Conrad

Reading Comprehension • Understand Point of View

WEEK 3

READING-WRITING BRIDGE 113

Academic Vocabulary • Word Study: Vowel Teams • **Read Like a Writer** • **Write for a Reader** • Spelling • Language and Conventions: Compound and Complex Sentences

WRITING WORKSHOP 119

Writer's Craft

WEEK 4

READING WORKSHOP

Genre | Poetry

Infographic: A Poetry Machine

Poetry Collection .... Poetry 129

by Kristine O'Connell George | by Drew Lamm and James Hildreth | by Karen O'Donnell Taylor | by Marilyn Singer

Reading Comprehension • Explain Sound Devices and Figurative Language

READING-WRITING BRIDGE 143

Academic Vocabulary • Word Study: Suffixes *-able*, *-ible* • **Read Like a Writer** • **Write for a Reader** • Spelling • Language and Conventions: Common, Proper, and Collective Nouns

WRITING WORKSHOP 149

Develop Structure

WEEK 5

READING WORKSHOP

Genre | Informational Text

Slideshow: A Painted Journey

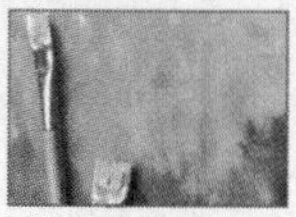

Picturesque Journeys .... Informational Text 159

by Yanitzia Canetti

Reading Comprehension • Analyze Text Structure

READING-WRITING BRIDGE 179

Academic Vocabulary • Word Study: VCe Syllables • **Read Like a Writer** • **Write for a Reader** • Spelling • Language and Conventions: Regular and Irregular Plural Nouns

WRITING WORKSHOP 185

Publish, Celebrate, and Assess

WEEK 6

Infographic: Compare Across Texts

PROJECT-BASED INQUIRY 192

Inquire: Hit the Road! • **Conduct Research:** Explore the Sites • **Collaborate and Discuss:** Argumentative Text • **Celebrate and Reflect**

REFLECT ON THE UNIT 207

UNIT 2

CONTENTS

Observations

WEEK 1

Genre | Informational Text

READING WORKSHOP

Infographic: How Scientists Study Ocean Life

from *Far from Shore* .... Informational Text **219**
by Sophie Webb

Reading Comprehension • Explain Author's Purpose

READING-WRITING BRIDGE **241**

Academic Vocabulary • Word Study: Open and Closed Syllables V/CV and VC/V • **Read Like a Writer** • **Write for a Reader** • Spelling • Language and Conventions: Subject-Verb Agreement

WRITING WORKSHOP **247**

Immersion and Introduction

WEEK 2

Genre | Informational Text

READING WORKSHOP

Map: Protecting Habitats

A Place for Frogs .... Informational Text **257**
by Melissa Stewart

Reading Comprehension • Analyze Text Structure

READING-WRITING BRIDGE **279**

Academic Vocabulary • Word Study: Final Stable Syllables *-le*, *-tion*, *-sion* • **Read Like a Writer** • **Write for a Reader** • Spelling • Language and Conventions: Principal Parts of Regular Verbs

WRITING WORKSHOP **285**

Develop Elements

WEEK 3

Genre | Realistic Fiction

READING WORKSHOP

Poem: Perfect Inspiration

from *Hatchet* .... Realistic Fiction **295**
by Gary Paulsen

Reading Comprehension • Analyze Point of View

WEEK 3

READING-WRITING BRIDGE 317

Academic Vocabulary • Word Study: *r*-Controlled Vowels • **Read Like a Writer** • **Write for a Reader** • Spelling • Language and Conventions: Principal Parts of Irregular Verbs

WRITING WORKSHOP 323

Writer's Craft

WEEK 4

Genre | Informational Text

READING WORKSHOP

Primary Sources: In the Words of Theodore Roosevelt

"Tracking Monsters" .... Informational Text **333**
by Mary Kay Carson

Reading Comprehension • Explain Relationships Between Ideas

READING-WRITING BRIDGE 351

Academic Vocabulary • Word Study: Prefixes *il-*, *in-*, *im-*, *ir-* • **Read Like a Writer** • **Write for a Reader** • Spelling • Language and Conventions: Perfect Verb Tenses

WRITING WORKSHOP 357

Develop Structure

WEEK 5

Genre | Argumentative Text

READING WORKSHOP

Video: Saving Natural Habitats

Let Wild Animals Be Wild* and *Don't Release Animals Back to the Wild .... Argumentative Texts **367**
by David Bowles | by René Saldaña Jr.

Reading Comprehension • Analyze Argumentative Texts

READING-WRITING BRIDGE 387

Academic Vocabulary • Word Study: Base Words and Endings • **Read Like a Writer** • **Write for a Reader** • Spelling • Language and Conventions: Active Voice

WRITING WORKSHOP 393

Publish, Celebrate, and Assess

WEEK 6

Infographic: Compare Across Texts

PROJECT-BASED INQUIRY 400

Inquire: Staying Alive! • **Conduct Research:** Evaluating Sources • **Collaborate and Discuss:** Informational Text • **Celebrate and Reflect**

REFLECT ON THE UNIT 415

UNIT 1

Journeys

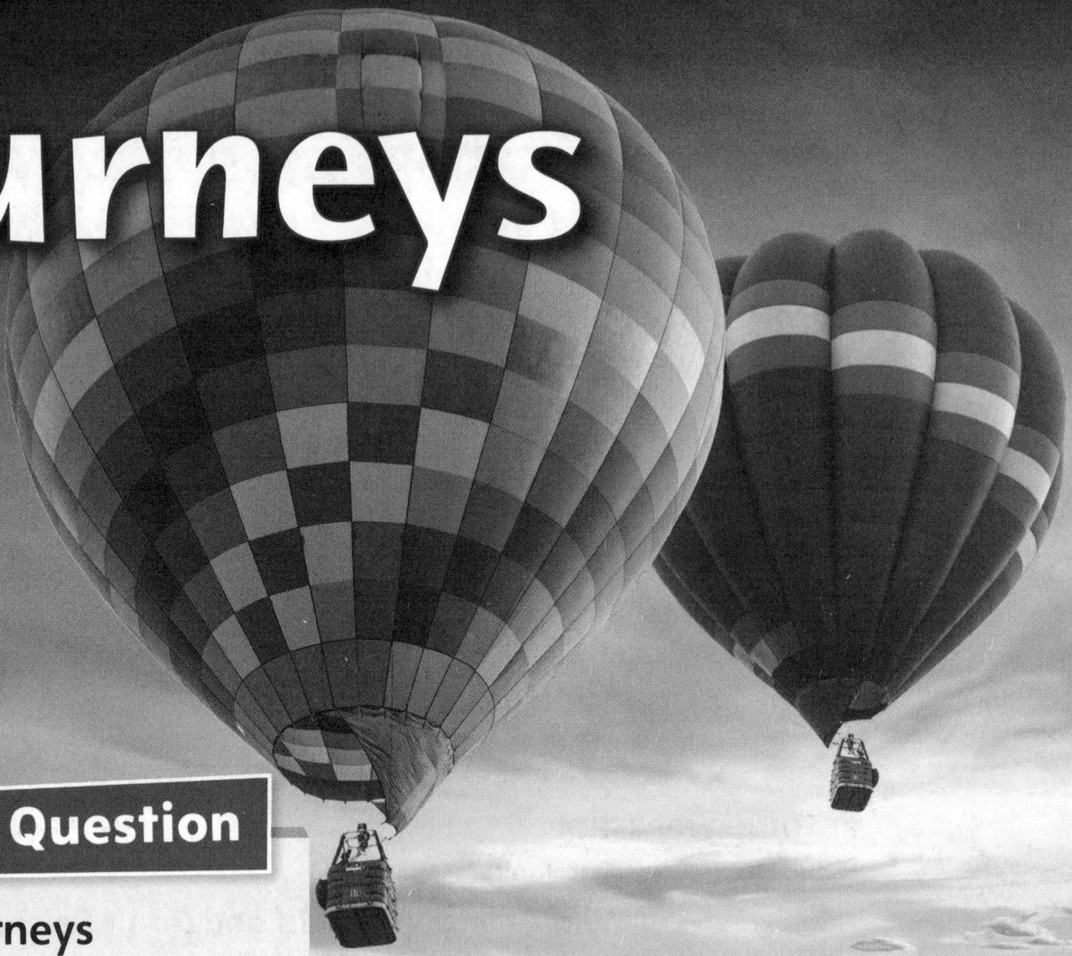

Essential Question

How do journeys change us?

WATCH

"Journeys"

TURN and TALK

What does the word *journeys* mean to you?

SAVVAS realize™

Go ONLINE for all lessons.

- VIDEO
- AUDIO
- INTERACTIVITY
- GAME
- ANNOTATE
- BOOK
- RESEARCH

Spotlight on Informational Text

READING WORKSHOP

Time Line: Immigration and Expansion in the United States

"The Path to Paper Son" and "Louie Share Kim, Paper Son" .... **Informational Texts**
by Grant Din | by Barbara D. Krasner

Infographic: The Places Scientists Will Go!

from *Life on Earth—and Beyond* .... **Informational Text**
by Pamela S. Turner

Map: The Age of Exploration

from *Pedro's Journal* .... **Historical Fiction**
by Pam Conrad

Infographic: A Poetry Machine

Poetry Collection .... **Poetry**
by Kristine O'Connell George | by Drew Lamm and James Hildreth | by Karen O'Donnell Taylor | by Marilyn Singer

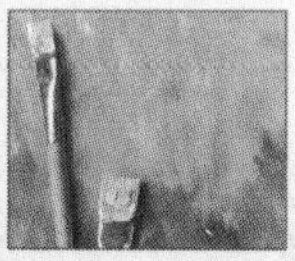

Slideshow: A Painted Journey

Picturesque Journeys .... **Informational Text**
by Yanitzia Canetti

READING-WRITING BRIDGE

- Academic Vocabulary • Word Study
- **Read Like a Writer • Write for a Reader**
- Spelling • Language and Conventions

WRITING WORKSHOP

Personal Narrative

- Introduce and Immerse • Develop Elements
- Develop Structure • Writer's Craft
- Publish, Celebrate, and Assess

PROJECT-BASED ASSESSMENT

- Inquire • Research • Collaborate

Independent Reading

One of the best ways to become a stronger reader is to do a lot of reading. You will read with your teacher in this unit. You will also read on your own during independent reading.

Follow these steps to help you select a book you will enjoy reading.

Step 1 Choose a book at the right level. Ask yourself:

- What is one book that was too easy for me? What made it too easy?
- What book was too challenging for me to read on my own? Why?
- How can I choose a book that I can read independently?

Step 2 Use this strategy to determine if the book is just right for you. Select a book and open it to any two pages. Answer the questions. If most of the answers are yes, you are ready to read.

Is this book right for me?

Read the pages you turned to and then ask yourself:

	YES	NO
Do I understand most of the words?	○	○
Do I understand most of the ideas?	○	○
Can I read the text smoothly?	○	○

Independent Reading Log

Date	Book	Genre	Pages Read	Minutes Read	My Ratings
					☆☆☆☆☆

Unit Goals

Shade in the circle to rate how well you meet each goal now.

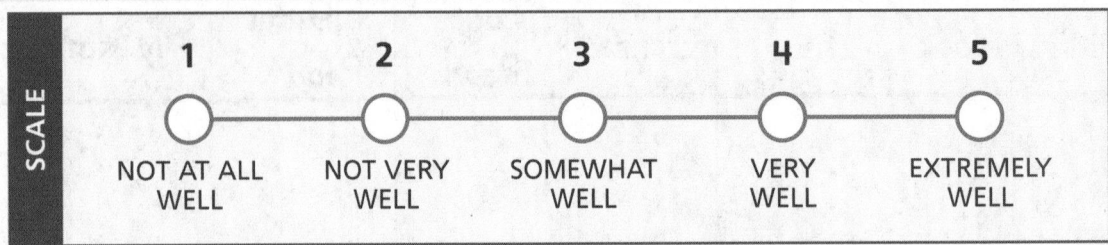

SCALE	1	2	3	4	5
	○ NOT AT ALL WELL	○ NOT VERY WELL	○ SOMEWHAT WELL	○ VERY WELL	○ EXTREMELY WELL

Reading Workshop	1	2	3	4	5
I know about different types of informational text and understand their structures and features.	○	○	○	○	○
Reading-Writing Bridge	**1**	**2**	**3**	**4**	**5**
I can use language to make connections between reading and writing.	○	○	○	○	○
Writing Workshop	**1**	**2**	**3**	**4**	**5**
I can use elements of narrative writing to write a personal narrative.	○	○	○	○	○
Unit Theme	**1**	**2**	**3**	**4**	**5**
I can collaborate with others to determine how journeys change us.	○	○	○	○	○

Academic Vocabulary

Use these vocabulary words to talk and write about this unit's theme, *Journeys*: *insight*, *wandered*, *passage*, *adventure*, and *curious*.

TURN and TALK Read the words and definitions in the chart. Make a list of synonyms, or words that have a similar meaning, for each academic vocabulary word. Share your list with a partner. Explain why you chose the words you did and how they relate to the academic vocabulary.

For example: *Strolled* is a synonym for *wandered*. To *stroll* is to walk without hurry.

Academic Vocabulary	Definition	Synonyms
insight	clear or complete understanding of a situation	
wandered	walked slowly or aimlessly	
passage	an entry or doorway	
adventure	an exciting experience	
curious	having an interest to learn about something	

INTERACTIVITY

IMMIGRATION and Expansion in the United States

1882: Congress passes the Chinese Exclusion Act to ban Chinese immigration.

1892: Ellis Island opens in New York to process immigrants coming from Europe.

1620: Pilgrims from England sail the *Mayflower* to North America to establish a new colony.

1848: Americans and immigrants rush to California when gold is discovered.

1830–1850: 2.5 million immigrants sail from Ireland and Germany to the United States.

1862: The Homestead Law grants land in the West to families who claim it. Settlers move farther and farther west.

WEEK 1

Weekly Question

What motivates people to leave a place they call home?

1910: Angel Island Immigration Station opens in California to process immigrants arriving from Asia.

1940: Angel Island closes.

1943: The Chinese Exclusion Act is repealed.

1954: Ellis Island closes.

Quick Write What stories do you know that are about people who leave their native homes? Which of those stories are the most powerful? Why?

Learning Goal

I can learn more about informational texts by analyzing main ideas and details.

Spotlight on Genre

Informational Text

An **informational text** gives factual information about a topic. It includes

- **Main ideas,** or the most important ideas about the topic
- **Details,** which support the main idea
- **Text features,** such as the title, headings, bold words, images, and other clues to main ideas

TURN and TALK Describe a nonfiction text that you read recently. Use the anchor chart to tell whether the text you read is an informational text. Then take notes on your class discussion.

My NOTES

To figure out the topic of a text, look at the title, headings, and pictures for repeated ideas.

INFORMATIONAL TEXT ANCHOR CHART

PURPOSE:

- To give information about a topic or explain a concept

ELEMENTS:

- Main ideas are the topic's most important ideas.
- Details support or tell more about main ideas.
- Text features offer clues to main ideas.

TEXT STRUCTURES:

- Cause and effect
- Compare and contrast
- Problem and solution
- Chronological or time order

Meet the Authors

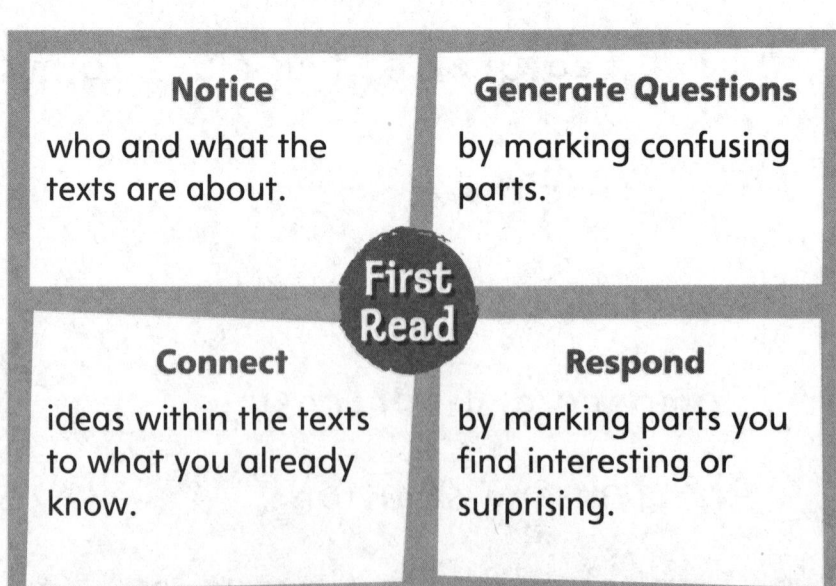

As a member of Angel Island Immigration Station Foundation, researcher **Grant Din** helps people learn more about their families' histories.

As a child, **Barbara D. Krasner** wrote stories and articles for her friends. Now she writes about history for magazines such as *Cobblestone* and *Highlights for Children*.

The Path to Paper Son and Louie Share Kim, Paper Son

Preview Vocabulary

As you read the texts, pay attention to these vocabulary words. Notice how they relate to the main ideas and details in the texts.

citizens **immigration**
opportunity **processing** **admitted**

Read

Before you begin, establish a purpose for reading. Readers of **informational texts** follow these strategies when they read a text the first time.

First Read

Notice who and what the texts are about.	**Generate Questions** by marking confusing parts.
Connect ideas within the texts to what you already know.	**Respond** by marking parts you find interesting or surprising.

The Path to **Paper Son**

by Grant Din

Louie Share Kim, **Paper Son**

by Barbara D. Krasner

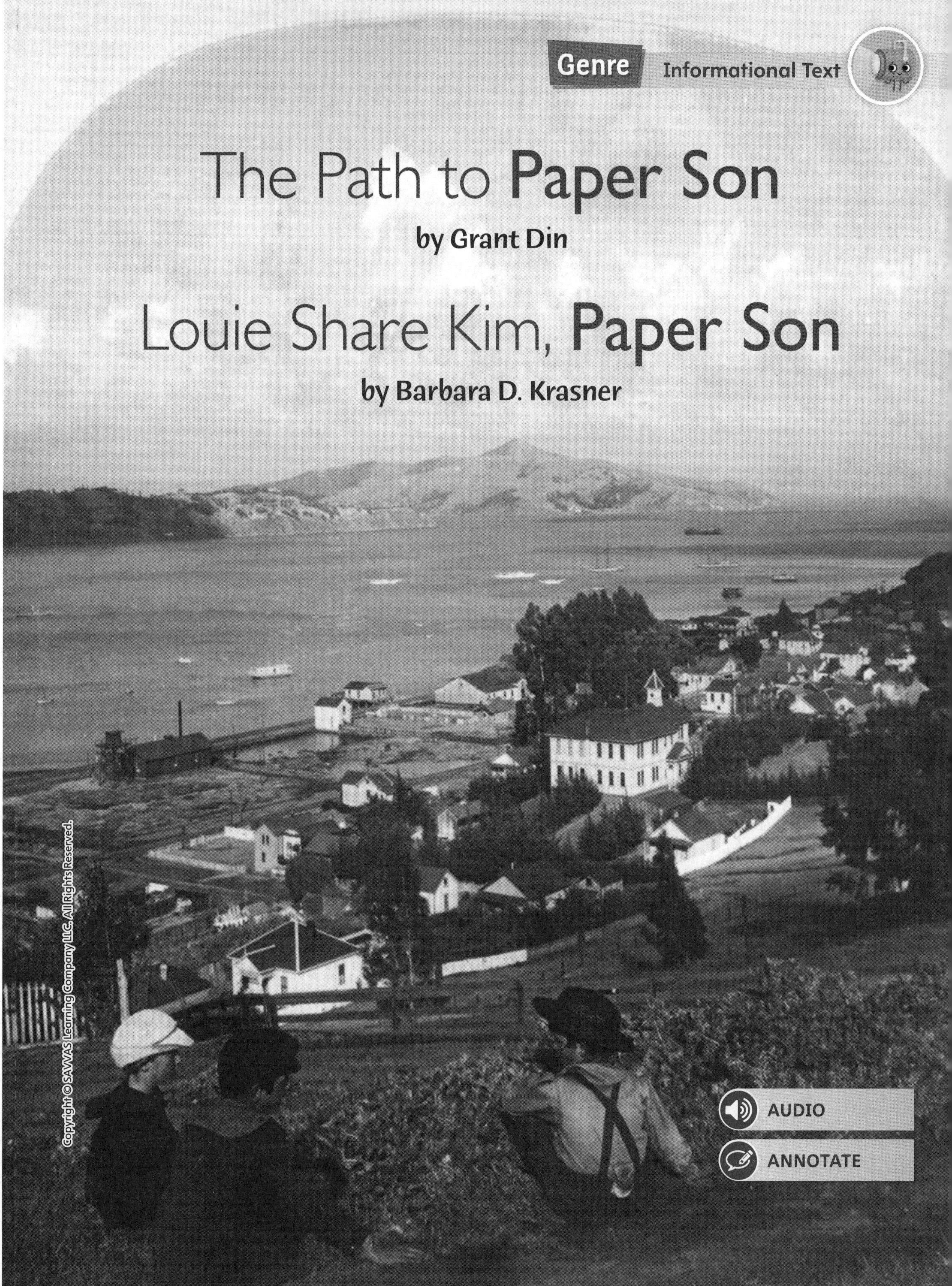

AUDIO

ANNOTATE

CLOSE READ

Analyze Main Ideas and Details

Underline sentences that give more information about why "paper sons" started.

citizens people who belong to a particular place

immigration the act of moving to a new country to live there

opportunity an agreeable situation or chance

The Path to **Paper Son**

by Grant Din

1 Most of the Chinese workers who came to the United States in the mid-1800s were men. Half of them were married, with wives, and sometimes children, who had been left behind in China. The Chinese Exclusion Act of 1882 prohibited Chinese laborers from sending for their families to join them in the United States. But merchants and U.S. citizens were allowed to do so. So each time a member of those groups returned to China for a visit, they often reported the birth of a son or two to the immigration authorities when they came back. The claim created immigration slots, which could be used to bring another Chinese to America.

2 In 1906, a major earthquake and fire destroyed much of San Francisco (below), including the city's Hall of Records. With the city's birth records destroyed, some Chinese saw an opportunity. They claimed that they had been born in San Francisco and that they had a wife and so many sons in China.

3 Sometimes the son was truly related, and sometimes the "son" might be a nephew or another relative. Often, the identity was sold to an unrelated person who lived near the "father's" Chinese village. When a "paper son" bought an identity, he also purchased a coaching book or notes that provided both the questions and answers that might be asked during immigration processing. The paper son's job was to memorize the answers.

4 Paper son documents were worth thousands of dollars. Families borrowed money to make it possible for a child to make the trip. It often took several years of hard work to repay the debt.

Did You Know?

In 1868, the 14th Amendment to the Constitution established that anyone born in the United States is granted U.S. citizenship. In 1898, American-born Chinese Wong Kim Ark won a U.S. Supreme Court case that reaffirmed that law. After he made a trip to China, the U.S. government denied his readmission into the country. He appealed his case, and his birthright citizenship was upheld.

CLOSE READ

Use Text Evidence

Highlight text evidence that supports a main idea.

processing a series of steps in a legal action

Vocabulary in Context

Context clues are words and phrases around an unfamiliar phrase that help readers understand the phrase.

Underline context clues that help you understand the meaning of the phrase *birthright citizenship*.

Louie Share Kim, **Paper Son**

by Barbara D. Krasner

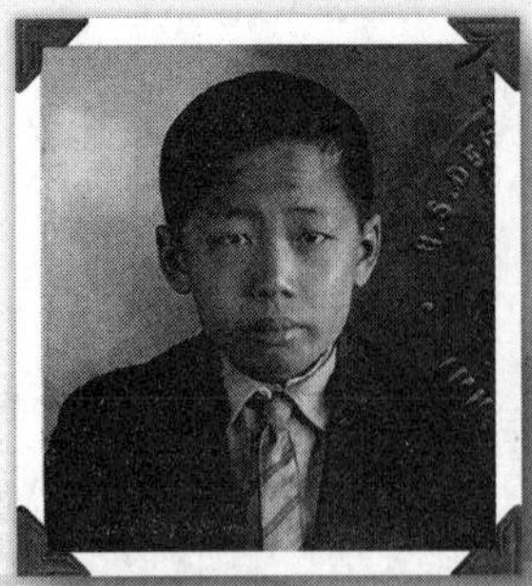

Louie Share Kim, age 14

Louie Share Jung, paper father to Share Kim

CLOSE READ

Use Text Evidence

Look at the images. **Highlight** words and phrases in the text that show how the images support the main idea.

1 Fourteen-year-old Louie Share Kim arrived at the Angel Island Immigration Station from Guangdong Province, China, in 1916. He had traveled alone on a journey that took nearly a month to cross the Pacific Ocean. He had little schooling, no job skills, and no place to live, and he did not speak any English. Yet his family pinned all their hopes on him to become a success in America. His father made sure he even looked American in his passport photograph by making him wear a suit and tie.

2 But Louie Share Kim really had two fathers—or so it seemed. The Chinese Exclusion Act, in effect from 1882 to 1943, stopped all Chinese laborers from entering the United States. Only diplomats, merchants, students, teachers, visitors, and those claiming U.S. citizenship were able to enter from China. To get around the law, many immigrants from China claimed to be related to a merchant or a U.S. citizen—on paper only.

Angel Island Immigration Station might have looked like this when Share Kim arrived as a child.

3 Share Kim became a "paper son" of Louie Share Jung in America. Share Jung was a U.S. citizen born in San Francisco who frequently traveled to China. Share Kim's father made arrangements to have Share Jung claim Share Kim as his son. In the village where their two families lived only two houses away from each other, everyone was related. Share Jung had known Share Kim since birth.

4 At Angel Island, officials detained Share Kim. They interrogated him and Share Jung. They asked question after question about their family history and their village's layout. Once satisfied with the answers, Share Kim was allowed entry to America. He received his Certificate of Identity, which stated he was admitted as the "son of a native."

CLOSE READ

Analyze Main Ideas and Details

Underline information that helps you analyze the challenges of the "paper son" immigration process.

admitted granted access to a place

Share Kim's wife and children were detained at Angel Island.

5 When Share Kim was 20 years old, his real father wrote him a letter from China. "Dear Number One Son," the letter began, referring to Share Kim as the eldest son. "It is time to come home." Now considered a "son of a native," Share Kim could visit his village in China and know that he would be readmitted into the United States. He arrived in China on a Tuesday. He was married on Saturday to a woman chosen by his parents and whom he had never seen before. They had a son who died as a baby.

6 Share Kim returned to America to work. In 1924 and in 1929, he returned to China to visit his village and see his wife. They had two children, Wanda and Sherman. After each visit, Share Kim returned to the United States to work. In 1935, he decided to bring his family to America. He and his wife offered a 12-year-old boy in the village the opportunity to go with them. They gave the boy the name John. John became their paper son.

7 Share Kim knew there would be another interrogation. Officials detained and questioned all new immigrants. He put together a book for his wife so they could coordinate their stories and make certain that they gave the same answers during questioning. The coaching book contained information about names and birth dates of all family members, the location of the home village and its environment, dates of Share Kim's travels to China, and more. Any wrong answers could lead to deportation. As expected, Share Kim's wife and children were detained at Angel Island. Officials questioned each member of the family, even six-year-old Sherman, and they brought Share Kim in a second time for questioning.

CLOSE READ

Analyze Main Ideas and Details

Underline details that support the main idea that the immigration process was complicated and challenging for paper sons.

CLOSE READ

Use Text Evidence

Highlight details in the text that support a main idea about the opportunities and risks for paper sons.

8 Sam Louie, the youngest son of Share Kim who was born later in San Francisco, says, “The interrogation was a nervous process for everyone.” Louie is a retired educator and volunteer at Angel Island Immigration Station. In July 2015, the Angel Island Immigration Station Foundation hosted a family history/reunion day event. Portraying his father, Louie shared his story. He says, “Many Chinese, including my father, claimed to be ‘a son of a native’ so they could come to America to seek a better life for themselves and their family. They were, in fact, only sons on paper, an affidavit the ‘father’ signed—thus the term *paper son*.”

9 Louie showed his father’s Certificate of Identity. He explains that for Share Kim to claim his birth record, he had to find two witnesses who would testify that they knew him as a child. Louie says, “The witnesses had to be white because Chinese were not trusted.”

10 Share Kim had a “twin” paper brother. But when the two boys were placed next to each other, it seemed clear they were not twins at all. Share Kim was much taller. The “twin” was deported back to China, where he died two years later.

11 Some Chinese scholars estimate that 80 percent of Chinese in America had a paper son in their family history. Louie adds, “I knew as a child growing up that I was never to reveal to others that my father was a paper son for fear that we might all get deported.”

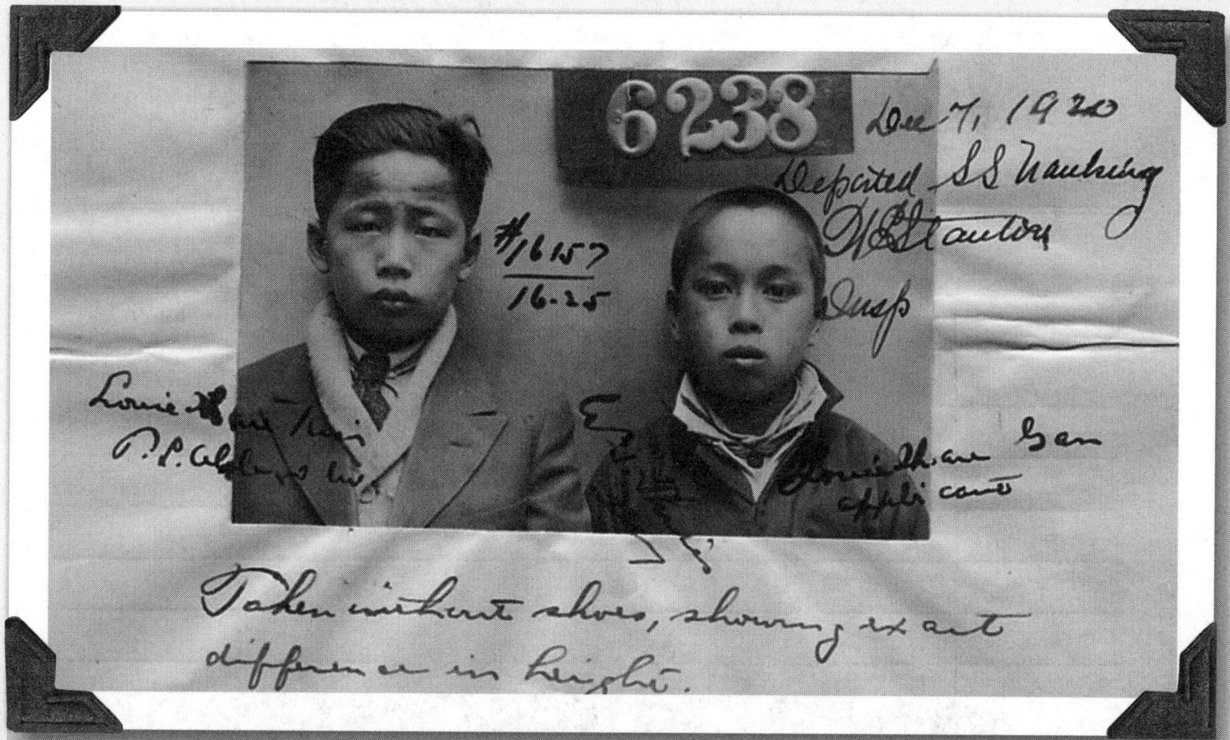

The lack of resemblance between Share Kim (left) and his “twin” brother made officials determine that they were not related.

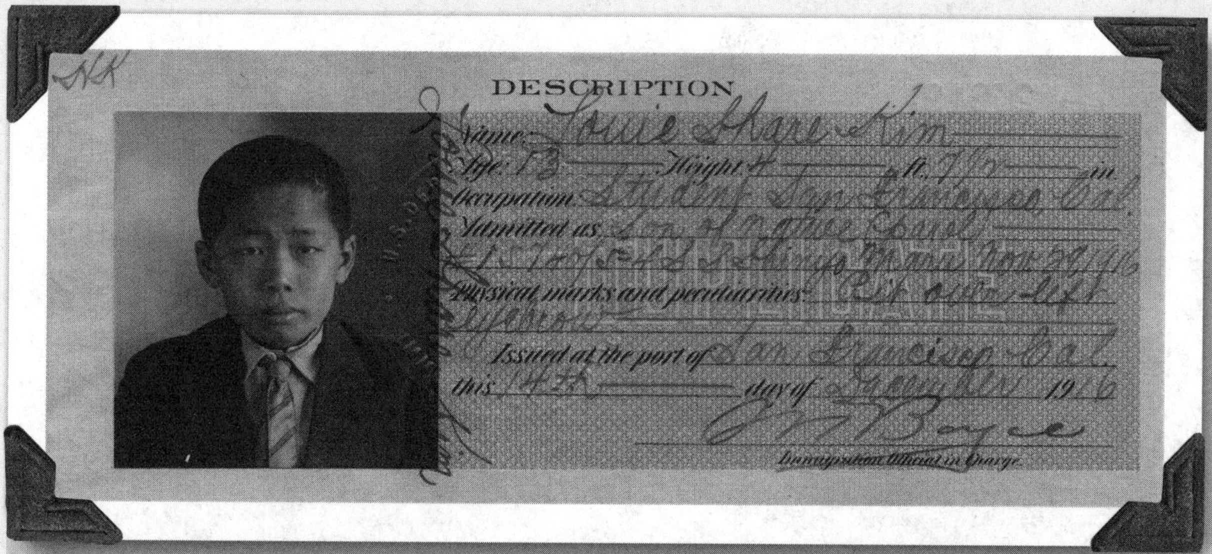

Share Kim’s Certificate of Identity makes note of a “pit over left eyebrow” under “physical marks and peculiarities.”

12 "My parents never talked to me about their immigration experience," he says. "I never even knew they were detained at the Angel Island Immigration Station until after my mother passed away at the age of 98 in 2003." Louie conducted research at the National Archives and Records Administration in San Bruno, California. He found a transcript of the interrogation of his mother and siblings during their detainment. The transcript was 42 single-spaced typed pages.

13 Louie says, "Many of my friends and relatives said their parents never talked about their immigration experience either. I suspect those experiences were painful, something they would rather forget."

Sam Louie shares his family's story as a volunteer at the Angel Island Immigration Station.

CLOSE READ

Vocabulary in Context

Underline context clues that help you understand the meaning of the word *transcript*.

Develop Vocabulary

An informational text uses academic and domain-specific words and phrases to explain a topic. These words help the reader build knowledge around a topic.

My TURN Write a sentence for each word. Each sentence should include the vocabulary word and explain how it relates to the topic of immigration.

citizens

opportunity

immigration

Immigration is the act of moving to a new country to live there.

processing

admitted

Check for Understanding

My TURN Look back at the text to answer the questions.

1. How do you know that "The Path to Paper Son" and "Louie Share Kim, Paper Son" are informational texts? Give three examples.

2. What do you think the author's purpose was for writing "The Path to Paper Son"? What do you think the author's purpose was for writing "Louie Share Kim, Paper Son"? How do you know?

3. What can you conclude about Sam Louie's parents' immigration experience based on information in the selection? Use text evidence.

4. Compare Louie Share Kim's two immigration experiences. How were they similar? How were they different?

Analyze Main Ideas and Details

Main ideas are the most important ideas about a topic. **Details** and other evidence support the main ideas.

1. **My TURN** Go to the Close Read notes in "The Path to Paper Son" and "Louie Share Kim, Paper Son" and underline the parts that help you understand the main ideas and details of both texts.

2. **Text Evidence** Use the parts you underlined to complete the chart.

	"The Path to Paper Son"	"Louie Share Kim, Paper Son"
Main Idea	Chinese immigrants used the "paper son" system to come to the United States.	
Details		

Analyze how the details support the main ideas.

Use Text Evidence

Identify and analyze the author's main ideas and supporting details to better understand the text. Check that the main ideas you identify can be supported by **text evidence**, or the actual words of the text.

1. **MyTURN** Go back to the Close Read notes and highlight text evidence that helps you identify main ideas.

2. **Text Evidence** Use your highlighted evidence to support your analysis of both texts.

"The Path to Paper Son"

Main Idea	Text Evidence
Documents for paper sons were expensive.	

"Louie Share Kim, Paper Son"

Main Idea	Text Evidence

Analysis:

Reflect and Share

Talk About It "Paper sons" were among many Chinese immigrants who left their home country to start new lives in the United States. Consider all the texts you have read this week. Talk about why people leave their home countries. Before you share your thoughts, think about what others have said and why they might feel as they do. Respond thoughtfully. Ask relevant questions based on others' views.

Retell Texts Retell specific ideas in ways that maintain the meaning and logical order of each text. Speak clearly and naturally.

- Allow others to add details and ask relevant questions about the topic.
- Respond with questions and comments that are useful, to the point, and based on what your classmates say.

Use these sentence frames to guide your retelling:

First, a paper son had to ________.

Finally, Louie Share Kim ________.

Weekly Question

What motivates people to leave a place they call home?

Academic Vocabulary

Learning Goal

I can develop knowledge about language to make connections between reading and writing.

Related words are forms of a word that share roots or word parts. They can have different meanings based on how the word is used, such as *immigrate*, *immigrant*, and *immigration*.

MyTURN For each sentence,

1. **Use** print or digital resources, such as a dictionary or thesaurus, to find related words.
2. **Add** a related word to the second column.
3. **Complete** the sentence with the correct related word.

Word	Related Word	Sentence with Related Word
insight	insightfully insightful	The author wrote an insightful article about Chinese immigrants.
curious	curiosity ____________	Rashid's ____________ about his mother's job led to a tour of her office.
passage	passenger passageway ____________	Lin walked through the narrow ____________ between rooms.
wandered	wander wanderer ____________	He was known as a ____________ who liked to explore new places.
adventure	adventurous adventuresome ____________	Maria's love of skydiving showed her ____________ personality.

Suffixes *-ic, -ism, -ive*

A **suffix** is a word part added to the end of a word or word part. Suffixes change the meaning or part of speech of a word.

The word *secret* means "information that is kept from someone." If you know what *secret* means, you can figure out the meaning of the word *secretive*. *Secretive* means "keeping information to oneself" or "hiding something."

My TURN Read each word part and meaning. Then use your knowledge of suffixes to write a definition for each word.

athlete a person who exercises a lot	+	*-ic* associated with	=	*athletic* **associated with exercise**
hero a brave person	+	*-ism* act or process	=	*heroism*
exclus- leave out	+	*-ive* doing something	=	*exclusive*

Read Like a Writer

Authors choose text structures to support their purposes for writing. A cause-and-effect text structure explains what happened and why. A chronology, or time-order, text structure shows a sequence of events.

Model! Reread paragraph 1 of "The Path to Paper Son."

1. **Identify** Grant Din explains what happened in China and the United States as a result of the Chinese Exclusion Act of 1882.
2. **Question** What structure does he use to organize the text?
3. **Conclude** Grant Din explains the causes and effects of Chinese immigration to the United States.

Reread paragraph 5 of "Louie Share Kim, Paper Son."

My TURN Follow the steps to explain the text structure.

1. **Identify** Barbara D. Krasner presents information by ____.
2. **Question** What structure does she use to organize the text?
3. **Conclude** Barbara D. Krasner uses ______________ to ____.

Write for a Reader

Use your task and audience to choose a text structure for a writing assignment.

Writers use text structures to present ideas in a logical way. Writers of historical texts often explain important events using the cause-and-effect or the chronology text structure. The cause-and-effect text structure explains what happened and why. Signal words that show a cause-and-effect structure include *because, as a result,* and *effect*. The chronology text structure presents events in the order they happened. Chronology signal words include *first, then,* and *finally*.

My TURN Think about how the text structures chosen by Grant Din and Barbara D. Krasner affect you as a reader. Now choose a historical event to write a short paragraph about. Decide on a text structure for your paragraph.

1. Introduce the historical event you will write about. Explain why you chose the text structure you did.

2. Write a paragraph about the historical event you chose. Be sure to use signal words that are appropriate to the text structure you use.

Spell Words with Suffixes *-ic, -ism, -ive*

A **suffix** is a group of letters added to the end of a word that can change the word's meaning or part of speech. For example, adding *-ic* to the noun *hero* changes the noun to the adjective *heroic*.

When you add *-ic* or *-ive* to a word that ends in e, drop the e. For example, *defense* changes to *defensive*.

My TURN Read the words. Spell and sort the words in alphabetical order.

SPELLING WORDS

heroic	dramatic	organism	deflective
heroism	artistic	capitalism	executive
comic	historic	federalism	perspective
atomic	tourism	secretive	narrative
kinetic	realism	defensive	representative

Simple Sentences

A **simple sentence** tells one complete idea. It has one independent clause, or a subject and a verb. A simple sentence begins with a capital letter and ends with an end punctuation mark. A statement without a subject or a verb is called a fragment. Writers edit to avoid fragments. A sentence that has two independent clauses connected by a comma is called a comma splice. Writers can use end punctuation to separate a comma splice into two simple sentences. There are four kinds of simple sentences.

	Use	Example
Declarative	tells something	Ana plays soccer every Saturday.
Interrogative	asks a question	Are you playing soccer this Saturday?
Exclamatory	shows strong feeling	I love soccer!
Imperative	gives a command or makes a request	Go to soccer practice on Saturday.

My TURN Edit this draft for fragments and splices. Then revise to include one interrogative sentence, one exclamatory sentence, and one imperative sentence.

The Pilgrims. Left England in 1620 to practice religious freedom. They sailed across the Atlantic Ocean, the *Mayflower* landed on Cape Cod instead of Virginia. The trip was stormy and difficult. The journey. Lasted for 66 days. There are books in the library about the Pilgrims.

Analyze a Personal Narrative

Learning Goal

I can use elements of narrative writing to write a personal narrative.

A **personal narrative** tells about an experience in the author's life.

My TURN Use a personal narrative you have read to fill in the chart.

The **narrator** is the author, the person the personal narrative is about.

Who is the main person in the text? What did you learn about him or her?

A **topic** is what the author is writing about.

What event or experience is the writer writing about?

The **setting** is when and where the events happened.

Where do the events take place?

Outline the **sequence of events,** or what happens and in what order.

First

Next

Last

Know the Narrator

The narrator of a personal narrative is the author. An author uses details and dialogue to show the thoughts, feelings, and actions of the people involved. Use these details to understand the narrator's relationships with other people in the narrative.

My TURN Think about a personal narrative you have read. Write what you learned about the author and any other important people. Include text evidence in your response.

Name

Text Evidence
He or she says
He or she does
He or she thinks or feels

What does the author show through words and actions?

Analyze Setting and Sequence of Events

A **sequence of events** in a personal narrative is the real experiences the author tells about. The **setting** is where and when the events take place. The setting may affect the events.

My TURN Work with a partner. Read a new personal narrative from your classroom library. Explain the setting and the sequence of events in the personal narrative.

Setting

Where do the events happen?

When do the events happen?

Events

What happens, and in what order?

What is the main problem or conflict the writer experiences?

What does the writer learn or do as a result of the experience?

Brainstorm a Topic

Before you begin writing, consider your task, purpose, and audience.

My TURN Answer the questions and brainstorm details as you prepare to write your personal narrative.

Task What are you being asked to do?

Purpose What is the purpose of your personal narrative: to inform, entertain, or persuade?

Audience Who will read your personal narrative? What questions might your readers have? How do you want readers to react?

Authors think of ideas before they begin drafting their writing. One way to gather ideas is by **brainstorming**.

The **topic** is what you write about. A topic for a personal narrative is often an event or experience that is important to the writer.

Brainstorm details about one experience you could write about. Highlight your topic.

Plan Your Personal Narrative

Authors sometimes **freewrite** to generate ideas for their stories. Thinking of many ideas at once can help you focus on the most interesting or meaningful events and experiences in your personal narrative.

My TURN Follow the freewriting steps to find ideas for your personal narrative.

BEFORE YOU BEGIN

- Think about the topic you chose to write about.
- Consider your purpose for writing: to persuade, to inform, or to entertain.
- Think about who your audience is.

START WRITING

- Begin writing about your experience.
- Continue writing until the timer goes off.
- Write every idea that comes into your head.
- Write ideas, and do not worry about writing complete sentences.
- Do not stop to fix spelling or grammar at this point.

REVIEW YOUR FREEWRITE

- Reread your freewrite.
- Highlight the best ideas to include in your personal narrative.
- Use the best details as you continue to plan.

DISCUSS YOUR PLAN

- Work with your Writing Club to discuss your writing plan.
- Talk about how the freewrite helped your ideas start to flow.

INTERACTIVITY

THE PLACES Scientists Will Go!

Scientists travel to barren deserts like the Atacama Desert in Chile to search for signs of life.

Deserts rely on little rain to sustain life. The Atacama Desert is considered the driest desert in the world. It averages only 1 millimeter of rainfall per year!

Scientists travel to Antarctica to study the kinds of life that can survive in extreme cold. Near the coast, Antarctica averages about 10°F (–12°C). In the mountains, the temperature drops as low as –76°F (–60°C).

Weekly Question

What can scientists discover by traveling to distant places?

Scientists use unmanned space probes to virtually travel to far places in space. On December 2, 1973, *Pioneer 10* sailed by Jupiter. On August 25, 2012, *Voyager 1* traveled beyond the gravitational pull of the sun and into interstellar space.

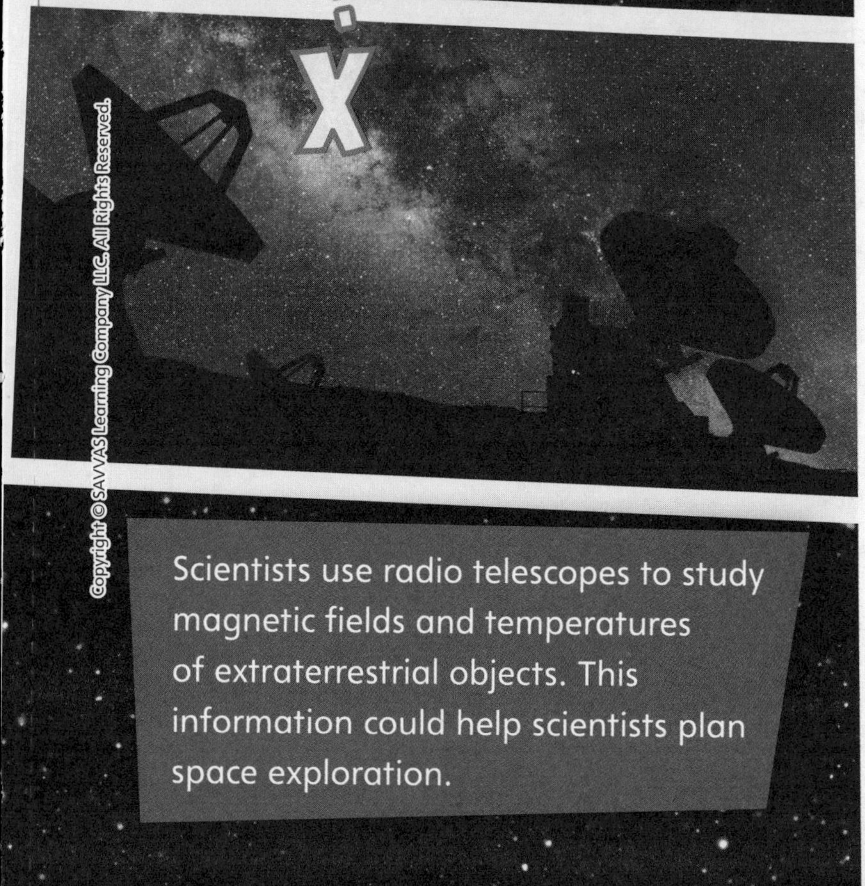

Scientists use radio telescopes to study magnetic fields and temperatures of extraterrestrial objects. This information could help scientists plan space exploration.

TURN and TALK What distant place would you like to visit? What do you think you would discover there? Share your answers with a partner.

Learning Goal

I can learn more about informational texts by analyzing text features.

Spotlight on Genre

Informational Text

Informational texts develop a main idea and support it with details. These texts often use **text features** to organize and add information.

- **Headings** appear at the beginning of a section of text.
- **Photographs, illustrations, and maps** help readers picture the topic. Visuals often include **captions** that explain the images.
- **Sidebars** give readers additional information about the topic.

Establish Purpose The **purpose**, or reason, for reading informational texts is to learn more about a subject. Readers could also read to learn how to complete a specific task.

Text features emphasize important ideas.

TURN and TALK With a partner, discuss a purpose for reading an informational text. Then describe a text you read recently that has text features. Use the anchor chart to determine which text features were included and why.

My PURPOSE ______________________________

____

____

____

____

TEXT FEATURE ANCHOR Chart

heading — To organize related information

PHOTOGRAPH — To show what Something or Someplace looks like

MAP — To show the GEOGRAPHY of a place

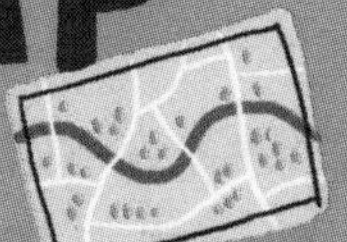

CAPTION — To describe what is shown in a Photograph, MAP, or illustration

Sidebar — To add more INFORMATION related to the TOPIC

Meet *the* Author

Pamela S. Turner spent her childhood reading, exploring nature, and riding horses on her friend's farm. Curiosity and love of nature led Turner to write on a variety of subjects, from ocean predators in *Prowling the Seas* to explorer George Schaller in *A Life in the Wild*.

from

Life on Earth—and Beyond

Preview Vocabulary

As you read *Life on Earth—and Beyond*, pay attention to these vocabulary words. Notice how they relate to the concept of scientific exploration.

astrobiologists **microbes**

colony **sensors** **radiation** **rovers**

Read

Before you begin, establish a purpose for reading. Follow these strategies when you read an informational text.

First Read

Notice how text features, such as headings, help you better understand the topic.

Generate Questions to help you clarify information and deepen your understanding of the text.

Connect this text to other texts you have read. How are the texts similar and different?

Respond by talking about the text with a partner.

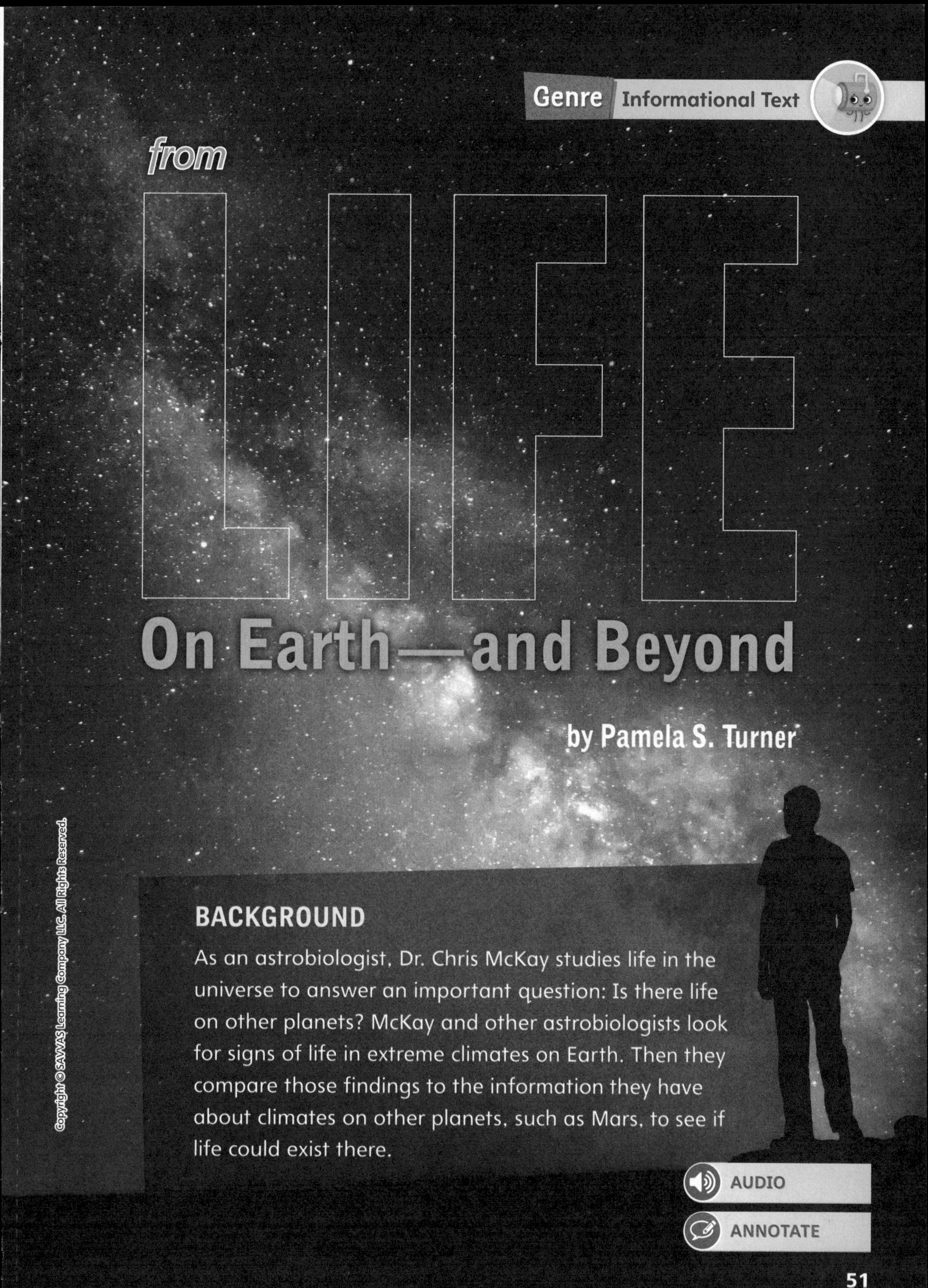

Genre Informational Text

from LIFE On Earth—and Beyond

by Pamela S. Turner

BACKGROUND

As an astrobiologist, Dr. Chris McKay studies life in the universe to answer an important question: Is there life on other planets? McKay and other astrobiologists look for signs of life in extreme climates on Earth. Then they compare those findings to the information they have about climates on other planets, such as Mars, to see if life could exist there.

AUDIO

ANNOTATE

Make Inferences

Highlight details from the caption and headings that help you make inferences about the Dry Valleys.

Between a Rock and a Cold Place

The Dry Valleys, Antarctica

Can life survive in a very cold, dry place?

1 At the very bottom of the globe, in a land of ice and snow, there are great curving valleys of bare earth: Antarctica's Dry Valleys. It's a harsh place. In April, the beginning of the Antarctic winter, the sun goes down and doesn't come up again until September. For months the Dry Valleys are locked in frozen darkness. There isn't a single scraggly weed or tiny insect. The Dry Valleys are almost as lonely as outer space.

The Antarctic Dry Valleys (the dark places in this satellite photo) are the largest ice-free areas in Antarctica.

2 Yet the Dry Valleys fascinate astrobiologists like Chris McKay. "The Dry Valleys are like Mars," explains Chris. "Both are cold and dry. It hardly ever snows in the Dry Valleys, and when it does, the air is so cold that very little snow ever melts. Mars is even colder and drier."

3 Chris set off to visit the Dry Valleys in January 2005, during the Antarctic summer. Just getting to such a remote spot was an adventure.

CLOSE READ

Analyze Text Features

Underline details that tell what the map adds to your understanding of the text.

astrobiologists scientists who study life in the universe

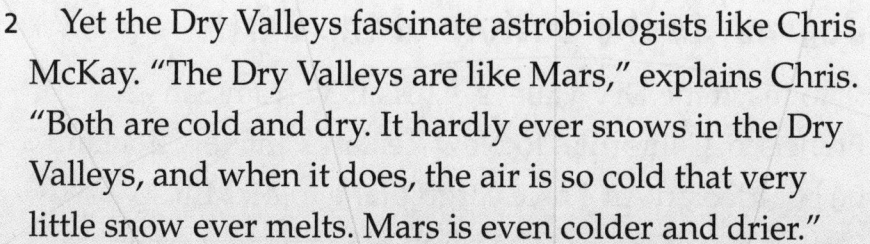

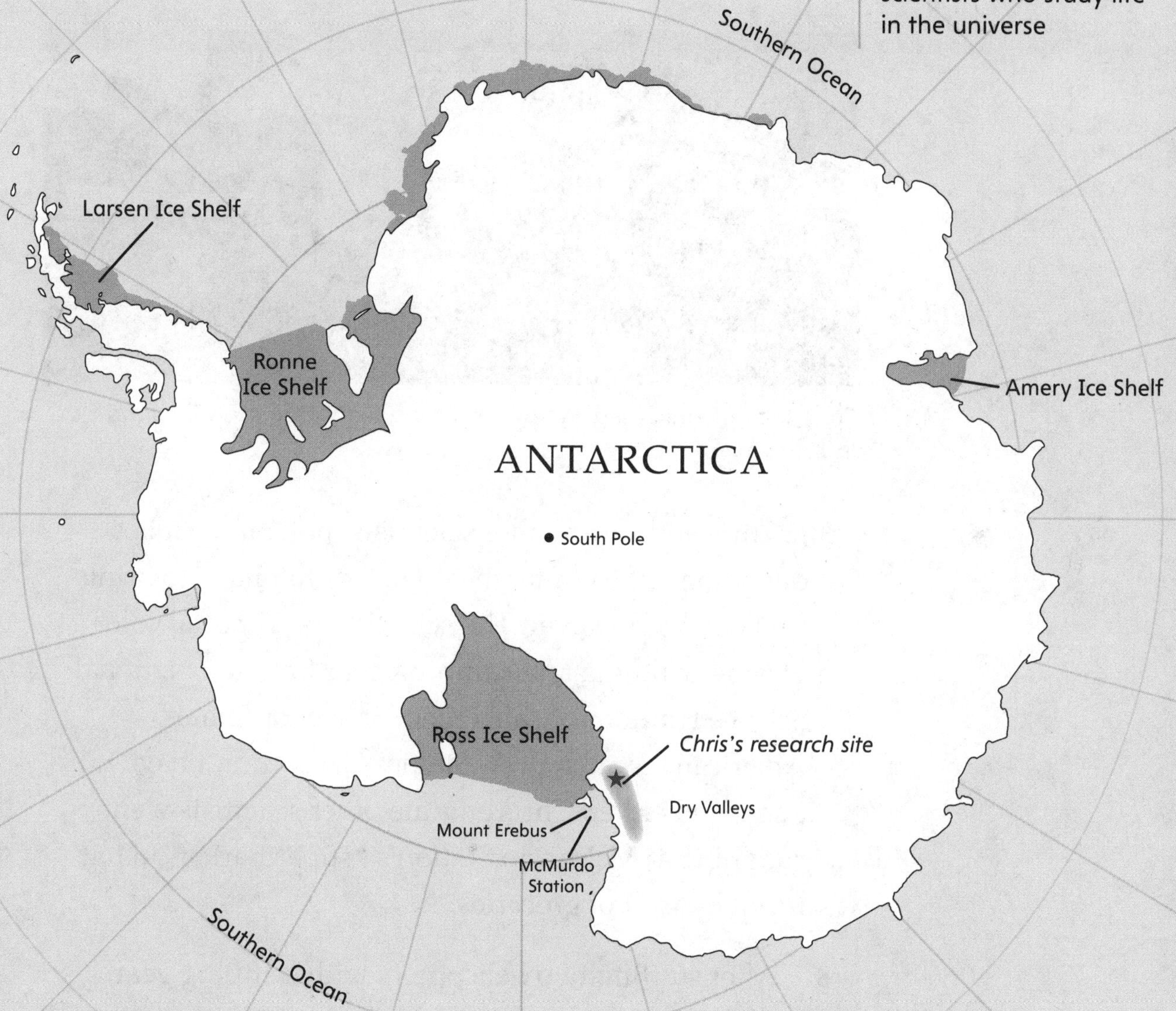

Along the edges of Antarctica are huge ice shelves (thick, floating platforms of ice). The Ross Ice Shelf, near McMurdo Station, is the size of France. The Antarctic Dry Valleys are also nearby.

Analyze Text Features

Underline details that explain the heading "Journey to the Bottom of the Earth."

Journey to the Bottom of the Earth

4 To reach the Dry Valleys, Chris flew from San Francisco, California, to New Zealand. In New Zealand he boarded an Air Force cargo plane to McMurdo Station in Antarctica. The cargo plane had no reclining seats or meal service. No windows either. "It was eight hours of being cramped and cold, and so noisy you had to wear earplugs," Chris later recalled.

Chris's team boards a cargo plane for the flight from New Zealand to Antarctica.

5 Chris and seven other scientists took many boxes of equipment to Antarctica. They didn't have to bring everything, however. The scientists had special cold-weather clothing and camping gear from the National Science Foundation, an agency that coordinates American research in Antarctica. They didn't have to pack food either. Chris and the other scientists went shopping at McMurdo Station's "supermarket": a big metal hut full of groceries.

6 After stuffing two helicopters with camping gear, equipment, food, and water, the scientists flew to the Dry Valleys. They landed atop a giant lump of sandstone called Battleship Promontory. It would be their home for the next two weeks.

Little Green Men

7 Early on his first morning in the Dry Valleys, six-foot-six-inch Chris wormed his way out of his extra-long sleeping bag. There was plenty of light outside. The sun is up twenty-four hours a day during the Antarctic summer. However, the sun's rays didn't give off much warmth. Even during the summer the Dry Valleys were as cold as Montana in winter.

8 Chris dressed quickly and made his way through the scientists' tent camp. The chilly wind cut like a razor, even through down-filled clothing.

9 The camp was a little "tent city." There was a science tent, a kitchen tent, a toilet tent, and the "suburbs" (the sleeping tents). Solar panels powered the kitchen tent, fondly nicknamed Café Battleship. Chris treated his companions to pancakes with canned cherries on top. Cleaning up was easy. The scientists just wiped everything with paper towels and let the dishes freeze. Nothing rotted or spoiled in the cold, dry air.

This is the camp on Battleship Promontory. At the end of the trip, helicopters flew out every piece of trash and human waste.

CLOSE READ

Make Inferences

Highlight details in the text and caption that help you make inferences about how the scientists camped on Battleship Promontory.

This is the view from Chris's tent. In 2005 there was more snow than usual.

CLOSE READ

Analyze Text Features

Underline details on both pages that help explain why the author included the image of the 2005 snowfall.

microbes the smallest living things

colony a group of animals living in one place

sensors devices that detect changes in light, moisture, or other physical conditions

10 Chris has been making these camping trips to Antarctica for twenty-five years. He knows there are creatures hidden in the Dry Valleys that can survive some of the world's worst weather. Their secret? They live *inside* rock.

11 "Solid" rock isn't always solid. Many rocks are honeycombed with little spaces, or pores, that seem like huge caverns to super-small creatures called microbes. Microbes (also called microorganisms) are the tiniest of all living things. They are so small that they can't be seen without a microscope.

12 After breakfast Chris headed to the nearby sandstone cliffs. He examined the sandstone carefully. Chris spotted little blotches on the rock. A colony of microbes was living in pores just under the surface. With a hammer and chisel he carefully chipped off a chunk of rock to take back to his lab at NASA. On previous visits Chris had drilled tiny holes into the sandstone and attached sensors. The sensors measured the light and moisture inside the rocks year-round. Chris's sensors showed that the microbes hidden in the rocks survived on tidbits of summer sunlight and a few drops of snowmelt.

13 Looking carefully, Chris also spied a wet spot on the rock. "When that happens there are microbes cheering, 'Yeah! Wet snow!'" Chris later explained. "They are living in little rock greenhouses. They 'wake up' for a few days in the summer, when the sun is shining and a little moisture seeps down through the pores in the rock. They grow a little and then go back to sleep for the rest of the year."

14 Chris chipped off another rock sample. Just under the rock's surface was a thin green line—a minute "forest" of microbes (cyanobacteria and fungi). These microbes were real survivors. "If life exists on Mars, it might look something like that," Chris later explained. "Those little green critters are the best Martians we have. And everyone knows Martians are little and green!"

15 A shelter of rock or dirt would be very important for any Martian life. The atmosphere on Mars is too thin to block dangerous radiation from the sun. If any life exists on Mars, it would need to be shielded from solar radiation by rock or soil. But microbes hiding inside rocks or underground aren't easy to find. So Chris used the Dry Valleys as a testing ground for microbe-detection machines.

CLOSE READ

Make Inferences

Highlight details from the text on both pages and the captions that help you infer why microbes in Antarctica might look like those on Mars.

radiation dangerous energy rays that cannot be seen

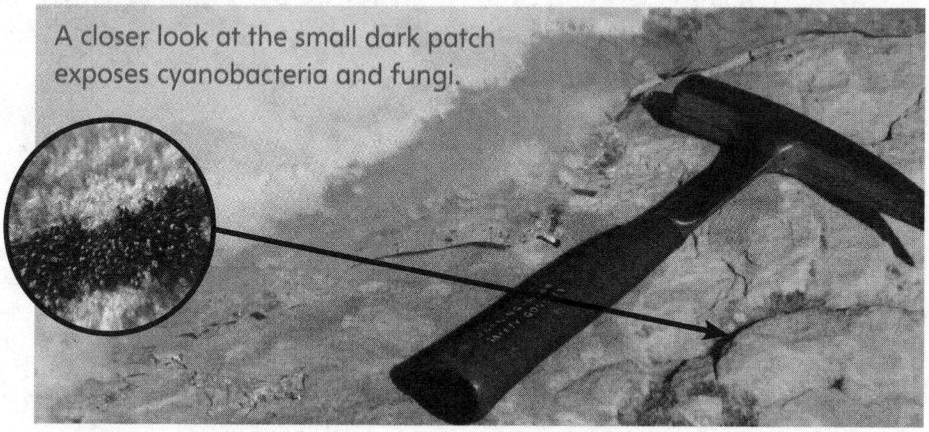

A closer look at the small dark patch exposes cyanobacteria and fungi.

Snowmelt reaches the microbes that are hidden inside the rock.

CLOSE READ

Analyze Text Features

Underline details from the sidebar that tell how it relates to the main topic: scientists study life in extreme places on Earth to see if life could exist on other planets.

What Is Life?

You'd think the answer is easy. Living things eat (take in energy) and give off waste, right? But a car "eats" gasoline and gives off heat and exhaust gases. A car isn't alive.

Let's add the ability to reproduce. A car can't make baby cars.

That doesn't work either. A fire eats wood and oxygen and gives off heat, carbon dioxide, and smoke. It can reproduce, too. A single spark can grow into a whole new fire.

Let's add the ability to evolve. Fire can't do this. Fire is fire. But all species of living things—from bacteria to bean plants to bears—evolve. They adapt over time in response to changes in their environment. So now we have it: a living thing eats, gives off waste, reproduces, and evolves.

Sorry, but there is one major glitch: viruses. Viruses are very small, very simple microbes. They cause many human diseases, including AIDS and the common cold. Viruses take in energy, give off waste, and evolve. Flu viruses evolve so quickly that scientists must develop new flu vaccines every year to fight the latest version of the virus.

But viruses can't reproduce by themselves. A virus must invade the cell of a living thing (such as a bacterium, plant, or animal) and hijack the cell's machinery to make more viruses.

So is a virus just a fancy bit of chemistry? Or is it possible for something to be half-alive?

Scientists are still arguing over these questions. There's no easy answer. That's life!

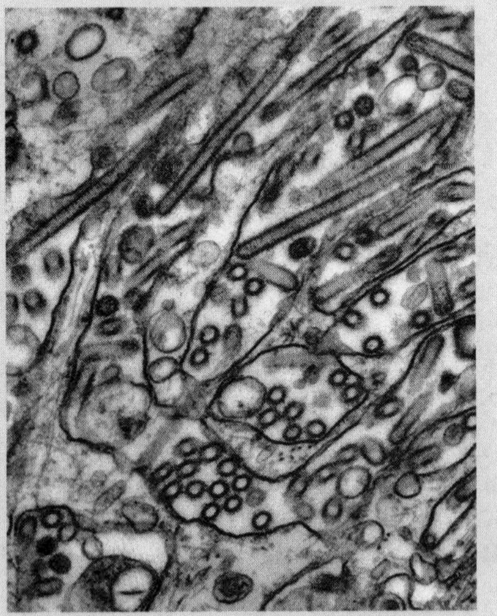

The gold circles and rods are the deadly H5N1 "bird flu" virus.

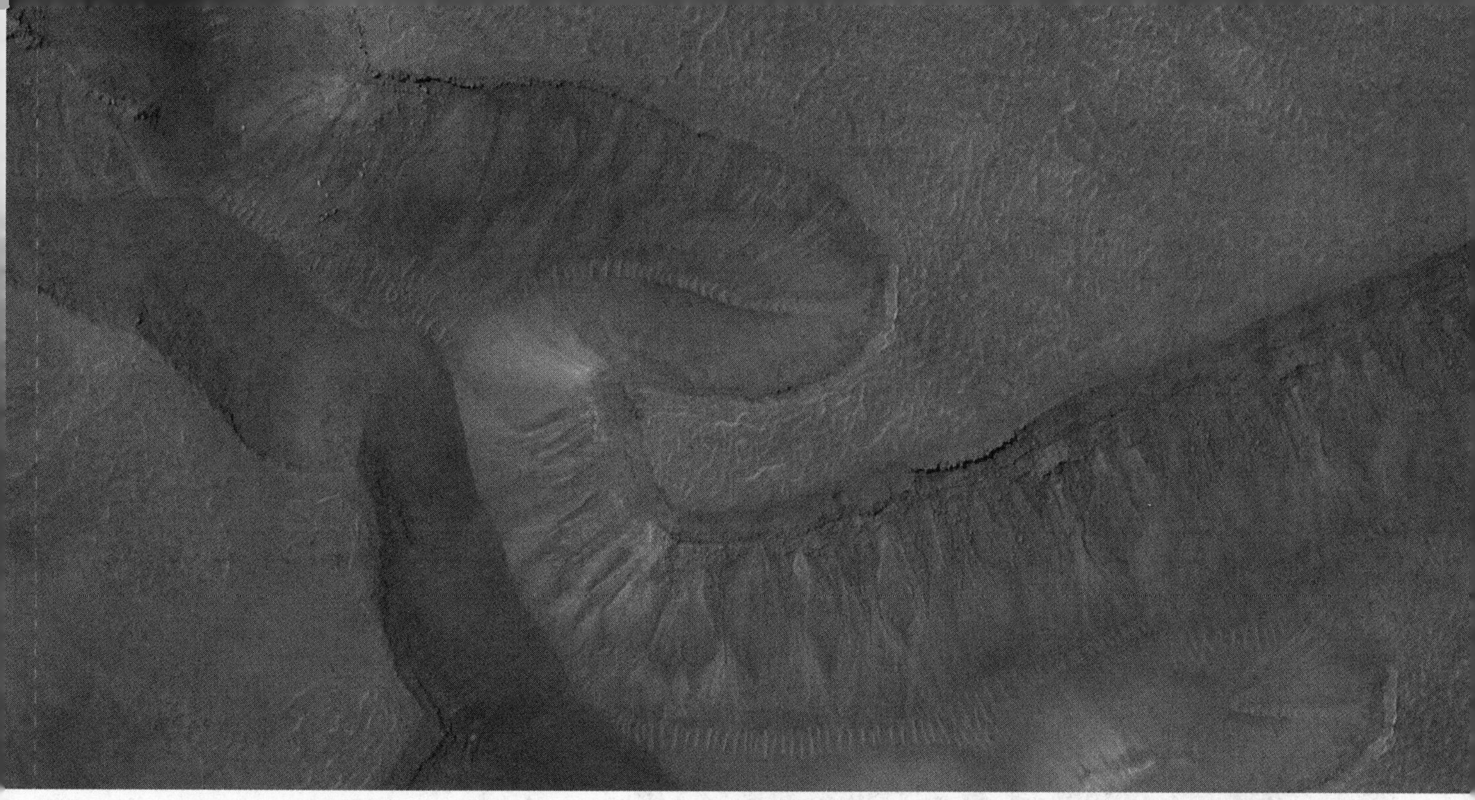

These are valleys on Mars. The average temperature on Mars is minus 80°F (minus 60°C), but the temperature can reach 70°F (20°C) during the Martian summer.

Machines for Mars and Beyond

16 The team brought a gas chromatograph, a spectrometer, and four types of ultraviolet (UV) lasers to test in the Dry Valleys. Each machine used a different technique for sensing hidden microbes. The gas chromatograph sensed gases given off by microbes. The spectrometer looked for the kind of light absorbed by microbes. The UV laser sensed the "glow" given off by microbes when the UV laser shone on them.

17 At least that's what was *supposed* to happen. But the gas chromatograph didn't work at all, despite hours of tinkering. Of the six machines Chris and the other scientists brought to Antarctica, only two, the spectrometer and one UV laser, were good at finding microbes. Even recording test results was difficult. The ink froze in Chris's pen!

CLOSE READ

Make Inferences

Highlight details that help you make an inference about what kinds of machines astrobiologists need.

Analyze Text Features

Underline details in the caption that help you understand how the spectrometer might be used on a NASA mission.

18 Chris was pleased that two machines worked. Science is all about testing new things and ideas. Sometimes things work out, and sometimes they don't.

19 A spectrometer or UV laser may travel on a future NASA mission. The machines may land on a planet that—like the Dry Valleys—seems too cold and too dry for life. Yet "little green men" might surprise us.

Kevin Hand, Robert Carlson, and Henry Sun test a spectrometer on rock containing hidden life

20 Chris can't wait to find out. He's been wondering what's out there ever since he found a dusty old telescope and pointed it into the night sky.

Bug-eyed Guys with Flying Saucers

Scientists think that aliens on other planets are most likely to be microbes, not bug-eyed guys with flying saucers. Why is this?

Microbial life is the simplest kind. Complex animals take much longer to evolve. As a result, microbial life should be far more common in the universe than complex life.

Simple, hardy microbes are also able to live in environments that are too harsh for complex life. That means many more possible homes are out there for alien microbes than for bug-eyed guys with flying saucers.

CLOSE READ

Vocabulary in Context

Context clues are words that surround an unfamiliar word and help you understand its meaning.

An antonym can be a context clue. An antonym helps you understand a word by identifying what it is *not*.

Underline an antonym near the word *complex* that helps you determine the word's meaning.

Make Inferences

Highlight details that help you make an inference about the purpose of Mars rovers like the one pictured.

rovers vehicles used to explore a planet's surface

Is Life Liquid?

Atacama Desert, Chile

Can life exist in a hot, dry place?

21 In January 2004 two robotic rovers landed on Mars. *Spirit* rolled through Gusev Crater. On the opposite side of the planet, *Opportunity* puttered around a dusty plain called the Meridiani Planum. NASA sent the rovers to Mars to find out if the planet once had liquid water—enough liquid water for life to exist. In searching for aliens, NASA's motto is Follow the Water.

22 As *Spirit* and *Opportunity* were humming around Mars, forty million miles (sixty-four million kilometers) away Chris and his NASA colleagues were exploring the Atacama Desert in South America. They weren't "following the water." They were looking for spots with as little water as possible.

An artist's idea of what a rover looks like on Mars

Very Little Rain on the Plain

23 To get to the Atacama, Chris and several other scientists and students spent a day flying from San Francisco to Antofagasta, Chile. From Antofagasta they drove two hours through the desert to a research station. (It took *Spirit* and *Opportunity* seven months to get from Earth to Mars!)

24 The research station was just a desert shack that housed a kitchen and laboratory. Water was brought in by truck. The scientists pitched their tents along a line of scrubby trees left over from an agricultural experiment. The trees were the only bits of green for miles around.

This is an aerial view of the scientists' camp. The scientists slept in tents at their research station in the Atacama.

25 Soon after arriving Chris checked his weather sensors. It had rained a few weeks before. "It was the biggest rain since 1994—about a fifth of an inch," recalled Chris. "For the Atacama, that's a flood!"

26 When Chris first visited the Atacama in 1994, he set up sensors to measure rainfall. For two years his sensors didn't record a single drop of rain. Chris thought they were broken, but they weren't. The lack of water was good news. Chris had found the driest desert in the world. The Atacama is even drier than Antarctica's Dry Valleys.

27 "There are lots of places where people say it doesn't rain, like the Gobi Desert in Mongolia, or the Australian outback," explained Chris. "But the Atacama is truly the driest place we've found." In fact, if the sky over the Atacama were reddish instead of blue, the super-dry desert would look a lot like super-dry Mars.

CLOSE READ

Vocabulary in Context

Underline context clues that help you define *housed* in paragraph 24.

CLOSE READE

Analyze Text Features

Underline text details on both pages that help you understand what the photograph shows.

Looking for Life in the Atacama

28 Chris and his colleagues tested the Atacama's soil and rocks for evidence of life. They tried some of the same soil experiments used by the *Viking* spacecrafts when they visited Mars in 1976. "If *Viking* had landed in certain areas of the Atacama, its tests would have said Earth is a dead planet," said Chris.

29 Chris tried other experiments. He brought rocks from other deserts and put them in the Atacama. On the underside of the rocks were microbes adapted to living in very dry places. The Atacama killed even those hardy microbes.

30 The Atacama isn't entirely dead, though. Some of the Atacama soil Chris collected did have live microbes. "We wondered how they survived," said Chris. "Did they grow in the Atacama? Or were they blown in by the wind, and we found them just before they died?"

CLOSE READ

Make Inferences

Highlight details in the captions that help you support an inference about how the balloon's pump works.

31 To find out if the microbes fell from the sky, Chris needed to take samples of the air over the Atacama. If the microbes were blown into the Atacama by the wind, the air would have about the same amount of microbes no matter where in the Atacama Chris took a sample. The conditions on the ground below—less dry or super-dry—shouldn't affect the number of microbes up in the air.

32 Chris brought along a helium balloon. The balloon was hard to handle in the desert wind. It bounced around like a crazed ping-pong ball. "It went every direction but up!" recalled Chris.

33 A small pump hung from the balloon. Once the bucking balloon was in the air, Chris turned the pump on using a remote-control device. The pump sucked a bit of air into a sealed dish. The balloon was pulled down, the dish removed, and a new one inserted. Later all the sealed dishes were brought to the lab and checked for microbial life.

A small pump hanging from the green balloon sucks in air, which will be checked for microbial life.

Chris holds the air-sampling balloon to keep it from flying off.

Make Inferences

Review the images. Then **highlight** text details you can use to make inferences about the similarities in the climates of the Atacama and Mars.

While Chris was in the Atacama, NASA rovers were scrambling around Mars. At left is a ridge in the Atacama; at right is a photo of a Martian ridge taken by the *Spirit* rover.

34 Chris found that the air over the less dry areas of the Atacama had microbes, while the air over the super-dry spots had no microbes at all. The balloon tests suggested that the Atacama microbes weren't visitors carried by the wind. Chris thinks that in the less-dry parts of the Atacama, microbes grow in the soil. The dirt is then kicked up into the air by the wind. That would explain why the amount of microbes in the air was the same as the amount of microbes in the dirt below.

35 One thing is clear, however: in the very driest parts of the Atacama, nothing can survive. There does seem to be a limit to life on Earth. "At first I hoped I could find a microbe in the Atacama that was somehow adapted to life without liquid water," said Chris, "but it seems that where there is no liquid water, there is no life."

36 There may be no liquid water on Mars now, yet the Mars rovers *Spirit* and *Opportunity* proved that once upon a time Mars *did* have liquid water—lots of it. *Spirit* found rock that had once been soaked in water. *Opportunity* discovered wavy bands of rocks formed by a long-lost sea. Scientists think Mars's surface had water for hundreds of millions of years. That's enough time for life to have evolved. So where might we find traces of ancient Martians?

37 Chris thinks that evidence of early Martian life may be in a natural underground freezer on Mars. A natural underground freezer just like the one in Siberia.

Water, the Host with the Most

Unless lost in a desert, we take water for granted. After all, it falls from the sky, and we flush it down the drain. But liquid water is a remarkable substance. Water is the essential molecule in the chemistry of life on Earth.

Imagine that life is a big party, and the most important elements of life (carbon, oxygen, nitrogen, hydrogen, and phosphorus) are the guests. Water is the host.

Water is the one who gathers all the guests together and introduces them to each other. Water makes sure everyone's comfy—neither too hot nor too cold. Without water, the chemicals necessary for life couldn't find each other, mix with each other, and react with each other. Life would never happen.

In the party of life, water is the life of the party!

From space you can see that Earth is a big, water-covered sphere.

CLOSE READ

Analyze Text Features

Underline details from the sidebar "Water, the Host with the Most" that tell how it relates to the main topic of the text.

Develop Vocabulary

Authors use specific terms in scientific texts to help readers understand scientific concepts. They use these words to explain ideas and clarify relationships between ideas.

My TURN Make connections between vocabulary words by answering the questions. Be sure to use the vocabulary words in your answers.

colony and **microbes**

1. In the Dry Valleys, where does Chris find a **colony** of **microbes**?

astrobiologists and **rovers**

2. What did the **astrobiologists** discover from the **rovers** exploring Mars?

sensors and **microbes**

3. How do weather **sensors** help scientists locate **microbes**?

Check for Understanding

My TURN Look back at the text to answer the questions.

1. What examples from the text helped you determine that the passage from *Life on Earth—and Beyond* is an informational text?

2. Choose a sidebar feature and explain why the author includes this text feature. Use text evidence to support your answer.

3. What conclusion can you draw about life on Mars based on information from the text?

4. Apply concepts from the text to develop a brief argument for or against additional funding for Chris and his team.

Analyze Text Features

Authors use **text features** to organize and clarify information. When you read, analyze text features to better understand the author's purpose and the main ideas in the text.

1. **My TURN** Go to the Close Read notes in *Life on Earth—and Beyond* and underline the parts that relate to and help you understand the text features.

2. **Text Evidence** Use the parts you underlined to complete the chart. Then analyze the effect of the text features.

Text Feature	How the Text Feature Helps Me as a Reader
heading	
photograph	
sidebar	
map	
Analyze the Effect of Text Features:	

Make Inferences

Readers make **inferences** to figure out information that is not stated directly. To make an inference, put together what you already know with what you read in the text and text features. Use evidence to support your understanding.

1. **My TURN** Go back to the Close Read notes and highlight evidence that helps you make inferences.

2. **Text Evidence** Use your highlighted text and what you already know to support an inference you made.

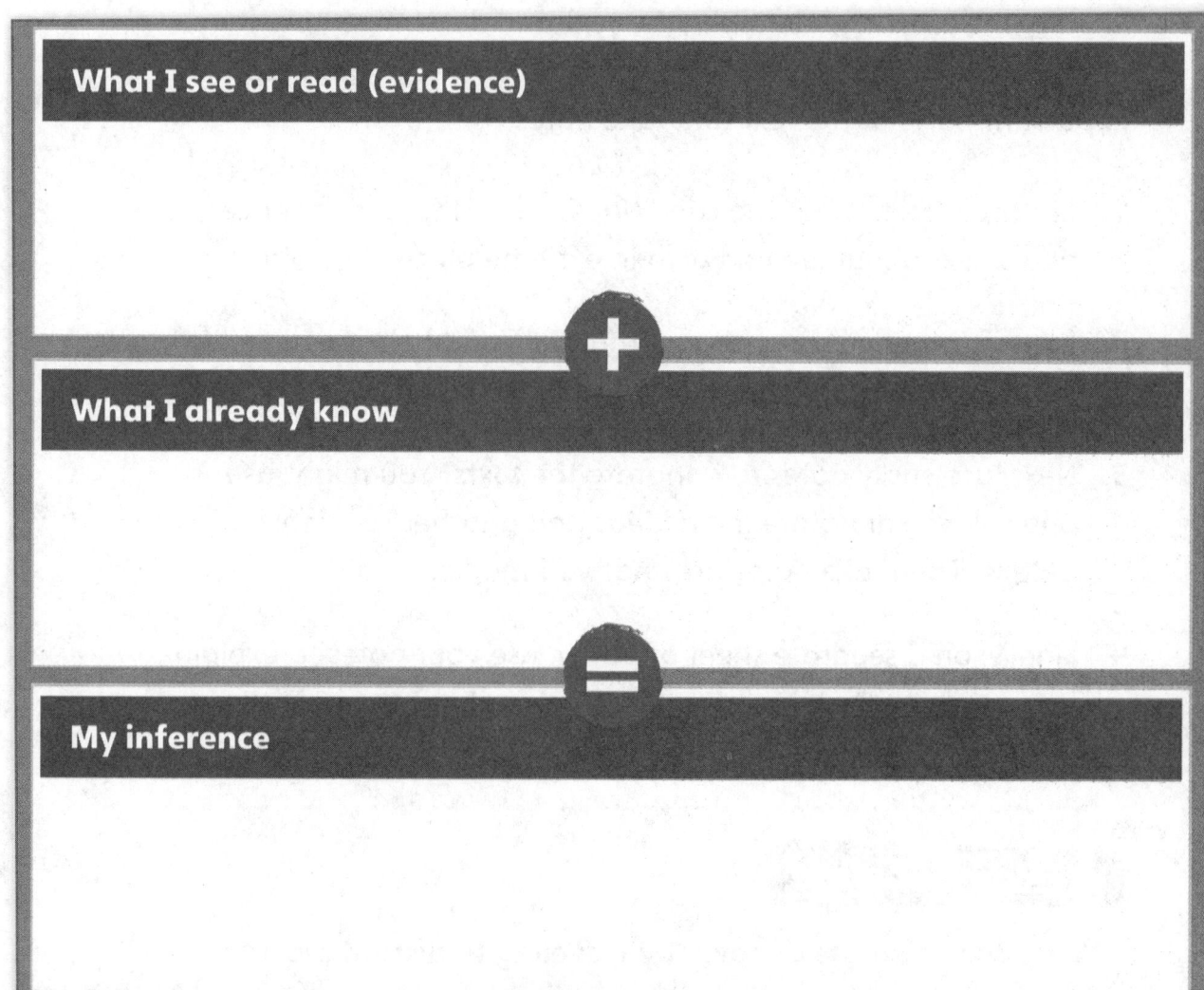

What I see or read (evidence)
+
What I already know
=
My inference

Reflect and Share

Write to Sources In *Life on Earth—and Beyond*, Dr. Chris McKay studies life in extreme places on Earth to see if life might exist on other planets. How might learning about Earth help us learn more about the universe? Use examples from the texts you read this week to write and support a response.

Interact with Sources When you read an informational text, identify the facts and details in the text and determine how they are organized. One way to do this is to annotate, or mark up, important parts of the text and take notes.

1. Choose a text about the conditions needed for life in space and a text about life on Earth in extreme places.
2. Identify passages in each text that tell you about possible life in the universe and life on Earth.
3. Next, use sticky notes to annotate the texts. You might use one color to annotate main ideas and another color for details. Then take notes on what you marked.
4. Finally, on a separate sheet of paper, use your notes to explain how studying Earth helps us learn more about the universe.

Weekly Question

What can scientists discover by traveling to distant places?

Academic Vocabulary

Learning Goal

I can develop knowledge about language to make connections between reading and writing.

Words that have the same or similar meanings are **synonyms.** Words that have opposite meanings are **antonyms.** Finding synonyms and antonyms can deepen your understanding of a word's meaning.

My TURN For each word,

1. **Read** the definition.
2. **Write** at least one synonym and one antonym.
3. **Use** a print or digital resource, like a thesaurus, as needed.

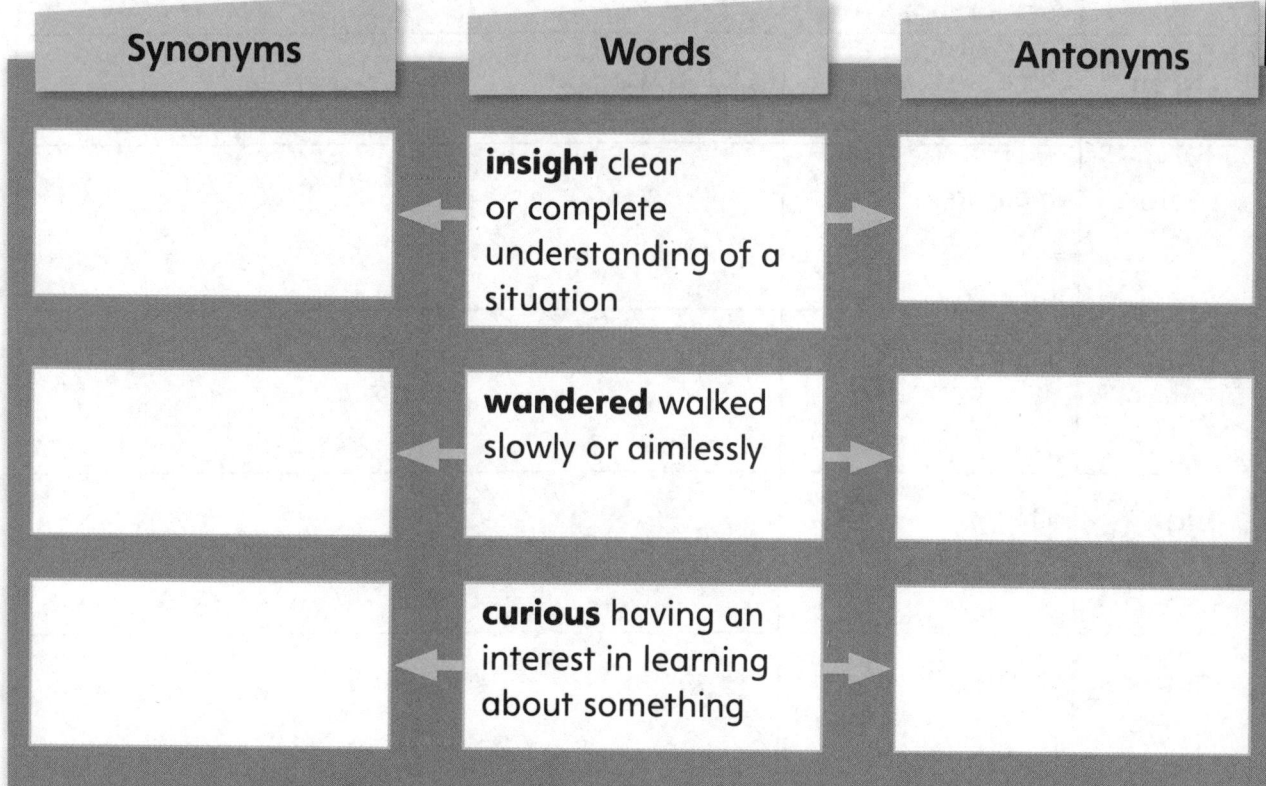

Synonyms	Words	Antonyms
	insight clear or complete understanding of a situation	
	wandered walked slowly or aimlessly	
	curious having an interest in learning about something	

Greek Roots

Words in English often come from words in other languages. For example, the English word *spectrometer* in paragraph 16 of *Life on Earth—and Beyond* comes from the Greek root *meter*, which means "measure." *A spectrometer* is an instrument that measures light wavelengths. Other common Greek roots include *chron*, *photo*, *bio*, *geo*, and *logy*.

My TURN Complete the chart by writing a word that includes each root. Then write the definition of each new word. On another sheet of paper, use three of the words with Greek roots in sentences.

Root	Root Meaning	Word	Definition
chron	time	chronological	in time order
meter	measure		
photo	light		
bio	life		
geo	earth		
logy	study of		

Read Like a Writer

Authors choose text features to achieve specific purposes, such as to organize their ideas or add information about a topic.

Model! Look back at the photographs near paragraph 15, and reread the captions.

1. **Identify** Pamela S. Turner includes a photograph; an inset, or close-up; and two captions.
2. **Question** Why does she include these text features?
3. **Conclude** Pamela S. Turner includes text features to help readers visualize what microbes are and where they live.

Reread paragraphs 18 through 20. Look at the text features.

My TURN Follow the steps to analyze the passage. Describe how the author achieves the purpose of informing through the use of text features.

1. **Identify** Pamela S. Turner includes the following text features:

   ____

   ______________________________.

2. **Question** How do these text features help you understand the text?

3. **Conclude** The text features help readers understand ideas in the text

   because ______________________________

   ______________________________.

Write for a Reader

Authors use text features to achieve a purpose. Text features might organize or clarify information. They may group related ideas or add more information about a topic. For example, an image might convey a main idea more clearly than words alone.

My TURN Analyze how Pamela S. Turner's use of text features in *Life on Earth—and Beyond* affects you as a reader. Explain how you can use text features to influence readers for a specific purpose.

1. If you were writing about Mars exploration, what text features would you include? Why?

2. Compose a passage about Mars exploration using information from the text and some of your own research. Include text features to organize your ideas and add information.

Spell Words with Greek Roots

Many words in English are formed by adding word parts to **Greek roots,** such as *chron, meter, photo, bio, geo,* and *logy.* For example, adding the prefix *eco-* to the root *logy* creates a word that means "the study of the environment." Sometimes a letter is dropped from or added to the root to form the new word.

My TURN Read the words. Spell and sort the words by their Greek roots. You may use some words twice.

SPELLING WORDS

meteorology	parameter	symmetry	photocell
photocopy	chronology	geocentric	biosphere
ecology	symbiotic	chronological	speedometer
geometric	photogenic	odometer	geology
synchronize	geography	chronic	photon

chron

meter

photo

bio

geo

logy

Independent and Dependent Clauses

A **clause** is a group of words that has a subject and a verb. **Independent clauses** can stand alone as sentences. **Dependent clauses** have a subject and a verb, but they cannot stand alone.

A **complex sentence** is made up of one independent clause and one dependent clause. If the independent clause comes last, use a comma after the dependent clause.

independent clause

When Clara went outside, she noticed the rainbow.

dependent clause

Often, dependent clauses begin with words such as

after	*until*	*although*
if	*when*	*because*
since	*though*	*while*

My TURN Edit this draft by using at least four words from the list to change independent clauses to dependent clauses, changing two sentences to one. Use a comma to separate clauses in most sentences.

Antarctica is covered with ice. It is as dry as many deserts. Many scientists conduct research there. Its climate is unique. Its environment is so unusual. Antarctica fascinates many people. You like remote places. Maybe you could travel there someday.

Develop an Engaging Idea

Learning Goal

I can use elements of narrative writing to write a personal narrative.

Writers focus ideas for a personal narrative by thinking about their memorable or interesting experiences. They include vivid details to help readers learn or feel something.

My TURN Read the About the Author features in texts from your classroom library. List details about where those authors found their engaging ideas.

Author	Author
Details	Details

Experiences

Author	Author
Details	Details

My TURN Use your notes to help you focus on an engaging idea for your own personal narrative.

Develop Specific Details

You can make a personal narrative more engaging by including specific and vivid details about your experiences. Make details more vivid by using precise action verbs, concrete nouns, and descriptive adjectives.

Sam **gets** the apple.	Sam **jumps** to pick the apple.
The knife's **sharpness** is good.	The knife's **edge** is sharp.
The **very big** elephant picked up the peanut.	The **enormous** elephant picked up the peanut.

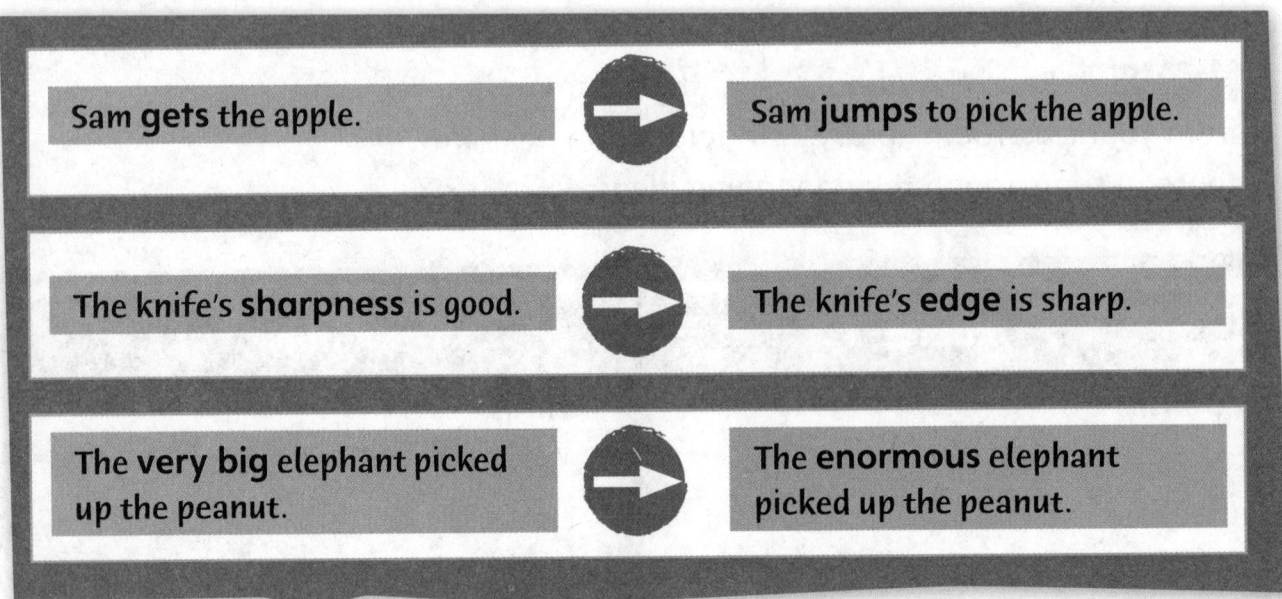

My TURN Rewrite each sentence, replacing the underlined verbs, pronouns, nouns, and adjectives with more precise words to provide more specific details.

1. That girl is in line for the big rollercoaster.

2. They are not very friendly dogs.

3. We were about to go many miles.

My TURN In your writing notebook, develop a draft of a personal narrative using specific details.

Develop Sensory Details

Sensory details appeal to the five senses. These details help readers see, hear, smell, taste, and feel the writer's descriptions. Sensory details help readers feel as if they are experiencing the story.

Original Sentence

The horse jumped over the wall and landed on the other side.

Sentence with Sensory Details:

The **chestnut** mare **flew** over the **cold stone** wall, and her feet **thudded** on the **dirt** where she landed.

My TURN Compose sentences on the topic. Use sensory details. Share your sentences with a partner. **Topic:** Your favorite place to visit

1. **Sights** ______________________________

2. **Sounds** ______________________________

3. **Touch/Textures** ______________________________

4. **Tastes** ______________________________

5. **Smells** ______________________________

My TURN In your writing notebook, develop a draft of a personal narrative using sensory details.

Develop Point of View

In a personal narrative, the writer is the narrator. You tell the events from your own point of view. Your point of view is your thoughts about a subject.

My TURN Write a sentence about your own experience with each topic below. Use first-person point of view.

A place you have been

A conflict or problem you have solved

A goal you have achieved

My TURN In your writing notebook, compose a personal narrative that gives your point of view. Use appropriate pronouns.

To write from your own point of view, use pronouns *I*, *me*, *my*, *us*, *we*, and *ours*.

Compose with Dialogue

A writer can provide details and develop experiences through **dialogue**, or words that are spoken between people in the narrative. Set off dialogue with quotation marks and text that tells which person is speaking.

My TURN Rewrite the following paragraph as dialogue between two people. The first example has been done for you.

We finally got to the Grand Canyon! Josie wanted to get as close to the edge as we could. I told her that I had never seen anything so beautiful. She said that she couldn't believe how far down the bottom of the canyon was. We agreed that it was hard to believe that a river could have created such an incredible place.

"We finally got to the Grand Canyon!" I said.

" ," suggested Josie.

" ," I told her.

" !" she exclaimed.

" ," I said.

" ," she agreed.

My TURN In your writing notebook, compose a personal narrative using dialogue to develop experiences, events, and situations. Share your work with your Writing Club.

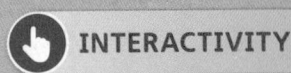

INTERACTIVITY

The Age of EXPLORATION

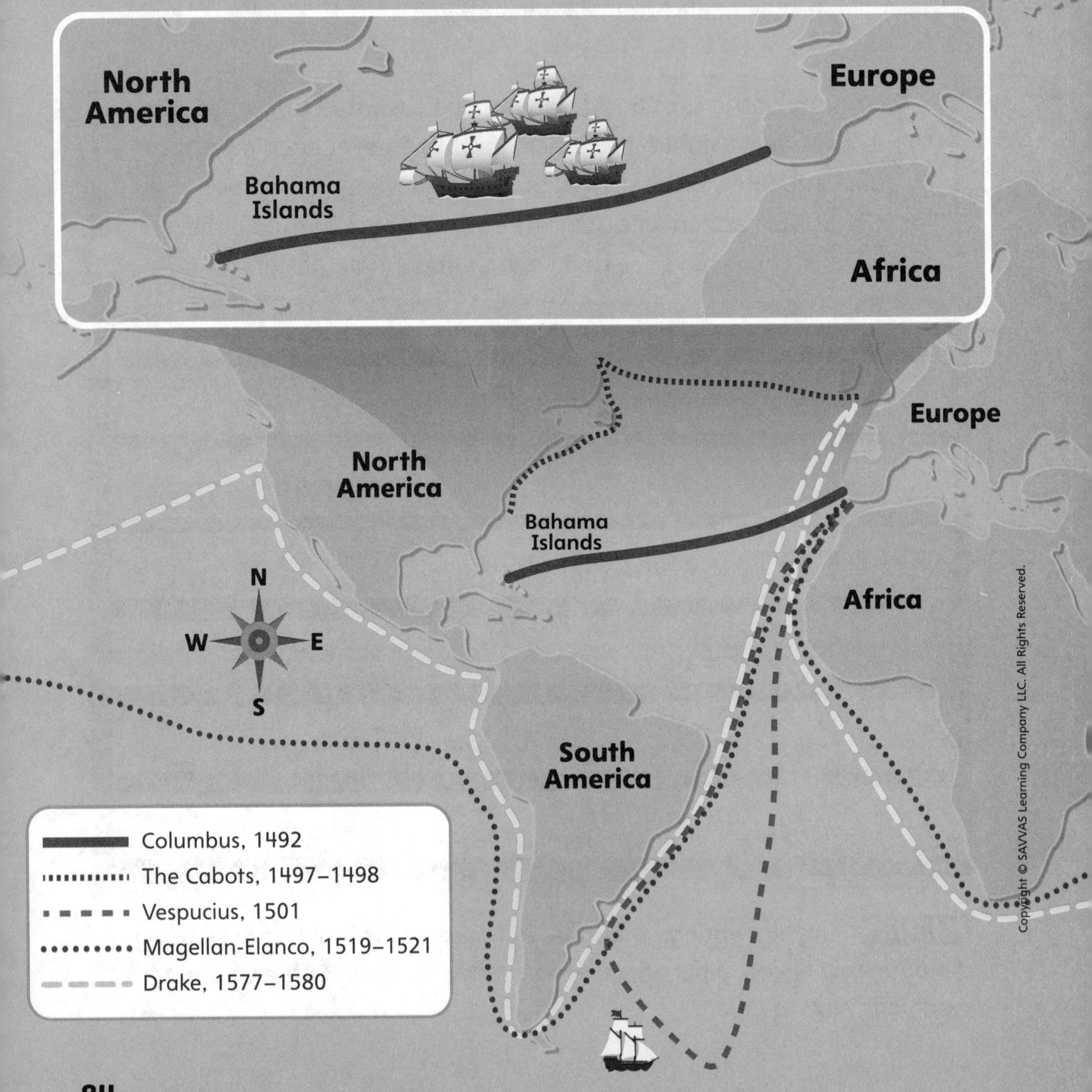

Christopher Columbus and his crew sailed west from Spain in 1492. Columbus hoped to find a more direct trade route to India, China, and other Asian trading partners. He wanted to improve on known routes that required sailing around Africa. Instead, after a long journey across the Atlantic Ocean, the crew found themselves in an area they did not know existed. This map shows the route they took on that famous voyage. It also shows subsequent routes taken by other European explorers as they continued to seek the wonders of the world.

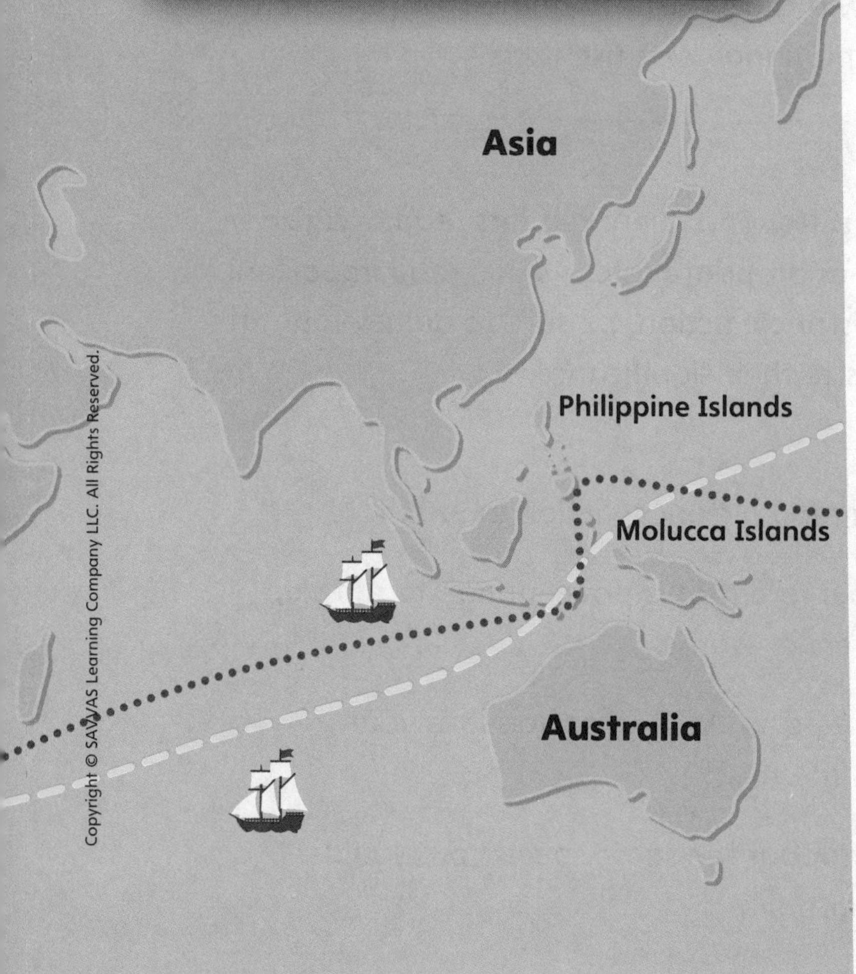

WEEK 3

Weekly Question

What can people learn from visiting unknown lands?

TURN and TALK What would you like to learn by visiting a new place? Discuss your answer with a partner.

Learning Goal

I can learn more about the theme *Journeys* by analyzing point of view in historical fiction.

Historical Fiction

- **Historical fiction** tells made-up stories based on real people, places, or events from the past.
- **Characters** are people who do actions in stories. Sometimes characters in historical fiction are based on real people. Sometimes they are made up.
- **Setting** is where and when a story takes place. Setting is important in historical fiction. These stories happen in real places or real time periods.

TURN and TALK Historical fiction includes facts about real people, places, and events to tell a story. How is that similar to and different from the way informational texts use facts?

Be a Fluent Reader Fluent readers read accurately and at an appropriate rate. As you read important ideas in historical fiction, be sure to adjust your rate to emphasize their significance.

When you read historical fiction aloud:

- Read at a rate that is slow enough to not skip any letters or words.
- Do not read so slowly that you lose your place in the text.
- Read at about the same speed you would speak normally.

Historical Fiction Anchor Chart

WHO?

- Fictional characters
- Some characters may be based on real people

WHAT?

- Realistic plot that mixes fact with fiction
- Plot inspired by real historical events
- Chronological, or time order, structure

WHERE?

- A place that actually exists
- Setting supported by facts

WHEN?

- The past
- A specific and historically significant time period

WHY?

- To entertain and to inform

Meet *the* Author

Pam Conrad wrote several award-winning books. Her books help readers imagine Columbus's voyage, understand the challenges of life on the American prairie, and explore how one New York town changed through the decades. Her book *Our Home: The Stories of Levittown* was a finalist for the Newbery Medal in 1995.

from

Pedro's Journal

Preview Vocabulary

As you read *Pedro's Journal*, pay attention to these vocabulary words. Notice how they relate to the idea of a journey.

tide **course**

leagues **fathoms** **jaunts**

Read

Before you begin, establish a purpose for reading. Active readers of **historical fiction** follow these strategies when they read a text for the first time.

First Read

Notice how the plot develops.	**Generate Questions** about the purpose you set for reading to deepen your understanding of the text.
Connect this text to what you know about the world.	**Respond** by discussing how this text answers the weekly question.

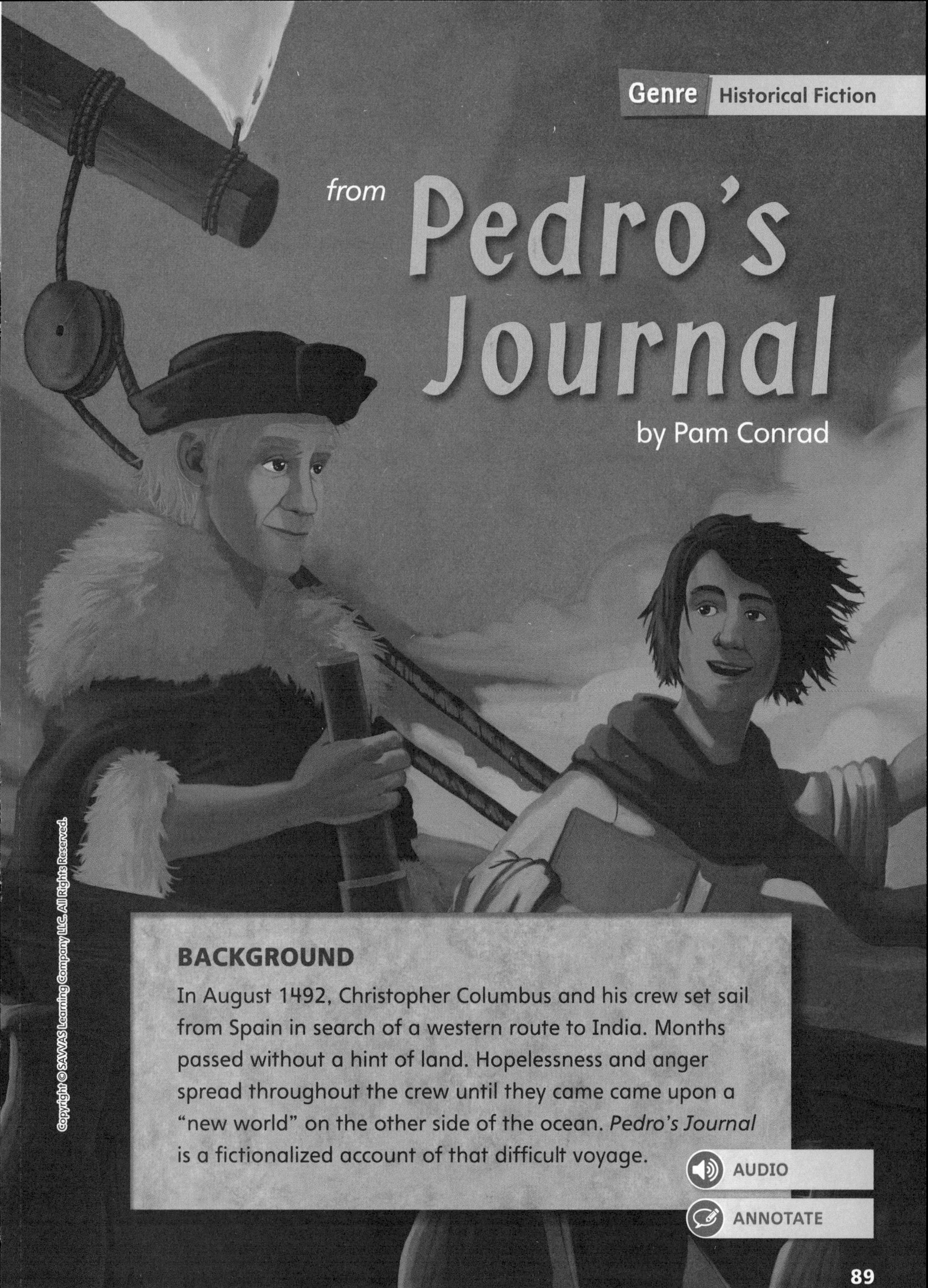

Genre Historical Fiction

from Pedro's Journal

by Pam Conrad

BACKGROUND

In August 1492, Christopher Columbus and his crew set sail from Spain in search of a western route to India. Months passed without a hint of land. Hopelessness and anger spread throughout the crew until they came came upon a "new world" on the other side of the ocean. *Pedro's Journal* is a fictionalized account of that difficult voyage.

AUDIO

ANNOTATE

CLOSE READ

Understand Point of View

Underline words that show that the main character, Pedro, is the narrator of the story.

August 3

1 The ship's roster of the *Santa María* has me down as Pedro de Salcedo, ship's boy. And the captain of this ship, who calls himself "Captain General of the Ocean Sea," has hired me not for my great love of the sea, nor for my seamanship, but because I have been taught to read and write, and he thinks it will be useful to have me along.

2 Last night when I boarded the *Santa María* with forty others and made ready to begin this uncertain journey to India, I saw my mother standing alone on the dock wrapped in her black shawl. She lifted her hand to wave, and I turned away quickly. I have never been away from our home. I have never been on a ship as great as this one. I dedicate this journal, this parcel of letters and drawings, to my dear mother, who has lost so much and who I pray will not lose me as well—me, her young boy whom she calls *Pedro de mi corazón,* Pedro of my heart.

3 We are a fleet of three ships, the *Niña* and *Pinta* with us, and this morning in the darkness, with no one watching or waving good-bye, we left the harbor at Palos and headed out for the sandbar on the Saltes River. There we waited for tide and wind and then made way for the Canary Islands. We are to be the first ships ever to run a course west to the Indies, Marco Polo's land where palaces are built of gold, where mandarins wear silk brocade and pearls are the size of ripened grapes.

CLOSE READ

Understand Point of View

Underline the words that indicate Pedro is joined by other characters.

tide the rise and fall of the ocean

course the direction of travel

CLOSE READ

Understand Point of View

Underline details in first-person point of view that show Pedro's confidence in his skill.

4 A couple of the men are seasick and are already mumbling that we will never see this India our Captain General is so certain he will find. Me, I have no knowledge of maps or charts or distant journeys. I am only a ship's boy. There are three of us, and I am beginning to suspect that we will do all the work no one wants to do. But already the Captain favors me and has called upon me to write and to copy certain of his writings. I believe he is testing me and will find I am capable and write a good hand.

5 The Captain told me he was pleased to see my stomach is as strong as my handwriting and has encouraged me to sketch some of the things I see around me. Perhaps I am a natural seaman, although I admit that looking over the side of this creaking ship into the swelling water can fill me with terror.

September 10

6 Everyone seemed crazy all day. No one is doing his job well. Even the helmsman steered improperly and took us north instead of west. I thought the Captain would string up the whole crew to the mast. "What do you think you are doing?" he shouted. "Steering a ferryboat across the River of Seville?" I've seen him go into white rages and then pace his small cabin saying his Hail Marys.

7 We finally lost sight of land as we sailed west. Some say it will be a long time before we see it again. If at all. A couple of the men were crying, and the Captain shamed them and then promised them all sorts of riches and fame. He has said that the first man to spot land will receive a reward of 10,000 maravedis.

8 The men listen to him sullenly, and I see them exchange glances. They don't believe him, and after what I saw this morning, I wonder if they should. I noted that the morning's slate said we made 180 miles, and yet the Captain recorded only 144 in his official log that the men see. I believe he is trying to make the crew believe that we are closer to home than is true.

9 But 10,000 maravedis! Ah, think of all I could buy for my mother. Even now I can picture a beautiful dress, a rich dress that she could wear to Mass at Easter. I will keep a sharp eye. I will be the first to spot land!

CLOSE READ

Use Text Evidence

Highlight evidence that helps you understand the crew's reactions to being far from land.

CLOSE READ

Use Text Evidence

Highlight evidence that shows Pedro's observations of other characters' behavior.

leagues units of distance

October 10

10 This has been the worst day of all for the Captain. I am certain of this. We have doubled all previous records of days and leagues at sea, and we've gone way past the point where he originally said we would find land. There is nothing out here. Surely we are lost. And everyone is certain now as well.

11 This morning the men responded slowly to orders, scowling and slamming down their tools and lines. They whispered in pairs and small groups on deck and below. The air was thick with mutiny and betrayal, until finally everything came to a dead stop. The wind howled through the shrouds, and the men just stood there on deck and did not move aside when Columbus came.

12 "Enough," one of the men said to his face. "This is enough. Now we turn back." They were mad

13 The other men grumbled their assent and nodded, their fists clenched, their chests broad. And they remained motionless and unmoved while Columbus paced the deck, telling them how close he figured we must be, that land could be right over the next horizon. He told them again of the fame and fortune that would be theirs if they could only last a little longer. And they laughed at him, the cruel laughter of impatient and defeated men.

14 "All that aside," he added, "with the fresh easterly wind coming at us and the rising sea, we can't turn a course back to Spain right now. We would stand still in the water."

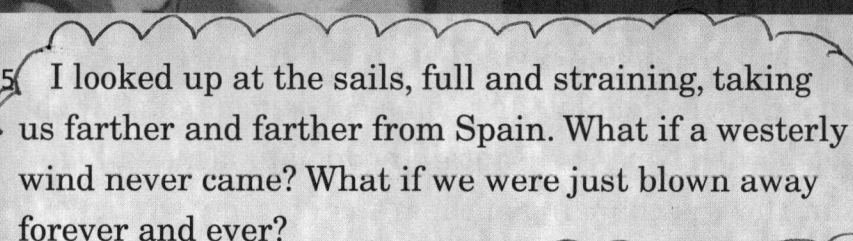

15 I looked up at the sails, full and straining, taking us farther and farther from Spain. What if a westerly wind never came? What if we were just blown away forever and ever?

16 "Let me offer you this," Columbus finally said. "Do me this favor. Stay with me this day and night, and if I don't bring you to land before day, cut off my head, and you shall return."

17 The men glanced at each other. Some nodded. "One day," they said. "One day, and then we turn around."

18 "That is all I ask," Columbus said.

19 Later, when I went down to the cabin with the log, the Captain's door was bolted shut, and when I knocked he didn't answer, so I sat outside the door with the heavy journal in my lap and waited.

CLOSE READ

Understand Point of View

Underline a detail that shows how Pedro reacts to challenges on the journey.

CLOSE READ

Understand Point of View

Underline parts of Pedro's description that reflect the crew's hopefulness.

October 11

20 Through the day, the day that was to have been our last day traveling westward, many things were seen floating in the water, things that stirred everyone's hopes and had the men once again scanning the horizon. We saw birds in flocks, reeds and plants floating in the water, and a small floating board, and even a stick was recovered that had iron workings on it, obviously man-made. Suddenly no one wished to turn around. There was no further word on it.

21 At sunset, I led the prayers and the men sang the *Salve Regina*. Then the Captain spoke to the seamen from the sterncastle, doubling the night watch and urging everyone to keep a sharp lookout. No one asked about turning back. Then the Captain added a new bonus to his reward of 10,000 maravedis. He added a silk doublet, and some of the men joked with each other. Next the Captain nodded to me, and I sang for the changing of the watch, but my words were lost in the wind that was growing brisker and in the seas that were growing heavier and sounding like breakers all about us. The men dispersed to their watches and their bunks, and the Captain paced the deck. I don't know why, but this night I stayed with him. I stayed still by the gunwale, watching over the side. Once in a while he would stand beside me, silent, looking westward, always westward.

CLOSE READ

Use Text Evidence

Highlight a detail that shows that Pedro knows how the crew feels about finding land.

22 Then, an hour before moonrise, the Captain froze beside me. "Gutierrez!" he called to one of the king's men on board, who came running. He pointed out across the water. "What do you see?"

23 Gutierrez peered into the west. "I don't see anything," he said. "What? What? What do you see?"

24 "Can't you see it?" the Captain whispered. "The light? Like a little wax candle rising and falling?"

25 The man at his side was quiet. I was there beside him, too, straining my own eyes to the dark horizon.

26 Suddenly another seaman called out across the darkness, "Land! Land!"

27 "He's already seen it!" I shouted. "My master's already seen it!" And the Captain laughed and tousled my hair.

28 "*Tierra*! *Tierra*!" It was heard all across the water from all three ships.

29 I am below now in the Captain's cabin writing, while in the light of the rising moon, with our sails silver in the moonlight, we three exploring ships are rolling and plunging through the swells towards land. Tomorrow our feet will touch soil, and I can assure my dear mother in the hills of Spain that no one will get much sleep on board the *Santa María* tonight!

Understand Point of View

Underline a detail that only Pedro experiences when Columbus leaps out of the boat.

fathoms units of length that measure the depth of water

October 12

30 A lush green island was there in the morning, and our three ships approached it carefully, maneuvering through breakers and a threatening barrier reef. We could see clear down to the reef in the sparkling blue waters as we sailed through. And, ah, it is truly land, truly earth, here so far from Spain. The *Santa María* led the way into the sheltered bay of the island and got a mark of only five fathoms' depth. We anchored there and barely paused to admire the breathtaking beauty. Small boats were prepared, armed, and lowered, and in these some of us went ashore. Out of respect, all waited while Christopher Columbus leaped out of the boat, his feet the first to touch this new land. (I wondered what my mother would say if she knew her son had lost the 10,000 maravedis to the Captain, who claimed it for himself.)

31 The Captain carried the royal banner of our king and queen, and as everyone else scrambled out of the boats and secured them in the white sand, he thrust the banner into the earth and then sank down to his knees and said a prayer of thanksgiving for our safe arrival in India. Others dropped to their knees around him. Diego was beside me, and he clapped his hand on my shoulder. I knew he was happy to be on land again. I was, too, although I have been at sea so long that even on land the ground seems to buckle and sway beneath my feet.

CLOSE READ

Vocabulary in Context

Context clues are words and sentences around an unfamiliar word that help readers understand the word.

Underline context clues that help you define *solemn* in paragraph 32.

32 The Captain made a solemn ceremony and formally took possession of the land for the king and queen, naming it San Salvador. We all witnessed this, and then little by little we noticed something else—there were people stepping out from the trees, beautiful, strong, naked people, with tanned skin and straight black hair. My mother would have lowered her eyes or looked away, as I have seen her do in our home when someone dresses, but I could not take my eyes off them. Some had boldly painted their bodies or their faces, some only their eyes, some their noses. They were so beautiful and gentle. They walked towards us slowly but without fear, smiling and reaching out their hands.

33 The sailors watched them in wonder, and when these people came near, the crew gave them coins, little red caps, whatever they had in their pockets. Columbus himself showed one native his sword, and the native, never having seen such an instrument before, slid his fingers along the sharp edge and looked startled at his fingers that dripped blood into the sand.

34 Everyone was smiling and so friendly. Close up, we could see how clear and gentle their eyes were, how broad and unusual their foreheads. The Captain especially noted and said to one of his men, "See the gold in that one's nose? See how docile they are? They will be easy. We will take six back with us to Spain."

35 I think at this, too, my mother would have lowered her eyes.

Leah
october 18

CLOSE READ

Understand Point of View

Underline parts of Pedro's description that show his point of view about how the natives feel about the crew members.

October 16

36 So much has happened. There is so much to remember and record, and so much I do not think I want to tell my mother. Perhaps I will keep these letters to myself after all. The natives think that we are angels from God. They swim out to us, wave, throw themselves in the sand, hold their hands and faces to the sky, and sing and call to us. The crew loves it, and no one loves it better than Columbus. He lifts his open palms to them like a priest at Mass. I sometimes wonder if he doesn't believe these natives himself just a little bit.

37 They come right out to the ship in swift dugouts that sit forty men, and sometimes as they approach us the dugout tips, but in minutes they right it and begin bailing it out with hollow gourds. All day long the Indians row out to see us, bringing gifts of cotton thread, shell-tipped spears, and even brightly colored parrots that sit on our shoulders and cry out in human voices. For their trouble we give them more worthless beads, bells, and tastes of honey, which they marvel at.

38 The six native men Columbus has taken aboard are not very happy. One by one they are escaping, which I cannot help but say I am happy for. One jumped overboard and swam away, and another jumped overboard when a dugout came up alongside us in the darkness. Some of the crew seized another man coming alongside in a dugout and forced him

on board. Columbus tried to convince him of our good intentions through sign language and broken words and more gifts of glass beads and junk, and the man rowed back to some people on the shore. They stood talking to each other and pointing at our ship. Columbus smiled and was convinced they know we are from God. Me, I am not so sure they will believe it for much longer.

CLOSE READ

Use Text Evidence

Highlight parts of Pedro's description that make Columbus appear dishonest.

CLOSE READ

Understand Point of View

Underline a detail that shows that Pedro knows how Diego feels.

December 3

39 We are anchored in a quiet harbor in scattered showers. It has been raining for days without the slightest breeze or gust. Many of the men went ashore to wash their clothes and themselves in the river. Two men wandered into the jungle and returned to tell us they had come upon a village where hanging from a post was a basket with a man's head in it. I don't think I will go looking in any baskets I find.

40 One day I went ashore with Diego, Columbus, and a native who is working as an interpreter for us. The Captain gave Diego a bag of brass rings, glass beads, and bells and told him to see what trading he could do. Diego agreed, but I could tell he does not like to do this. A group of natives joined us, but these were not so friendly, and they had little to trade. Their eyes were distrustful, and their bodies were painted red, with bundles of feathers and darts hanging from them. When we finished our meager trade, they gathered at the stern of our small boat in the river, and one began making a speech we could not understand. The others began to shout in response.

Columbus stood by looking pompous and arrogant as he waited, but the interpreter with us turned pale and began to shake. He told the Captain to go back to the *Santa María* at once, that they were planning to kill us.

41 I hopped right in the boat to go back, but Diego didn't move and Columbus laughed. He interrupted the village speechmaker and drew his sword from his scabbard. With a gentle smile on his face, he showed him the steel glistening in the sun, sliced clear through a leather strap the speechmaker bore around his neck, and the man's beads tumbled into the sand. Next the Captain had one of his men demonstrate his crossbow. At this the crowd of natives turned and ran into the trees. Our interpreter was still not comforted. He jumped into the boat beside me and, trembling, beckoned us to get aboard and get back to the ship, quickly.

42 The Captain was slow about it. He talked of how he admired the workmanship of these natives, but how cowardly they were: "They are so timid, ten of our men could frighten away thousands of them." I said nothing. The Captain expects nothing of me. I just watched silent Diego's back straining and bulging in rhythm as he helped row us back to the *Santa María*.

CLOSE READ

Use Text Evidence

Highlight words and phrases Pedro uses to describe the natives' fear of the Captain.

CLOSE READ

Understand Point of View

Underline sentences that tell you Pedro thinks Columbus is arrogant.

jaunts short, enjoyable journeys

December 13

43 It is difficult to keep a journal now that we are so busy, traveling from island to island and up and down rivers and in and out of harbors. There are no longer endless empty jaunts into the western sky. But one thing has not changed. The crew continues to grumble. They are saying this is not Asia at all, that this whole trip has been a costly failure. They say they will be laughed at when we finally return home. There are no silks, no treasures, and just tiny trinkets of gold. All we will bring back are spools of rough cotton thread, a few rustic spears, and some natives who grow quieter and thinner with each day they spend on board the *Santa María*.

44 Columbus goes on naming everything he touches. He sees a cape of land and he says, "I christen you Cabo de la Estrella," or "Hail, Cabo del Elefante." "I name you Cabo de Cinquin," or "Isla de la Tortuga." "And you I name Puerto de San Nicolas." I am surprised he doesn't name the birds as they fly by. Every time his feet touch land he thrusts a cross into the sand and claims it for the king and queen of Spain.

CLOSE READ

Use Text Evidence

Highlight the words and phrases Pedro uses to describe the special bond between the native women.

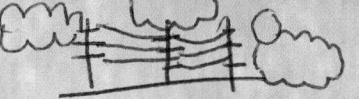

45 The natives no longer greet us with gifts and song. Now when they see us they run. I am glad for this. Except yesterday three sailors ran after them and brought back to the ship a most beautiful young girl. Columbus wanted to talk to her and convince her that we are harmless and wish only to trade. There seemed to be an instant tenderness between her and the other native women on board, whom I've written of before. She wanted to take the women with her when she left. Columbus refused, of course, telling her to go back to her people and tell them he means no harm. The women touched hands and spoke to each other in quiet whispers. Once she was gone, the Captain turned to me and said, "Did you see the gold ring in her nose?"

46 The next day he sent a party to search for her and her village, and they found the village, but it had been abandoned. The fires were still warm, but not a soul was tending them. Soon they found people hiding and persuaded them to come out. They reported they even saw the beautiful girl on the shoulders of her husband. But when they returned to the ship they did not bring gold or silks. More blessed parrots.

CLOSE READ

Use Text Evidence

Highlight a word that supports Pedro's feelings about going home.

January 28

47 How wonderful this feels to be heading home. We almost made one extra stop. One of the natives on board told the Captain of an island on our way where only women live, where it is believed men come only part of the year and then are kicked out along with boy children who are old enough to leave their mothers. It was not the women the Captain was interested in, but the fact that this may be the island Marco Polo wrote about in his voyage to the Orient. And this would be the proof Columbus needs to show we did indeed make the Indies.

48 He even turned in this direction for two leagues, but when he saw how disappointed the men were—how even the thought of an island full of women did not distract them from their desire to go home, or their uneasiness about the leaking boats—he turned back towards our homeland, and now the ships roll before the winds, winds that grow cooler and cooler with each passing day.

February 2

49 Tonight is the night of the full moon, and once again we are traveling through a throbbing meadow of seaweed, this time at a good speed with gentle winds pushing us along. Earlier, I was not able to sleep for the eerie noise the seaweed brings, the soft, enchanted swish against the hull, like a mother's hand soothing a baby's head, so I went above and found the Captain alone on deck, lit by the moon. His log entries these last days are concerned with the miles we make and the direction we sail, constantly plotting and striving to find his way back to Spain. I was uncertain at first what to do, but finally I came up beside him. I don't think he had even looked to see who I was, when he pointed off toward the north-northeast and said, "I believe there are islands off in that quarter. When we come back on our second voyage, I will make certain we visit them."

50 A second voyage. Suddenly the wind was too cold for me. The moon too bright. Below, I wrap myself tight in my blanket and struggle to write. The inkhorn in one hand, the quill in the other, I try to imagine myself growing to manhood on ships such as this, and I cannot. Oh, I cannot.

CLOSE READ

Understand Point of View

Underline details that show Pedro's reaction to the thought of a second voyage.

Fluency

Reread paragraphs 47–48. Read at an appropriate rate, or pace, that is neither too slow nor too fast.

Develop Vocabulary

In historical fiction, authors use precise words to help readers visualize people, places, and actions in a story. Sometimes those words have multiple meanings.

My TURN Read the multiple-meaning vocabulary words from *Pedro's Journal*. Then match each word with its correct definitions. Use a dictionary to confirm your answers.

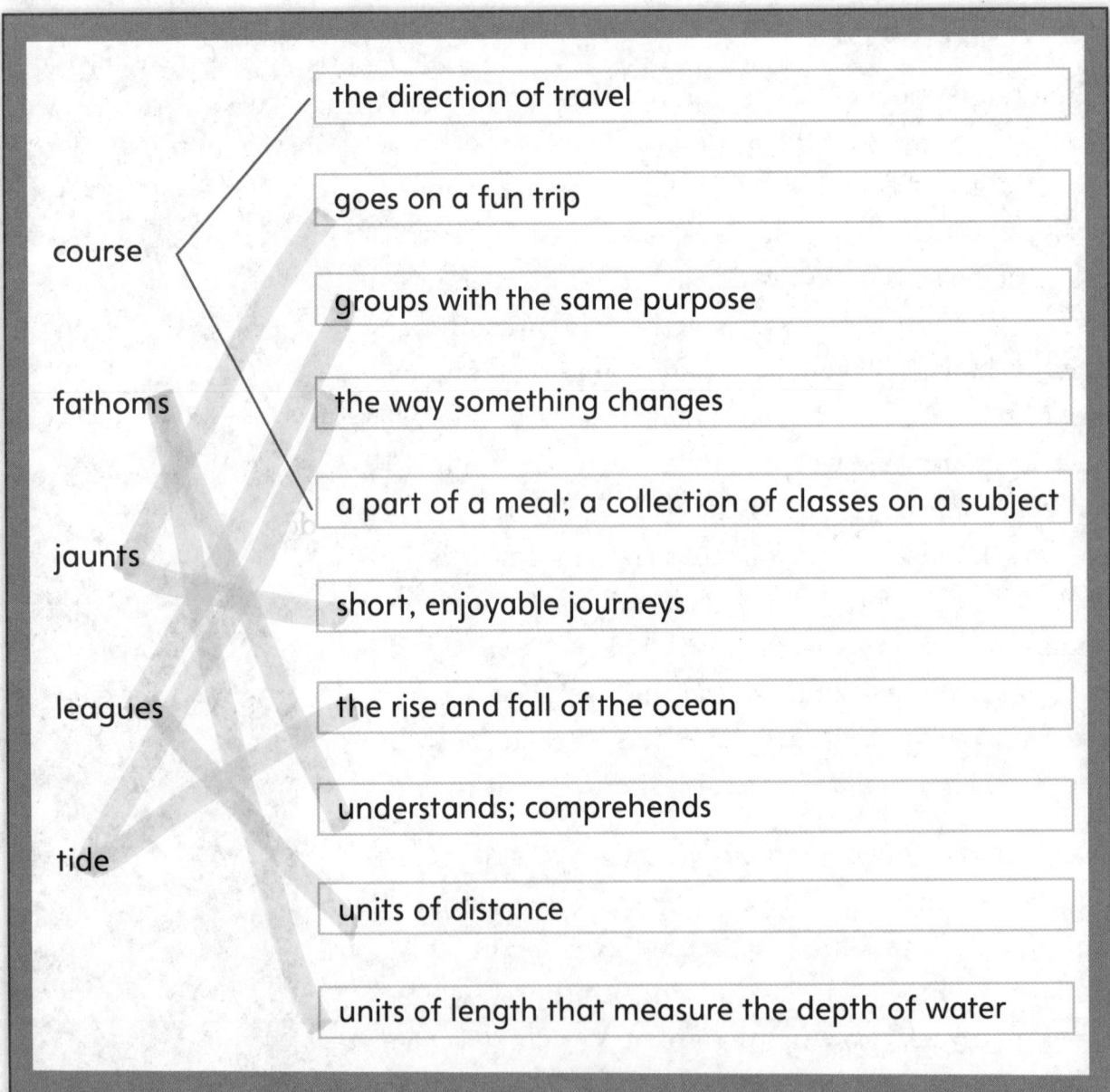

Words	Definitions
course	the direction of travel
fathoms	goes on a fun trip
jaunts	groups with the same purpose
leagues	the way something changes
tide	a part of a meal; a collection of classes on a subject
	short, enjoyable journeys
	the rise and fall of the ocean
	understands; comprehends
	units of distance
	units of length that measure the depth of water

Check for Understanding

My TURN Look back at the text to answer the questions.

1. What identifies this text as historical fiction?

The text is historical fiction because the character is not real, but the events of the story are.

2. How does the author create different moods in the October 10 and October 11 entries? Use text evidence.

On October 10th, the men were "Scowling and slamming down their tools". On October 11th, the men saw things floating in the water and were yelling "Land" and laughing.

3. How does Pedro feel about his first sea voyage? Why doesn't he want to join Columbus on a second trip? Use text evidence.

Pedro didn't enjoy his first sea voyage. He doesn't want to join Columbus because he does not want to "grow into manhood on ships such as this."

4. Pedro often imagines what his mother would think of his experiences. How do her imagined reactions influence his actions and decisions on the journey?

Pedro writes that his mom would not approve of Columbus. Because he cares about his mom so much, it influences him to make good decisions.

leah T.

Understand Point of View

Point of view is the perspective from which an author presents the actions and characters in a story. Readers experience a story through the thoughts, feelings, and actions of the narrator. The narrator may be a character in the story. First-person point of view uses the pronouns *I*, *me*, and *mine*. Third-person point of view uses the pronouns *he*, *she*, *her*, *him*, *his*, and *hers*.

1. **My TURN** Go to the Close Read notes in *Pedro's Journal* and underline the parts that help you identify who is telling the story. Consider what the narrator thinks and feels.

2. **Text Evidence** Use the parts you underlined to complete the questions and chart.

   Who is telling the story? Pedro

   How do you know? The Story uses words like I, me, we, and my and Shares his thought.

   From which point of view is the story told? 1st Person

Evidence from *Pedro's Journal*	Pedro's Thoughts, Actions, or Feelings
"The Caption told me he was Pleased to see my Stomach is as strong as my handwiti."	

Use Text Evidence

When reading, readers use **text evidence**, details stated in the text, to help them understand and interpret elements in a text.

1. **My TURN** Go back to the Close Read notes and highlight text evidence that helps you understand how point of view is revealed in *Pedro's Journal*.
2. **Text Evidence** Use the evidence you highlighted to complete the chart and support your response.

Text Evidence	How It Reveals Point of View
"Everyone seemed crazy all day. No one is doing his job well." "men were crying"	It shows Pedro's observations about the crew's reactions to being far from land.
The man Stood there by the deck and did not move a Side when columbas came	It shows observasios about the crews feelings twards columbas.
they laghed at him at th adounc and the crew lahafter	It Shows Pedros observasion how tired the man or Columbas.
I Sat outsid with my heavy Jurnal.	it Shows that he is being braged about how hevay Jarnol.

Reflect and Share

Write to Sources In this unit so far, you have read about real and fictional people who traveled great distances. Consider all the texts you have read this week. Was leaving home and traveling to a new place worth it? Use the following questions to help you write an opinion about if travel is worth the risk.

Use Text Evidence When writing an opinion essay, include text evidence to support your opinion statement, or claim.

On a separate sheet of paper, write a claim about whether travel is worth the risk. Then choose two texts you read this week. Identify a piece of text evidence from each text that supports your opinion. Use these questions to evaluate the evidence:

- Does this quotation clearly support my claim, or opinion?
- Will this quotation help me convince others that my opinion is valid?
- Are there better quotations to make my opinion even more convincing? If so, I will review my annotations and notes.

Replace evidence as needed. Finally, write a short paragraph that includes text evidence to express and support your opinion.

Weekly Question

What can people learn from visiting unknown lands?

Academic Vocabulary

Learning Goal

I can develop knowledge about language to make connections between reading and writing.

Words that surround an unfamiliar word are called **context clues.** Some common context clues are synonyms and antonyms. A synonym is a word with the same meaning as another word. An antonym is a word with the opposite meaning.

My TURN For each pair of sentences,

1. **Read** the sentences.
2. Use context within and beyond each sentence to **write** the clues that help you determine the relevant meaning of the boldfaced word.
3. **Tell** what type of context clue is used.

Sentences	Context Clues	Type of Context Clue
Travis understands the book. His **insight** will help us.	understands	synonym
Mrs. Hsu **wandered** through the park. However, other people walked quickly past the pond.		
Alex quickly walked through the **passage** into the hall. The doorway was small.		
The family leaves on an **adventure** next week. It will be another exciting trip.		
Maria felt indifferent about the new teacher. But Chris was **curious** about him.		

Vowel Teams

Vowel teams are two or three letters that together make one vowel sound. The letters can include vowels and consonants. A **digraph** is a single sound represented by two letters, such as *ai* in *strain* (long *a*). A **diphthong** includes two vowel sounds blended in one syllable, such as *oi* in *oil*.

Other vowel teams include *ea*, *ie*, *igh*, *ow*, *ou*, *oa*, and *oy*. Some vowel teams can be pronounced in several ways. For example, *ea* can have the long e sound *(reaching)*, the short e sound *(headed)*, the long *a* sound *(great)*, or the schwa sound *(ocean)*.

My TURN Read the words from *Pedro's Journal*. Highlight the vowel team in each word. Then underline the sound the vowel team makes.

shouted	blended *ow*	long *o*
tomorrow	blended *ow*	long o
friendly	short *e*	long e
slightest	short *i*	long *i*
yesterday	short *a*	long *a*
defeated	blended *ea*	long e
voyage	blended *oi*	long *o*
believe	long *e*	long *i*

Read Like a Writer

Authors choose precise words and descriptive details to help readers experience events in a story through the eyes of the narrator. These details also help develop the narrator's unique voice.

Model! Read the text from *Pedro's Journal*.

> Perhaps I am a natural seaman, although I admit that looking over the side of this creaking ship into the swelling water can fill me with terror.

1. **Identify** Pam Conrad includes these details to describe what Pedro thinks and feels.
2. **Question** What does this language tell me about Pedro's voice?
3. **Conclude** Pedro wants to be a sailor but is sometimes afraid of the sea.

Read the text.

> The six native men Columbus has taken aboard are not very happy. One by one they are escaping, which I cannot help but say I am happy for.

MY TURN Examine how the author's use of language contributes to voice.

1. **Identify** Pam Conrad uses the language ______________________________ .
2. **Question** What does this language tell me about Pedro's voice?
3. **Conclude** Pedro ______________________________ .

Write for a Reader

Use voice to emphasize individual feelings and actions!

The narrator's unique voice helps shape the story. Voice influences how readers "see" and understand story events through that narrator's eyes. The narrator's voice may reveal thoughts and feelings as well as the narrator's personality, age, and background.

My TURN Think about how Pam Conrad's use of voice in *Pedro's Journal* affects your understanding of Pedro and the story. Now identify how you can use voice to affect readers.

1. If you were trying to create a specific voice for a narrator in historical fiction, what language would you use? Think about the narrator's personality, age, and background.

2. Write a passage to show your narrator's voice through his or her thoughts and actions. Include descriptive details to help your reader "see" and feel what the character is experiencing.

Spell Words with Vowel Teams

Vowel teams are two or three letters that together make one sound. The same sound can be spelled using different vowel teams, such as the long e sound in *committee* and *zeal*. The same spelling can have different sounds, such as *ea* in *realm* and *zeal*.

Digraphs and diphthongs can also have the same spellings but different sounds, such as the *ow* sounds in *hollow* and *brown*. They can have different spellings, such as in *royalty* and *embroider*.

My TURN Read the words. Spell and sort them in alphabetical order.

SPELLING WORDS

zealous	cowardice	treasury	allowance
bayonet	realm	zeal	concealment
royalty	embroider	typhoon	treachery
committee	nautical	marshmallow	approach
leukemia	gauntlet	flounder	proclaim

Compound and Complex Sentences

A **compound sentence** includes two independent clauses joined by a comma and a conjunction such as *and, but,* or *or.* A sentence with two independent clauses connected by a comma but no conjunction is called a comma splice. Writers edit to avoid comma splices. A **complex sentence** has an independent clause and a dependent clause. A comma appears after the dependent clause if that clause is first.

Sentence Type	Description	Example
Simple	a single independent clause	Max ate an apple.
Compound	two independent clauses joined by a conjunction such as *and, but,* or *or*	Max ate an apple, and Jen ate a banana.
Complex	an independent clause and a dependent clause	Because Max ate the last apple, Jen ate a banana.

My TURN Edit this draft by combining simple sentences to create a complex sentence and two compound sentences, one of which fixes a comma splice. Include commas in your rewritten complex and compound sentences.

Pedro did not know much about ships. He knew how to read and write. This skill gave him advantages over other people. Pedro was chosen to be a ship's boy. The native people on the island greeted the explorers without fear, the captain took advantage of this generosity.

Develop an Introduction

Learning Goal

I can use elements of narrative writing to write a personal narrative.

A writer focuses a personal narrative with an **introduction**. The introduction

- has a hook, or interesting statement, that makes readers want to keep reading.
- establishes the situation or problem that sets events in motion.
- introduces the narrator and any other people important to the experience. In a personal narrative, the narrator is the writer.

MY TURN Focus your writing by developing the introduction of your personal narrative.

Hook
Problem
Narrator

MY TURN Compose the introduction of your personal narrative in your writing notebook.

Develop a Sequence of Events

Writers focus their narratives by putting events in a logical order. This helps readers follow the events and experiences in the text. In narratives, the sequence of events usually follows chronological order, or the order in which the events occurred.

MyTURN Focus the sequence of events for your personal narrative. List the main events in the order they happen.

First	
Next	
Then	
Finally	

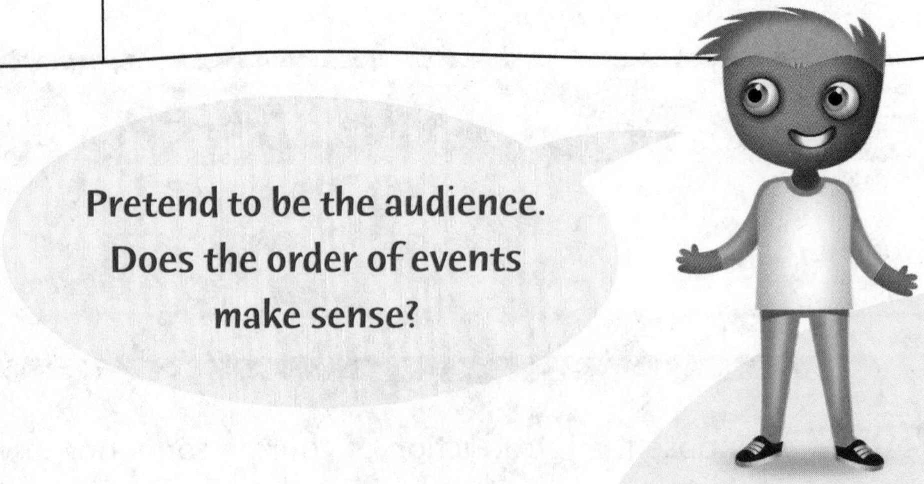

Pretend to be the audience.
Does the order of events
make sense?

Draft with Transitions

Writers use transitions to guide their readers through a text. These words and phrases make the events in a narrative clear and easy to follow.

Use specific transitions, such as time-order transitions, to show a logical sequence of events.

Beginning	first	once
	at first	before
Middle	then	second, third, and so on
	next	later
	in the meantime	earlier
	after	soon
End	finally	subsequently
	at last	in conclusion

Writers can use other time-order transitions throughout a narrative as needed to show relationships among events.

General Time-Order Transitions	about	during	following
	immediately	now	later
	meanwhile	sometimes	previously
	until	today	suddenly
	while	yesterday	when

MY TURN Use transitions to create a clear structure and sequence of events as you draft your personal narrative in your writing notebook.

Revise to Include Important Events

In personal narratives, writers do not include every event from their lives. They leave out irrelevant or uninteresting details and jump forward to the important parts that shape their narrative and message. They use transitions and new paragraphs to guide the reader.

My TURN Revise the paragraph below. Cross out irrelevant details and events. Add transitions and paragraph breaks (using the symbol ¶) to help readers follow along.

> I spent a lot of time getting pledges for our school's field day. On Monday, I got Mrs. James to pledge $1 per foot that I can jump in the long jump. Then I walked the dog and did my homework. On Tuesday, Mr. Fields pledged $2 for every half mile I can run. I helped him pick up leaves in his yard. On Wednesday, at my mom's office, her friend Ellen pledged $1 for every 10 jumps I can do with the jump rope. I was ready to compete on field day. More importantly, I was excited to help raise money for our local food pantry.

My TURN Revise your draft to include only the most relevant and meaningful details and events.

Start a new paragraph to show your readers you are shifting forward in time.

Develop a Conclusion

In the conclusion, a writer sums up his or her personal narrative. The conclusion helps readers focus on why the experiences or events were important to the writer. A conclusion may

- summarize the important events.
- show what the writer learned from the experience.
- teach a lesson or share an insight or message.

My TURN Compose the conclusion of your personal narrative in your writing notebook. Answer the questions to help focus your writing.

How can you sum up the events in your personal narrative?

Why were the events or experiences important to you?

What did you learn, or how did you change as a result of the events?

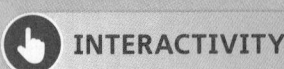

INTERACTIVITY

A POETRY Machine

Use the machine as a key to help you identify parts of the poem.

END RHYME

Rhyming words at the end of two or more lines of poetry

A birdie with a yellow bill . . .
Hopped upon my window-sill . . .

RHYME SCHEME

Pattern of end rhymes in a stanza

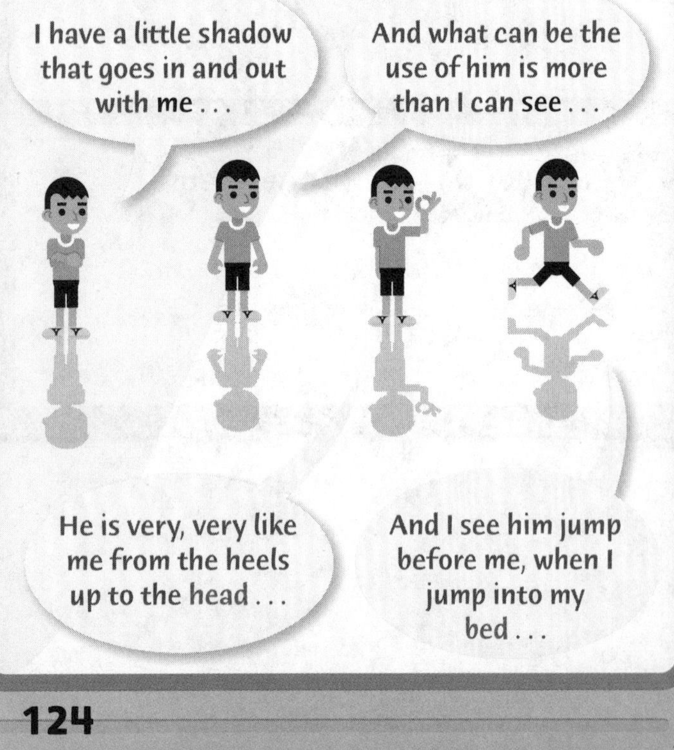
I have a little shadow that goes in and out with me . . .
And what can be the use of him is more than I can see . . .
He is very, very like me from the heels up to the head . . .
And I see him jump before me, when I jump into my bed . . .

INTERNAL RHYME

Rhymes inside a line of poetry

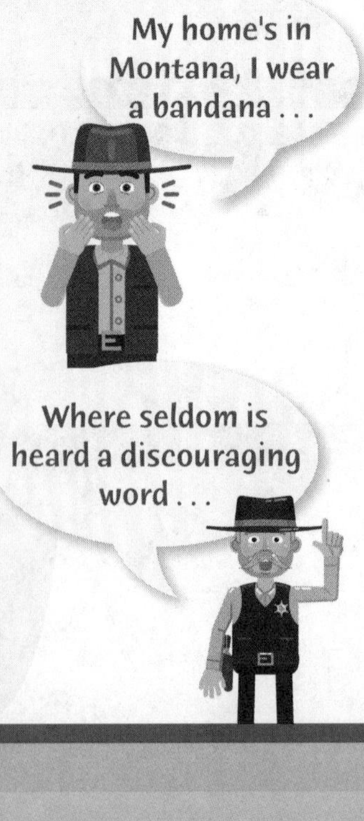
My home's in Montana, I wear a bandana . . .
Where seldom is heard a discouraging word . . .

ONOMATOPOEIA

Words that sound like what they mean

whirring

hissing

zipping

hush

SIMILE

Comparison of unlike things using *like* or *as*

From Florida's **fountains**
to Washington's **mountains** a
With **paddle**, in **saddle**,
adventurers **teem**. b
They **hike**, and they **bike**, and
they follow the footsteps c
Of hundreds of forebears
across field and **stream**. b

Each glistening sliver of light
in the **river** a
Dissolves in the ripples
like stars at **daybreak**. b
We push past the **hush**
of **lush** forested shorelines c
And murmur our thanks
for the journeys we **take**. b

WEEK 4

Weekly Question

What inspires people to start a journey?

TURN and TALK Where would you want to go on a journey? What thoughts and impressions would you include in a poem about your travels? Jot down notes to respond. Then use your notes to tell a partner about your plans.

Learning Goal

I can learn more about the theme *Journeys* by analyzing language in poetry.

Poetry

The words in **poetry** are arranged into lines and express ideas or feelings. They can include:

- **Rhythm**, or a pattern of sounds in language
- **Rhyme,** the repetition of sounds at the ends of words
- **Rhyme scheme,** the repetition of sounds at the ends of lines
- **Sound effects,** including repeated letter sounds and words that imitate sounds
- **Figurative language,** or language that expresses unusual, unexpected meanings

TURN and TALK Describe how poetry is different from informational texts. Use the chart to compare and contrast genres.

Be a Fluent Reader Fluent readers read poetry with accuracy, appropriate rate, and expression. As you read poems, adjust your rate and expression as needed to maintain the poem's rhythm.

When you read poetry aloud:

- Read at a comfortable pace.
- Do not read so quickly that you skip words or lose the poem's rhythm.
- Consider rhyming words, and emphasize words that create rhythm or other sound effects.

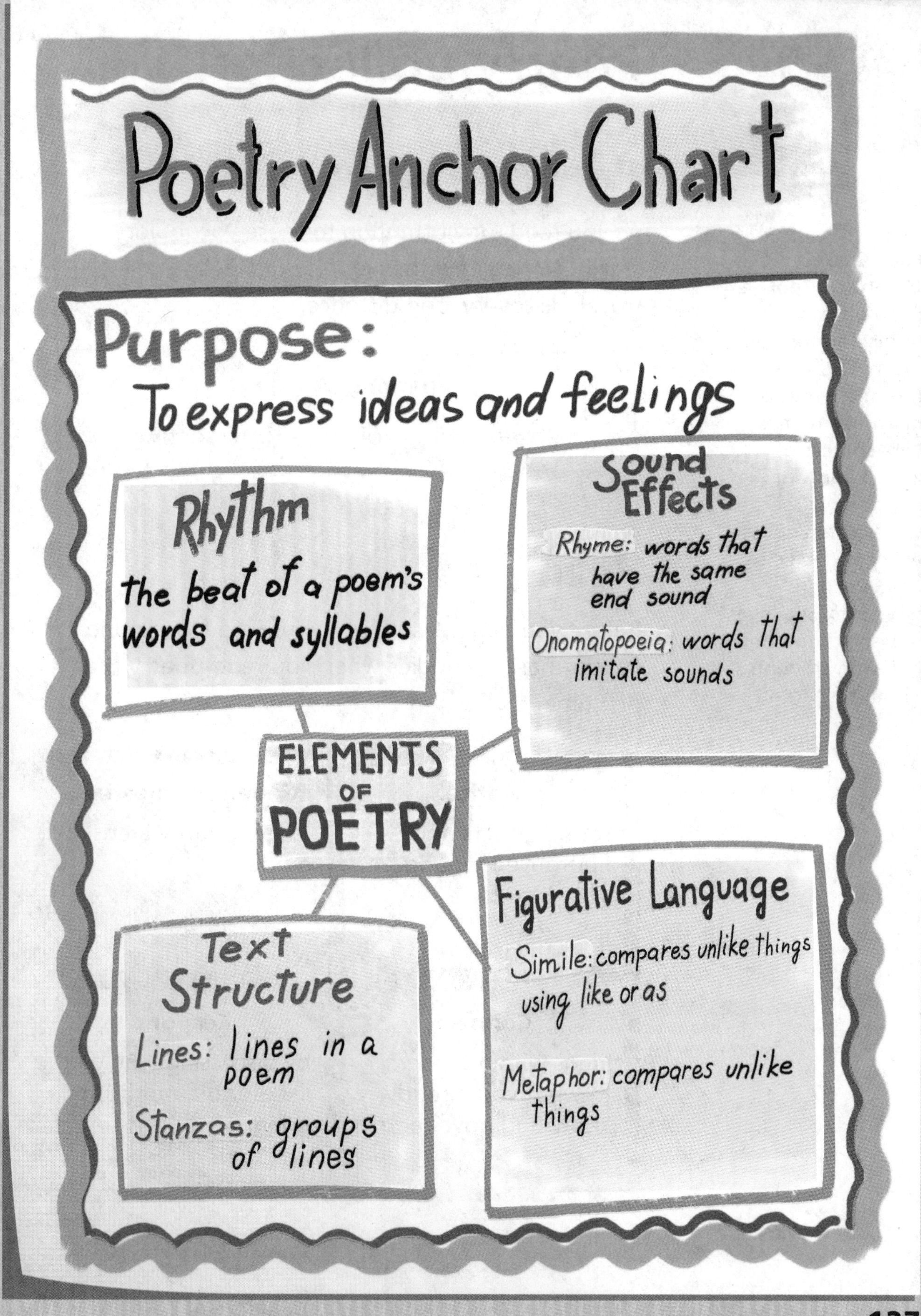
Poetry Anchor Chart
Purpose:
To express ideas and feelings
Rhythm
the beat of a poem's words and syllables
Sound Effects
Rhyme: words that have the same end sound
Onomatopoeia: words that imitate sounds
ELEMENTS OF POETRY
Text Structure
Lines: lines in a poem
Stanzas: groups of lines
Figurative Language
Simile: compares unlike things using like or as
Metaphor: compares unlike things

Meet *the* Author

Poet **Kristine O'Connell George** grew up in a family that moved often. She says that memories of her many homes "are sources of inspiration" for her poetry. George writes often about everyday objects, animals, and moments. She loves to visit schools and talk with students about writing.

Poetry Collection

Preview Vocabulary

As you read, pay attention to these vocabulary words. Notice how they emphasize feelings of travel, discovery, and distance.

peering **via**

traversed **girth** **intersecting**

Read

Before you begin, establish a purpose for reading. Follow these strategies when you read **poetry** the first time.

First Read

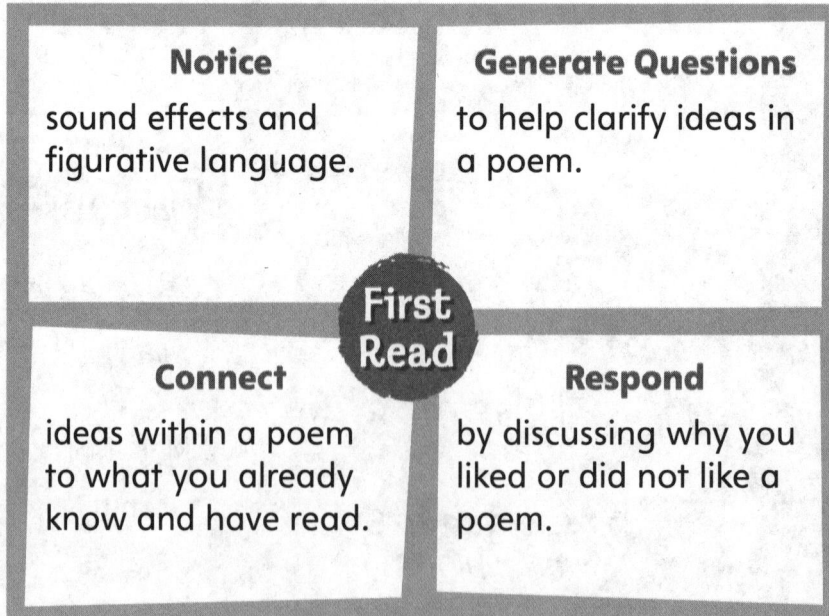

Notice sound effects and figurative language.	**Generate Questions** to help clarify ideas in a poem.
Connect ideas within a poem to what you already know and have read.	**Respond** by discussing why you liked or did not like a poem.

Poetry Collection

Learning the World
by Kristine O'Connell George

Latitude Longitude Dreams
by Drew Lamm and James Hildreth

A Map and a Dream
by Karen O'Donnell Taylor

Early Explorers
by Marilyn Singer

AUDIO

ANNOTATE

Explain Sound Devices

Read the poem aloud.

Underline punctuation that creates rhythm by signaling a quick or long pause. Explain the effect of these pauses.

Visualize

Highlight figurative words and phrases that help you create a mental image of an object the speaker holds.

peering looking closely at something that is hard to see

Learning the World

by Kristine O'Connell George

I'm memorizing oceans,
tracing rivers,
learning mountain ranges.
I'm memorizing capitals,
tracing countries,
learning crops and industries.

I'm smoothing out this map,
rolling it into a tube,
peering through one end,
wishing it were a telescope,
wishing I could see past my street,
wishing I could see
the whole world
spread beneath my feet.

N
W
E
S
Arctic Ocean
Europe
Asia
Africa
Atlantic Ocean
Antarctica
AMERICA
RICA

CLOSE READ

Explain Sound Devices and Figurative Language

Underline words that rhyme. Then underline a metaphor.

via by way of; by means of; through

traversed traveled through; moved across

girth distance around something; circumference

Vocabulary in Context

Context clues are words and phrases around an unfamiliar word that help readers identify the word's meaning.

Underline context clues near the word *traversed* to help you determine its definition.

Latitude Longitude Dreams

by Drew Lamm and James Hildreth

Magellan moved via stars
Steered his ship by celestial rays.
Columbus sailed on over the edge
Discovering lands and waterways.

They traversed their dreams, set their course
Voyaging over oceans and seas.
Etching earth with invisible designs
Crossing rivers, ice, and trees.

These lines that slide from pole to pole
Wrapping around the watery girth
Coordinate all of us on this globe
Our home, our ship, our planet earth.

Explain Sound Devices and Figurative Language

Underline the words that rhyme. Explain the effect of the rhymes.

Then underline the metaphor. Explain the effect of the metaphor.

intersecting crossing or overlapping

Visualize

Highlight words for features you could imagine seeing on a map. Explain how these mental images deepen your understanding of the poem.

A Map and a Dream

by Karen O'Donnell Taylor

Maps are more
than tiny lines
intersecting
lace designs . . .
More than names
and colored dots,
rivers, mountains,
tourist spots.
Maps are keys
to secret places
vast new worlds
and unknown faces.
I can trace each
graceful line . . .
Close my eyes
and in my mind
I can travel
anywhere . . .
A map, a dream
can take me there!

CLOSE READ

Explain Sound Devices

Read the poem aloud.

Underline details that show how the structure of the lines in the poem help create rhythm. Explain how this effect works.

Visualize

Highlight words that help you visualize walking.

Fluency

Reread "Early Explorers." Read at a comfortable pace so you can identify the poem's rhythm. You can pause to sound out an unfamiliar word, if needed.

Early Explorers

by Marilyn Singer

No place on earth
is ever undiscovered
Even in Antarctica
where whole mountains are hidden
under ice
penguins already laid shambling tracks
in the snow
before we traveled there
The hottest desert
the deepest jungle
where none of us have ever been
all have been crossed
and crossed again
by wings whirring or silent
feet furred or scaled
hoofed or bare
By adventurers we will never know
explorers who will never tell us
what wonders they have seen

E
Antarctica

Develop Vocabulary

In poetry, writers use literary language to connect ideas. Literary language is often more vivid and precise than everyday speech. Sometimes literary language is figurative, or nonliteral, as well.

My TURN Complete the sentences to identify the two ideas connected by each vocabulary word.

1. In "Learning the World," **peering** connects
   the speaker
   and the whole world.

2. In "Latitude Longitude Dreams," **via** connects
   ____
   and __________.

3. In "Latitude Longitude Dreams," **traversed** connects
   ____
   with __________.

4. In "A Map and a Dream," **intersecting** connects
   ____
   to __________.

Choose two vocabulary words and describe how the words are connected.

Check for Understanding

MyTURN Look back at the texts to answer the questions.

1. Identify characteristics of the texts that make them poems.

2. Compare how the speakers in the poems describe dreams in "Latitude Longitude Dreams" and "A Map and a Dream."

3. Based on the poems, what conclusion can you draw about how journeys affect people in similar ways?

4. Which poem best describes what it is like to be an explorer? Support your opinion with text evidence.

Explain Sound Devices and Figurative Language

Sound devices, such as rhyme and rhythm, add expression to a poem. Rhyming words have the same end sounds. Poets create rhythm, or a pattern of sounds, with punctuation, line breaks, and stanzas.

Poets also use **figurative language**, or words with meanings other than their literal definitions, to create different meanings. Metaphors, which compare unlike things without using *like* or *as*, are one type of figurative language.

1. **My TURN** Go to the Close Read notes in the poetry collection. Underline words that rhyme, elements that create rhythm, and metaphors.

2. **Text Evidence** Use the parts you underlined to complete the organizer. Give an example of each device and explain its purpose.

Poem with rhymes:

Examples of rhyming words:

Rhyme has the effect of:

Poem with rhythm:

Rhythm is created by:

Rhythm has the effect of:

Poem with a metaphor:

Metaphor compares:

Metaphor has the effect of:

Visualize

Readers visualize, or create **mental images**, based on a poet's word choices. Mental images in each line or stanza work together to deepen the reader's understanding of the poem. Figurative language, sound effects, and precise word choice all help readers visualize ideas in the text.

1. **My TURN** Go back to the Close Read notes and highlight evidence that helps you create mental images.

2. **Text Evidence** Use your highlighted text to help you describe your mental image to complete the chart. Then explain how the images in each stanza of "Latitude Longitude Dreams" help you visualize the poem.

Poem	Word Choice	My Mental Image
"Learning the World"		
"Early Explorers"		

The mental images in each stanza of "Latitude Longitude Dreams" work together by

Reflect and Share

Write to Sources In the poetry collection, several writers describe their thoughts on travel and exploration. What different sound devices and figurative language do they use? Choose two poems you read this week. Then use specific ideas from the texts to write and support a response.

Compare and Contrast Poets use figurative language and sound devices to describe similar topics.

On a separate piece of paper, use a Venn diagram to take notes about the sound devices and figurative language in poems you chose.

- Write about the first poem in the left circle.
- Write about the second poem in the right circle.
- Write what both poems share in the overlapping section.

Use your notes to write a response that compares and contrasts the figurative language and sound devices used to express similar ideas in the poems. Remember to use text evidence to support an appropriate response.

Weekly Question

What inspires people to start a journey?

Academic Vocabulary

Learning Goal

I can develop knowledge about language to make connections between reading and writing.

Figurative language gives words a meaning beyond their literal definition. **Idioms** are phrases or expressions whose meaning cannot be understood from the meanings of the individual words. Idioms can be used to express ideas in a unique or colorful way.

My TURN For each academic vocabulary word,

1. **Read** each idiom.
2. **Match** the word in the box with the idiom that best relates to the word's definition.
3. **Choose** two idioms. Then **write** a sentence that uses the idiom and its related academic vocabulary word.

WORD BANK

insight wandered passage adventure curiosity

IDIOMS

take an interest ______

all over the map ______

one sharp cookie ______

off the beaten path ______

right around the corner ______

______

______

______

______

Suffixes -*able*, -*ible*

A **suffix** is a word part that can be added to the end of a base word. A suffix changes a word's part of speech.

For example, the suffix -*able* changes a verb (*laugh*) into an adjective (*laughable*). The suffixes -*able* and -*ible* both mean "can be done."

MyTURN Read each word containing -*able* or -*ible*. Then write the word's meaning.

Base Word	Meaning
breakable	
collapsible	
likable	
noticeable	
reversible	

High-Frequency Words

High-frequency words are words that you will see in texts over and over again. They often do not follow regular word study patterns. Read these high-frequency words: *touch*, *practice*, *business*, *whose*, *yourself*, *woman*. Try to identify them in your independent reading.

Read Like a Writer

Poets use imagery to help readers create mental images. These images can help an author achieve a specific purpose, such as making the ideas in the poem more vivid and memorable.

Model! Read the lines from "Early Explorers."

> Even in Antarctica / where whole mountains are hidden / under ice / penguins already laid shambling tracks / in the snow

imagery

1. **Identify** The poet creates an image of penguins walking on ice and snow.
2. **Question** How does this image help me understand why "no place on earth is ever undiscovered"?
3. **Conclude** The image helps me imagine a huge place without any people but that is well traveled by animals.

Reread lines 7–10 from "Learning the World."

MyTURN Follow the steps to analyze the poem. Describe how the poet's use of imagery achieves specific purposes.

1. **Identify** The speaker creates an image of
   ______________________________.
2. **Question** How does this image help me understand the speaker?
3. **Conclude** The image of ______________________________
   emphasizes ______________________________
   ______________________________.

Write for a Reader

Writers use elements of craft, such as imagery, to give readers a deeper understanding of their topics. They create powerful images and ideas by choosing strong verbs, precise nouns, and descriptive adjectives and adverbs to describe sensory details.

My TURN Think about how the poets use imagery to help readers create mental images. Now identify how you can use precise word choices to help your readers create vivid mental images.

1. Draw a powerful image you would like to express in words. Illustrating a concept is a meaningful way of interacting with a text.

2. Create the same image in words. Use strong verbs, precise nouns, descriptive adjectives and adverbs, and other sensory details.

Spell Words with *-able, -ible*

When a word includes the word part ***-able* or *-ible***, there are no sound cues to show you which way to spell the word part. Practice writing the words to remember which form to use.

Adding *-able* or *-ible* as a suffix to a base word may require a spelling change. For example, the word *force* drops its *e* and uses the suffix *-ible* to form *forcible*.

MY TURN Read the words. Spell and sort the words by their word parts.

SPELLING WORDS

advisable	compatible	accountable	allowable
noticeable	workable	producible	irritable
admissible	forcible	considerable	combustible
reducible	justifiable	credible	perishable
available	digestible	tangible	edible

-able	-ible

Common, Proper, and Collective Nouns

A **common noun** names a general person, place, thing, or idea. It is usually not capitalized. A **proper noun** names a specific person, place, or organization. It usually begins with a capital letter. A **collective noun** names a group of people, places, or things.

	Common Noun	Proper Noun	Collective Noun
Person	bus driver	Mr. Tsuruda	staff
	singer	Keisha Johnson	choir
Place	school	Austin High School	class
	state	Texas	nation
Thing	cow	Bessie	herd
	star	Polaris	galaxy

My TURN Edit this draft to replace the underlined nouns with nouns mentioned in the parentheses.

In the early sixteenth century, people left the continent (proper) to explore the New World. Columbus, Ponce de León, and Cortés (common) traveled the coasts and interiors of this "new world." At first, the Aztec, Cherokee, and Iroquois (collective) welcomed the visitors. But soon the explorers (proper) were at war with the native peoples.

Use Adjectives

Learning Goal

I can use elements of narrative writing to write a personal narrative.

An **adjective** modifies, or describes, a noun or pronoun. Most adjectives answer the questions *What kind?*, *How many?*, or *Which one?*

Adjectives can compare nouns and pronouns.

Adjective	smart	intelligent	Rule
Comparative Compare 2 things	smarter	more intelligent	Short words: add *-er* Long words: use *more*
Superlative Compare 3 or more things	smartest	most intelligent	Short words: add *-est* Long words: use *most*

Some adjectives have irregular comparative and superlative forms that do not use *more* or *most* or an ending. These words do not follow rules, so authors learn to use the correct forms in their writing; for example, *good, better, best*.

My TURN Complete the sentences. Choose the correct form of each adjective.

1. Luis is the ______________ (good) skier in the state.
2. Even at the ______________ (young) age of fifteen, he has already won all of the ______________ (challenging) races of the year.
3. Luis is ______________ (fast) than Ralph, who was the ______________ (good) skier of last season.

My TURN Edit a draft of your personal narrative for correct forms of comparative and superlative adjectives.

Edit for Adverbs

An **adverb** tells how, when, or where something happens. It can describe a verb, an adjective, or another adverb. Adverbs add detail and description.

They **always** play **outdoors**.

Always and *outdoors* describe *play*.

A **conjunctive adverb** shows a relationship between ideas within a sentence. It can introduce an independent clause, connect two independent clauses, or link sentences with similar ideas.

The team played skillfully all season; **eventually**, they were going to win a game.

In sentences with two independent clauses, the conjunctive adverb is preceded by a semicolon and followed by a comma.

After a near miss, **however**, she finally caught the ball.

In fact, the goalie's last save was really very clever.

In other sentences, commas set off conjunctive adverbs.

My TURN Edit the paragraph below to have correct use of conjunctive adverbs and punctuation.

Sun-Joo studied hard for the exam however, when the day arrived, she worried that she might not remember everything. In contrast Josie was confident that her studying would help her succeed. Both students did well on the exam.

My TURN Edit a draft of your personal narrative to include conjunctive adverbs that create relationships between events. Use correct punctuation.

Edit for Indefinite Pronouns

Indefinite pronouns do not always refer to a specific person or thing. Some common singular indefinite pronouns include *someone, somebody, anyone, anybody, everyone, everybody, no one, nobody,* and *something*. Singular indefinite pronouns need a verb that agrees with singular subjects.

	Indefinite Pronoun	Verb
Someone left a coat at my house.	someone	left

Singular indefinite pronouns must agree with other pronouns.

Incorrect	Correct
Everybody is waiting for **their** score from the judges.	**Everybody** is waiting for **his** or **her** score from the judges.

Some plural indefinite pronouns include *few, several, both, others,* and *many*. Plural indefinite pronouns need a verb that agrees with plural subjects.

	Indefinite Pronoun	Singular or Plural	Verb
Others like the backstroke, but I prefer freestyle.	others	plural	like

MY TURN Edit for subject-verb agreement with each indefinite pronoun.

Everyone in this house need to clean their room. Girls, just look at all these toys on the floor! Many toys belongs in its boxes. Others goes in a closet. Nobody play outside until their room is clean.

MY TURN Edit your personal narrative for indefinite pronouns.

Revise by Adding Ideas for Clarity

After writers draft a narrative text, they reread for ideas or events that are vague, missing, or unclear. They revise by adding ideas to improve word choice.

My TURN Edit the draft to include ideas from the box so the story makes more sense. Only add those ideas that improve the story.

Ideas

younger	**My mom has good ideas.**	**said Mrs. Reyes**
exclaimed	**"I have an idea," Mom smiled.**	**volunteer**

"Mom," I said, "We learned today that it's good to do things to help other people. I decided that I want to help kids learn to read."

"What a fantastic idea!" Mom said.

"I don't know how to get started, though," I said sadly.

The next day after school, Mom and I walked to the second grade classroom and asked Mrs. Reyes if she needed help.

"What a wonderful idea, Emma! They'll think it's great that a big kid wants to read with them.

My TURN Revise a draft of your personal narrative by adding ideas for coherence and clarity. Focus on improving word choice.

Revise by Deleting Ideas for Clarity

After drafting a narrative text, reread to make sure it is clear and coherent. Sometimes this means deleting details that do not develop the setting, people, and events or help the reader understand the situation.

My TURN Read the paragraph below. Revise by deleting details that do not improve the story.

On Saturday morning, Aiden and I woke up early. We brushed our teeth and combed our hair. Then we woke up Dad. "It's time to go to the park!" we shouted as we jumped around. He groaned but eventually got up. My dad usually likes to wake up early. After a quick breakfast, we were finally ready to go. We decided we had spent too much time waiting around. Today wasn't just any day at the park. We were going to join a group of volunteers to pick up trash, plant flowers, and remove weeds. I like planting flowers. Aiden and I couldn't wait to get started.

My TURN Revise a draft of your personal narrative by deleting irrelevant or uninteresting ideas for coherence and clarity.

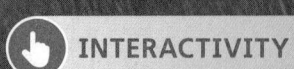

INTERACTIVITY

A PAINTED JOURNEY

View the images. Think about how they show a connection between *who you are* and *where you are*. What message about travel and journeys do the images convey? Consider how the images show the way location affects a person's point of view. Can a location change a person's ideas or feelings? What effects can people have on the places they visit?

United States government poster from the 1930s

'Now for the Painter,' (Rope.) Passengers Going on Board ('Pas de Calais'), 1827, J. M. W. Turner

Rain, Steam, and Speed—The Great Western Railway, 1844, J. M. W. Turner

WEEK 5

Weekly Question

How can new places change the way a person sees the world?

Across the Continent. "Westward the Course of Empire Takes Its Way," 1868, Currier & Ives

The Rail Road Suspension Bridge, Near Niagara Falls, 1856, Currier & Ives

Quick Write Think about a character from literature who visits a new place. How did the visit change him or her? Freewrite about your ideas.

Learning Goal

I can learn more about informational texts by analyzing text structure.

Spotlight on Genre

Informational Text

Text structure refers to the organization of ideas in a text. **Transition words** act as clues to text structure.

The most common text structures in informational text are

- **Chronological,** or time order
  first, then, finally, before, after, until
- **Comparison and Contrast,** similarities and differences *however, as well as, nevertheless*
- **Cause and Effect,** explains what happened and why
  because, thus, due to, therefore, since
- **Problem and Solution,** a conflict and its resolution
  reason, consequently, as a result, so that
- **Description,** details that create mental pictures
  for example, in fact, also, most important

Text structure = organization!

TURN and TALK Think about a book you read recently. How did the author organize the information? Did you notice any clues to text structure while reading? Use the chart to explain the book's text structure to a partner. On a separate sheet of paper, take notes on your discussion.

TEXT STRUCTURES

ANCHOR CHART

CHRONOLOGICAL ORDER

- Shows events or steps in order
- Shows a process or sequence

COMPARISON AND CONTRAST

- Compares two or more things to show similarities
- Contrasts two or more things to show differences

CAUSE AND EFFECT

- Why something happened (cause)
- What happened (effect)

PROBLEM AND SOLUTION

- Identifies a problem or concern
- Suggests possible solutions

DESCRIPTION

- Describes features or traits
- Classifies or categorizes information

Meet *the* Author

Cuban by birth, Swiss-Italian by heritage, and American by choice, **Yanitzia Canetti** has published more than 500 books! For her, writing is like breathing. Travel and art are her passions, too. She almost became an artist, but she was called to writing more.

Picturesque Journeys

Preview Vocabulary

As you read *Picturesque Journeys*, pay attention to these vocabulary words. Notice how they can help you talk and write about art.

inspired **express**
exhibit **imitated** **compositions**

Read

Before you read, **make predictions** about what you will learn in the text based on the text structure and genre. Record your predictions in the chart after the selection. Then follow these strategies as you read this **informational text** the first time.

First Read

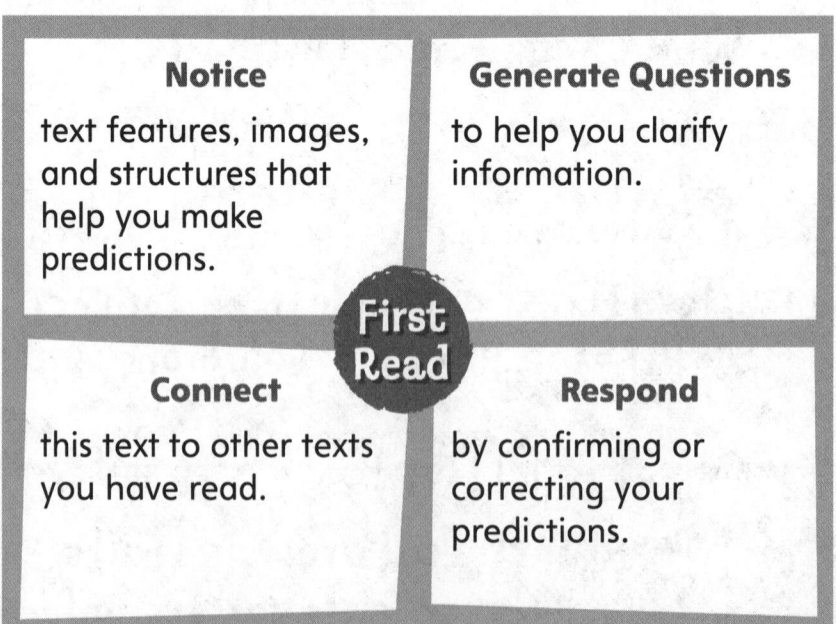

Notice
text features, images, and structures that help you make predictions.

Generate Questions
to help you clarify information.

Connect
this text to other texts you have read.

Respond
by confirming or correcting your predictions.

Genre Informational Text

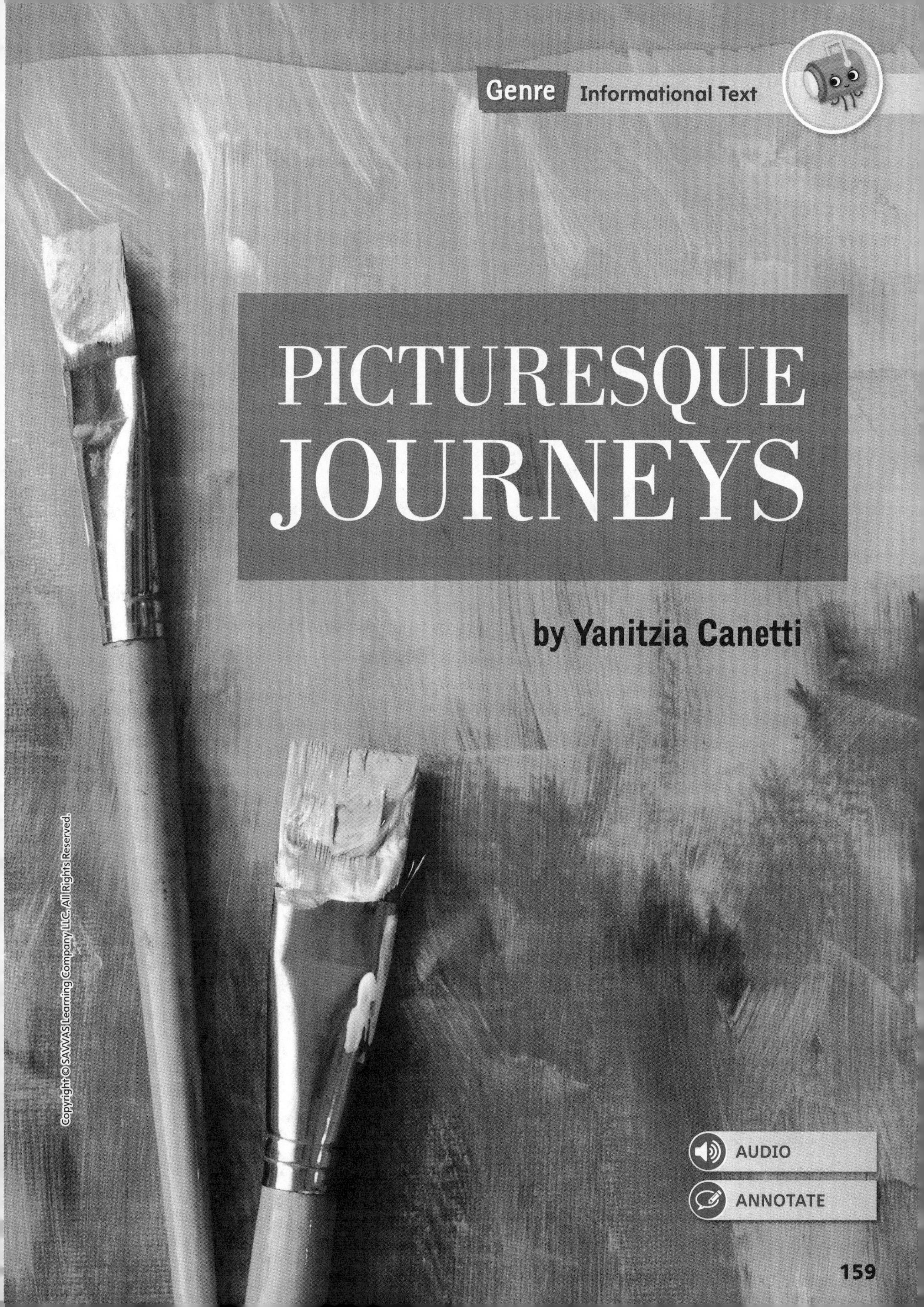

PICTURESQUE JOURNEYS

by Yanitzia Canetti

AUDIO

ANNOTATE

Confirm or Correct Predictions

Highlight the sentence that helps you predict how Kahlo's childhood experiences will affect her work.

inspired caused something to be created

1 Travel to distant places can have a powerful effect on people. This is especially true of artists. As the lives of the three artists featured here show, different locations have inspired some of the world's greatest painters to create their best works.

2 Many paintings by artists Frida Kahlo, Georgia O'Keeffe, and Paul Gauguin were strongly influenced by their journeys. Visiting or living in different places inspired the themes of their works and their colors and painting styles. In their art, these artists captured the landscapes and everyday scenes that inspired their imaginations and affected their art.

3 Frida Kahlo was born in 1907 in the town of Coyoacán, outside Mexico City, Mexico. Her father was Hungarian, and her mother was of Spanish and Mexican Indian descent. Kahlo's diverse background helped define both her identity and her vision of the world.

4 Kahlo showed her determined spirit from an early age. When she was six, she became ill with polio. It made one of her legs thinner and weaker than the other. However, this didn't slow her down. Kahlo still played sports, and she won several swimming competitions.

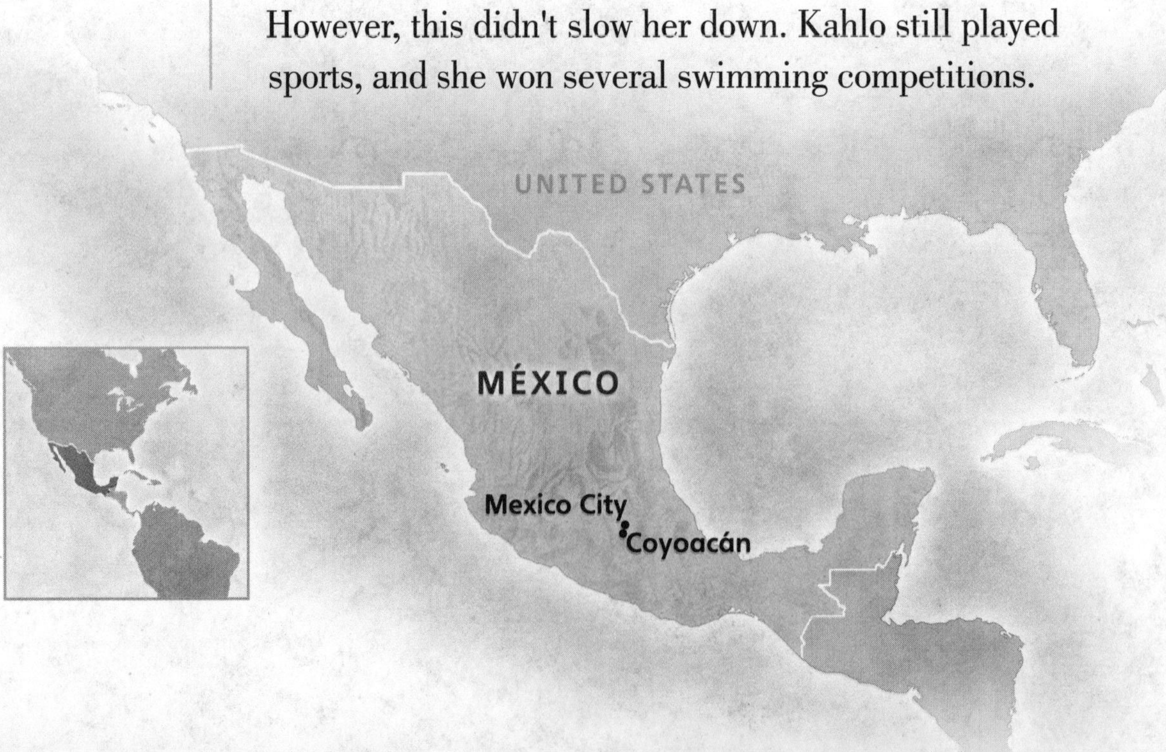

5 At age 18, Kahlo was in a bus crash and was seriously injured. She had to spend many months resting and recovering. Kahlo became bored lying in bed, staring at the ceiling. Her parents decided to give her a box of paints and an easel that she could use in bed. Kahlo began to paint everything she saw in her bedroom. Painting became her daily habit. Because she had a huge mirror in front of her bed, she started to paint images of herself. Kahlo would continue to create self-portraits throughout her life.

CLOSE READ

Analyze Text Structure

Underline the paragraph with a cause-and-effect chain about Kahlo becoming an artist.

6 After she recovered from the accident, Kahlo began going out and about again. One day, she passed by a building where the famous painter Diego Rivera was painting a huge mural. She decided to show Rivera some of her paintings and ask him for his opinion. Rivera agreed to take a look. He told her she was talented. That was the beginning of a long relationship between the two artists. A year after they met, Kahlo and Rivera married. Soon after they moved to the United States.

Self-Portrait with Thorn Necklace and Hummingbird, 1940, Frida Kahlo

Analyze Text Structure

Underline the most important detail in the paragraph. Consider why the author placed this detail where she did.

7 Kahlo and Rivera lived in San Francisco, California. But it was time spent in another American city—Detroit, Michigan—that began to influence Kahlo's paintings. She passed many hours alone in Detroit while Rivera painted murals for a North American company. She found that she greatly missed her homeland of Mexico. So Kahlo began to paint images that related to how she felt. No matter where she went, she painted what she could identify with most: herself.

Self-Portrait Along the Border Line Between Mexico and the United States, 1932, Frida Kahlo

8 Some of Kahlo's paintings contrast her memories of Mexico with the crowded city environment she found herself in. One example is her painting *Self-Portrait Along the Border Line Between Mexico and the United States.* Kahlo contrasts these places by showing herself standing between them. The painting represents her life divided between two worlds. Yet it's clear which world is more important to her.

9 In the painting, Kahlo is wearing a traditional Mexican dress and holding the Mexican flag. The Mexico side of the painting shows a traditional Mexican landscape. It has warm, earthy colors, exotic plants, and pieces of Aztec sculpture and mythology. The United States side shows a landscape dominated by technology. It's painted in dull grays and blues. The U.S. side includes an electrical power generator. In the painting, the generator draws its power from the roots of a plant on the Mexican side. It appears to supply power to the pedestal on which Kahlo is standing.

10 No matter where Kahlo lived, she made paintings that were like visual autobiographies. Every painting tells the story of something remarkable she lived through and how she felt about it. Her facial expressions, her clothing, and the colors and images around her help viewers understand what was happening at that moment in her life and in the world.

CLOSE READ

Vocabulary in Context

Context clues are words and phrases around an unfamiliar phrase that help readers determine the meaning of the phrase.

Underline context clues around the phrase *visual autobiography*. Based on the context clues, determine the phrase's definition.

Confirm or Correct Predictions

Highlight details that confirm or correct predictions you made about how Mexico became an important theme in Kahlo's painting.

Analyze Text Structure

Underline ideas that sum up how Kahlo's artistic style developed and why.

11 Kahlo missed her colorful and warm homeland. That's why in many of her paintings she portrays herself wearing jewelry and surrounded by objects that identify her cultural heritage. Her use of color, too, often expressed her yearning for home, as well as other powerful feelings. Yellow, for example, represents the sun and happiness of Mexico. But in some cases, it also represents illness or fear. Cobalt blue represents electricity and purity. Her paintings often include green, red, and white too. Those are the colors of the Mexican flag.

12 Even though she often lived in cities, Kahlo rarely painted urban scenes. She always preferred to paint the world she dreamed of returning to. Instead of skyscrapers and factory smokestacks, Kahlo painted tropical plants and animals from her homeland. For example, she often included monkeys and parrots in her paintings. These animals represented Mexico's past and present. They also represented Kahlo's dreams of a different life.

13 Much as she missed Mexico, however, Kahlo's travels had a major effect on the art she created. Travel helped her better understand her own identity and develop a distinct artistic style. That style made her one of the world's most famous artists, one who has influenced many others.

14 Like Kahlo, the American artist Georgia O'Keeffe was deeply influenced by her cultural background and her travels.

15 O'Keeffe was born in 1887 in the rural town of Sun Prairie, Wisconsin. Her parents were dairy farmers of Irish and Hungarian backgrounds. O'Keeffe grew up in a farmhouse, surrounded by trees, wildflowers, and grasslands.

16 O'Keeffe was surrounded by a big family, but she was quiet and independent. Growing up, she enjoyed spending long hours observing the natural environment.

17 When she was in eighth grade, O'Keeffe decided to become a painter. She took art lessons and began to focus on flowers as one of her favorite subjects. She was fascinated by their soft colors and irregular forms. This early experience strongly influenced her paintings years later.

Analyze Text Structure

Underline transition words that show the author is comparing two artists.

Analyze Text Structure

Underline places where O'Keeffe traveled that caused changes in her art.

express show or tell thoughts and feelings to others

exhibit a group of artworks or other objects arranged for public viewing

18 After high school, O'Keeffe decided to study painting at the Art Institute of Chicago, in Illinois. After further study in New York, she spent some time as a teacher at West Texas A&M University. There, she first saw the Palo Duro Canyon near Amarillo, Texas. It would become an important landscape in her paintings.

19 O'Keeffe's style and ideas about art took a turn in 1912 when she attended a summer school class at the University of Virginia. There, she was inspired by the ideas of Arthur Wesley Dow, who believed that artists should express themselves using color, lines, and shading. This was very different from the realistic style of painting, known as realism, that O'Keeffe had studied until then.

20 As a result, the young artist found a new way to share her feelings and ideas through her art. In 1915, she began a series of abstract drawings. Abstract art is a painting or other art form that doesn't try to show people, places, or things in a realistic way. The new style of these artworks represented her breakup with realism. Soon she became one of the first American artists to practice a purely abstract style of art.

21 The famous photographer and art gallery owner Alfred Stieglitz saw O'Keeffe's abstract drawings and was very impressed. In 1916, in New York City, Stieglitz opened the first exhibit of O'Keeffe's work. Eventually Stieglitz and O'Keeffe began a personal relationship as well. In 1924, Stieglitz and O'Keeffe were married, and they lived in New York.

Petunias, 1924, Georgia O'Keeffe

22 Living in New York City, O'Keeffe was captivated by skyscrapers. She made these tall buildings the subjects of such paintings as *The Shelton with Sunspots, N.Y.; City Night;* and *Radiator Building—Night, New York.*

23 O'Keeffe spent summers at her husband's family home, in the village of Lake George in the Adirondack Mountains of New York. While there, she began making large-scale paintings of nature at close range, as if she were looking through a magnifying glass. In 1924, she made her first large-scale flower painting, *Petunia, No. 2*. There were many more giant, expressive, and colorful flowers to come.

CLOSE READ

Analyze Text Structure

Underline an effect of living in New York City on O'Keeffe's art.

Red and Yellow Cliffs, 1940, Georgia O'Keeffe

CLOSE READ

Confirm or Correct Predictions

Highlight sentences that confirm or correct a prediction you made about how O'Keeffe's move to the desert will influence her artwork.

24 O'Keeffe's curious nature led her to travel often. In the late 1920s, she became fascinated with the landscapes of the Southwest. In the deserts of New Mexico, she found rough terrain with monumental rocks and animal bones that were partly buried in the arid ground. She also admired the distinct local art and the unique style of adobe architecture. Soon O'Keeffe began to spend almost all of her time in the Southwest. In New Mexico, she felt inspired and felt a new freedom to paint.

25 In 1934, O'Keeffe bought a home in New Mexico, in the desert she so often painted. Then, after 1946, O'Keeffe decided to move to New Mexico permanently.

26 O'Keeffe's famous paintings of New Mexico include *Black Cross, New Mexico* and *Cow's Skull with Calico Roses*. She said of the Southwest, "To me it is the best place in the world."

27 O'Keeffe took many exploratory drives across the Southwest. After one of her trips, she said, "Such a beautiful, untouched, lonely-feeling place. . . . It is a place I have painted before . . . even now I must do it again."

28 O'Keeffe continued traveling and discovering new places. Some of her artworks reflected these journeys. She painted lava bridges in Hawaii, the mountain peaks of Peru, and Mount Fuji in Japan. O'Keeffe was attracted to big, open spaces, so her work often includes paintings of clouds and endless skies.

29 O'Keeffe's paintings were of oversized flowers, cityscapes, rugged landscapes, remote hills, lonely crosses, and images of bones against the desert sky. Through them, O'Keeffe greatly influenced other artists of the twentieth century. Today her paintings can be found in museums all across the country, including one dedicated solely to her work, the Georgia O'Keeffe Museum in Santa Fe, New Mexico.

CLOSE READ

Analyze Text Structure

Underline a sentence that tells how journeys affected what O'Keeffe painted.

O'Keeffe lived and worked in Abiquiú from 1949 to 1984.

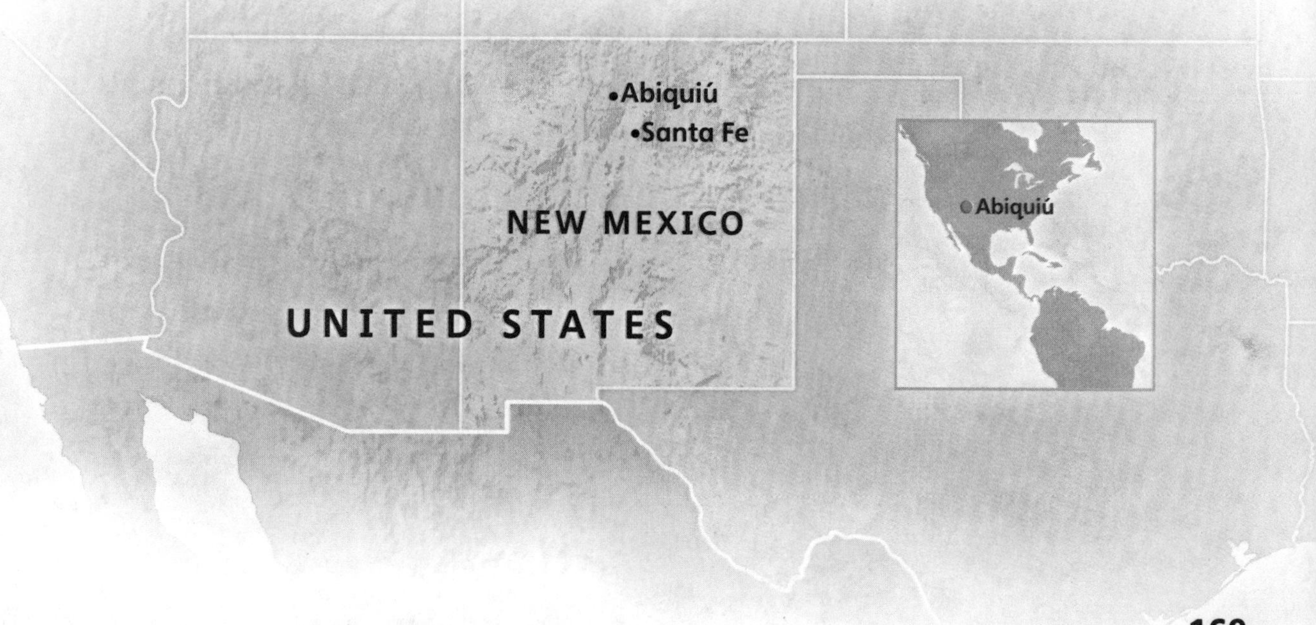

Confirm or Correct Predictions

Highlight the sentence that helps you confirm or correct a prediction you made about how location influenced Gauguin's work.

30 Like both Frida Kahlo and Georgia O'Keeffe, the French artist Paul Gauguin was greatly influenced by his cultural background and travels.

31 Gauguin was born in Paris, France, in 1848. His family left Paris to move to South America while he was still very young. Paul spent his childhood in Lima, Peru, surrounded by South American pottery and other objects that his mother loved. His mother also liked to dress in colorful traditional costumes of Lima. All of these things helped spark Gauguin's interest in art and creativity.

32 When Gauguin was seven, his family moved back to France. Ten years later, he joined the French Merchant Marine, traveling on ships that carry cargo and people from place to place. During this time, Gauguin sailed twice to Brazil. He discovered that he loved traveling and learning about other cultures. These passions would become important parts of his life and art.

33 After working for the Merchant Marine, Gauguin returned to France. He started a new way of life. He got a job as a stockbroker and married a Danish woman named Mette Gad. In 1873, he began painting as a hobby. He quickly showed great talent, and his paintings were displayed in major art shows.

34 In 1882, the stock market crashed in France, and Gauguin lost his job. He decided to take the risk of becoming a full-time painter. He moved to Brittany, in the north of France.

35 Gauguin felt that many French artists imitated each other rather than trying to create something new and different. He didn't want to imitate anyone. In Brittany, he started to move away from the Impressionist style that was so popular at the time. Impressionist art often used pastel colors and focused on the effects of light. Gauguin instead started painting scenes of Brittany's countryside in bold colors, with strong lines.

36 Sparked by Europe's growing interest in other cultures, especially Japanese culture, Gauguin continued to experiment in his own painting. He also began to travel outside France again, to find new inspiration for his art.

37 In 1887, after a brief trip to Panama, Gauguin visited the island of Martinique, in the Caribbean. The beauty of the Caribbean landscape amazed him. He also became friendly with people on the island. As the result of this experience, he started to include both tropical landscapes and symbols in his artwork. *Martinique Landscape* and *Among the Mangoes* are two of the paintings that Gauguin created during his stay on the Caribbean island. After he left the island, he used sketches he made in Martinique as the basis of many more paintings. The people of Martinique remained a popular subject in his artworks.

CLOSE READ

Analyze Text Structure

Underline what happened to Gauguin's art because of his journey to Martinique.

imitated copied; tried to do the same things others did

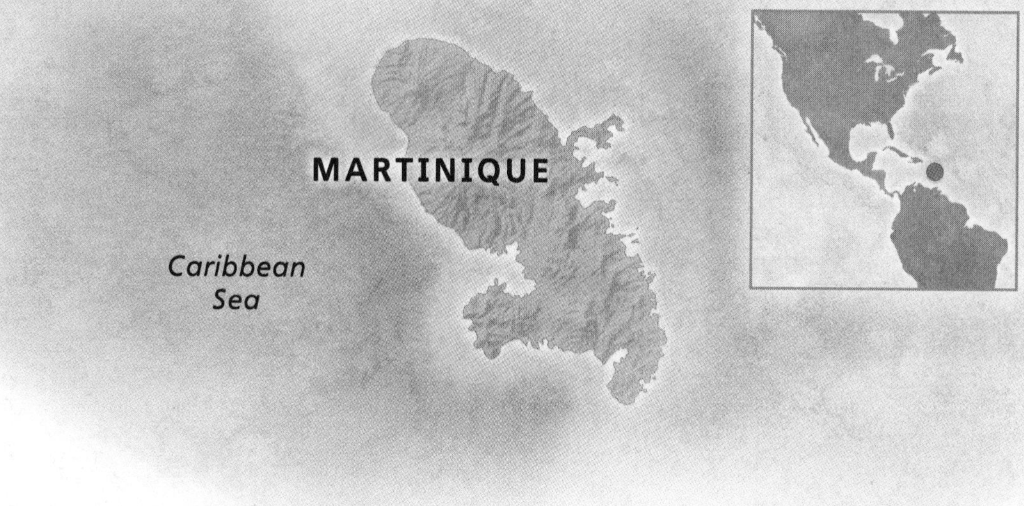

Analyze Text Structure

Underline the place Gauguin traveled to and the effect it had on his art.

38 Gauguin was eager to find another exotic destination that would inspire his creativity. He was tired of European culture. He found it artificial and dull. In 1892, he decided to sail for the island of Tahiti, also known as French Polynesia, in the South Pacific. He left his old life behind. He thought that this Polynesian island might offer him personal and creative freedom. He moved into a bamboo hut and started to paint the scenery and people of Tahiti. Along with new subjects, he experimented with new techniques and formats.

39 "I am leaving in order to have peace and quiet, to be rid of the influence of civilization," he wrote at the time. "I want only to do simple, very simple art. . . ."

compositions works of art, such as paintings and songs

40 Gauguin was fascinated by the strength and simplicity of art from Africa, Asia, and Latin America. In Tahiti, he strived to use these qualities in his own artworks. He used vivid colors and simple compositions to paint the tropical environment. Gradually, he began to focus more on the Tahitian people themselves. He painted many scenes of Tahitians doing everyday tasks, such as weaving baskets.

41 Gauguin also was inspired by the history and the stories of the Pacific Islands. He began to add elements of these stories, such as religious symbols, to his paintings. His style began to break away more and more from the traditions of European art. Soon, Gauguin's use of colors and lines was like no one else's.

Comings and Goings, Martinique (Allées et Venues), 1887, Paul Gauguin

42 Gauguin not only used intense, bright colors to reflect the landscape of the Polynesian Islands, but he also used colors with great freedom. For example, he painted grass red if he felt it should be red.

43 Near the end of his life, Gauguin moved to the more remote Marquesas Islands in the Pacific. He continued painting there until his death in 1903.

44 Gauguin had a huge influence on modern art. He inspired artists such as Vincent van Gogh, Henri Matisse, and Pablo Picasso, among others. Today he is known for his unique style and technique, as well as for his experiments with color, all of which were strongly affected by the places he visited and lived.

45 Frida Kahlo, Georgia O'Keeffe, and Paul Gauguin are among the many artists whose works have been influenced by their journeys. It is impossible to imagine how different these artists' lives, and art, would have been if they had never traveled.

CLOSE READ

Analyze Text Structure

Underline a reason Gauguin painted as he did.

Develop Vocabulary

In informational text, authors use domain-specific words that help tell about their topic or subject. In *Picturesque Journeys*, these words help readers learn about art and artists.

My TURN Find each word in context in *Picturesque Journeys*. Complete the chart to explain how each word relates to a cause or effect for the artists.

Word	Cause or Effect in Context
inspired	Journeys caused, or inspired, the themes, colors, and styles of the artists.
express	
exhibit	
imitated	
compositions	

Check for Understanding

My TURN Look back at the text to answer the questions.

1. How do you know *Picturesque Journeys* is an informational text?

2. A symbol is something that represents something else. What symbolism does the author explain in Kahlo's *Self-Portrait Along the Border Line Between Mexico and the United States*?

3. Summarize the text, listing the main ideas in order.

4. Synthesize information to compare and understand Kahlo's, O'Keeffe's, and Gauguin's styles.

N N

Analyze Text Structure

Text structure refers to the organization of a text. Authors may organize informational texts by putting the most important point first and supporting it with details, or by building to the most important point at the end.

Authors may also use structures such as cause and effect, problem and solution, or chronological order. Text structures help readers understand how information and ideas are related. A cause-and-effect text structure shows how facts, events, or ideas happen because of other facts, events, or ideas.

1. **My TURN** Go to the Close Read notes in *Picturesque Journeys*. Underline the parts that help you understand how different locations influence each artist's works.

2. **Text Evidence** Use the parts you underlined to complete the chart.

Artist	CAUSE: Place	EFFECT: How Place Affected Art
	Southwest	
	Her own bedroom	
	Tahiti	

Confirm or Correct Predictions

Before reading, readers preview the text to identify clues using structure, such as headings, sidebars, and captions, and genre, such as central ideas and details. They **make predictions,** or guesses, about the text. After reading, readers **confirm** that their predictions were correct.

1. **My TURN** Go back to the Close Read notes and highlight evidence that confirms or corrects the predictions you made before reading.
2. **Text Evidence** Use your highlighted text to confirm or correct the predictions you made about each artist.

My Predictions

1. **Kahlo:**
2. **O'Keeffe:**
3. **Gauguin:**

Text Evidence

1. **Kahlo:**
2. **O'Keeffe:**
3. **Gauguin:**

Confirmed or Corrected

1. **Kahlo:**
2. **O'Keeffe:**
3. **Gauguin:**

Reflect and Share

Talk About It Consider the texts you read this week. What places did you learn about? How do you think these places affect people's lives? Use these questions to prepare a presentation that gives your opinion about how traveling to different places can influence people.

Give a Short Presentation Before you begin your presentation, gather information to support your opinion. First, on a separate piece of paper, write a claim, or opinion statement. Then choose two or three texts. Record direct quotations from the texts that support your opinion statement. Be sure to include the name of the text, the author, and the page number.

Use these sentences to prepare for your presentation:

I think that ______________________________. Evidence from ____________________ says that ______________.

When giving your presentation,

- **speak** at a natural rate and volume.
- **speak** clearly and enunciate.
- **make eye contact** with the audience.
- **support** your opinion with specific facts and ideas from the text that are important to meaning.

Weekly Question

How can new places change the way a person sees the world?

Academic Vocabulary

Learning Goal

I can develop knowledge about language to make connections between reading and writing.

Parts of speech are categories of words. The way a word functions in a sentence determines its part of speech. A **noun** names a person, place, or thing. A **verb** shows a physical or mental action. An **adjective** describes a person, place, or thing.

My TURN For each item,

1. **Read** the sample sentence.
2. **Identify** the underlined academic vocabulary word's part of speech.
3. **Write** your own sentence using a synonym of the academic vocabulary word.

Sample Sentence	Part of Speech	My Sentence
José offered an unusual <u>insight</u> about bus safety.	noun	The detective shared her understanding of what happened.
Colin took his time as he <u>wandered</u> through the market.		
Shelley noticed the <u>passage</u> between the two rooms.		
Brinda planned a thrilling <u>adventure</u> for her next holiday.		

VCe Syllables

VCe syllables are syllables that contain a vowel, a consonant, and the letter *e*. When the VCe syllable appears at the end of a word, usually the first vowel has a long vowel sound, and the *e* is silent.

The word *imitate* in paragraph 35 of *Picturesque Journeys* has a VCe pattern of *a-t-e*. The *e* is silent, so the *a* has the long *a* sound, as in *date*.

My TURN Read the words from *Picturesque Journeys*. Then complete the chart by sorting each word by the sound of its VCe syllable.

Word Bank

institute	**became**	**remote**	**include**
create	**define**	**countryside**	**landscape**

Vowel Sound	Word Ending in VCe
long *a*	
long *i*	
long *o*	
long *u*	

Read Like a Writer

Figurative language helps authors achieve specific purposes, such as expressing ideas in imaginative ways. One example is a simile, which uses *like* or *as* to make a comparison between unlike things.

Model! Read the text about Frida Kahlo from *Picturesque Journeys*.

> No matter where Kahlo lived, she made paintings that were like visual autobiographies.

1. **Identify** Yanitzia Canetti uses a simile to describe Kahlo's paintings.
2. **Question** How does this figurative language help me understand Kahlo's work?
3. **Conclude** The simile helps me understand how personal Kahlo's paintings were.

Read the text about Georgia O'Keeffe.

> While there, she began making large-scale paintings of nature at close range, as if she were looking through a magnifying glass.

My TURN Follow the steps to analyze the passage. Describe how the author uses figurative language to achieve specific purposes.

1. **Identify** Yanitzia Canetti uses a simile to ______________________________

____

2. **Question** How does this help me understand O'Keeffe's work?
3. **Conclude** The simile helps me understand ______________________________

____

Write for a Reader

Figurative language helps readers think about ideas in new ways. Often, authors use similes and metaphors to draw interesting comparisons between unlike things. A metaphor, like a simile, compares ideas or objects, but it does not use *like* or *as*.

My TURN Think about how Yanitzia Canetti uses figurative language in *Picturesque Journeys*. How do the similes and metaphors she uses affect you as a reader? How do they affect your experience and understanding of the text? Now identify ways you can use figurative language to help readers better understand your own writing.

1. How could you use a simile or metaphor to clarify an idea about travel?

2. Write a short informational paragraph about a journey you have taken. Use figurative language, including similes and metaphors, to help readers understand your ideas.

Spell Words with VCe Syllables

VCe syllables can appear at the end of words. In most cases, the first vowel sound is long, and the *e* at the end is silent.

My TURN Read the words. Spell and sort them by the long vowel sound in the last syllable.

SPELLING WORDS

evaporate	elevate	coincide	oppose
improvise	intervene	delete	excavate
remote	devastate	serene	appetite
obsolete	liberate	centigrade	prosecute
evacuate	schedule	provoke	negotiate

long *a*	long *e*	long *i*	long *o*	long *u*

Regular and Irregular Plural Nouns

Plural nouns name more than one person, place, thing, or idea. **Regular plural nouns** are formed by adding *-s* or *-es*. Sometimes spelling changes, such as changing *y* to *i*, are needed before you add *-es*. **Irregular plural nouns** may take the same form as the singular noun or may require spelling changes.

Type	How to Form Plurals	Examples of Plurals
regular	+ s	*restaurants, valleys, lips*
regular	+ es	*lunches, dishes, cities*
irregular	same form as singular	*deer, sheep, series*
irregular	change spelling	*men, teeth, mice*

My TURN Edit this draft by choosing singular nouns in the paragraph and changing them to plural nouns. If the plural form of the noun is the same as its singular form, highlight it. Spell each word correctly.

Georgia O'Keeffe was one of the most influential woman in American art. She worked in many different style of painting during her career. She attended several university. After a summer school class, O'Keeffe created a series of different drawing. She also made large-scale canvas of flower and landscape of the Southwest.

Revise by Rearranging and Combining Ideas

Learning Goal

I can use elements of narrative writing to write a personal narrative.

When writers revise drafts, they **rearrange** ideas that are out of order. They **combine** ideas to show that they are related. They also change words and combine ideas to improve word choice. These changes help make writing coherent, or clear and logical.

My TURN Read the paragraph. Then follow the steps.

1. Rearrange the ideas in the paragraph so that the order makes sense.
2. Combine ideas to show relationships and improve how the writing sounds.
3. Rewrite the text on the lines.

My Visit to the Aquarium

We arrived at the aquarium. There were many things to see. We saw fish from the Amazon. My favorite thing was watching a beluga whale swim underwater. We saw fish from the Caribbean. We saw fish from the Arctic.

____

____

____

____

____

My TURN Revise a draft of your personal narrative by rearranging and combining ideas so your writing is clear and makes sense. Focus on improving word choice.

Edit for Subject-Verb Agreement

Writers edit to make sure their sentences are complete, or have at least one subject and one verb. They also use **simple and compound sentences.**

A happy dog	This fragment has only a subject.
Jumps up and down	This fragment has only a verb.
Maisy is a happy dog.	This complete simple sentence has one subject and one verb.
Maisy is a happy dog, so she jumps up and down.	This complete compound sentence has two independent clauses, each with a subject and a verb.

The subject and verb of a sentence must work together, or **agree.**

The dog jumps into the pool to save the boy. singular subject, singular verb

The dogs jump into the pool to save the boy. plural subject, plural verb

A compound subject needs a verb that works with a plural subject.

The sister and brother love their dog Sadie. compound subject, plural verb

My TURN Edit the paragraph for complete sentences with subject-verb agreement.

> Jorge and I spends the morning easing our way up the cliff. Each hold in the rocks appear so clearly that it seem as if the whole mountain of stones are urging us on. When we makes the summit. We each eats a snack, and we surveys the world. Only the mountain and the sky is our company.

My TURN Edit your personal narrative for subject-verb agreement. Use a variety of complete simple and compound sentences to add interest.

Publish and Celebrate

When a writer finishes writing, he or she publishes it so others can read it. To publish your work, share it publicly with your class.

My TURN Answer the questions about your writing experience. Write legibly, or clearly, in cursive so that others can easily read what you write.

The best personal narrative I wrote was

____

____

____

____.

My favorite line of dialogue was

____

____

____

____.

I would like to keep writing personal narratives because

____

____

____

____.

The next time I write a personal narrative, I will

____

____

____.

Prepare for Assessment

My TURN Follow a plan as you prepare to write a personal narrative in response to a test prompt.

1. **Relax.**
   Take a deep breath.

2. **Make sure you understand the prompt.**
   Read the prompt. Underline what kind of writing you will do. Highlight the topic you will be writing about.

   Prompt: Write a personal narrative essay about an experience in which you found a creative way to work with someone whose background is different than yours.

3. **Brainstorm.**
   List three personal experiences you could write about.
   Highlight your favorite.

4. **Plan out events in your personal narrative.**
   Pick the most interesting experience. Then put the events describing it in order.

5. **Write your draft. Remember to include an introduction and a conclusion.**
   Use your own paper to write your essay.

6. **Revise and edit your personal narrative.**
   Read your essay again to yourself. Check for subject-verb agreement when you use compound subjects and indefinite pronouns.

Assessment

My TURN Before you write a personal narrative for your assessment, rate how well you understand the skills you have learned in this unit. Go back and review any skills you mark "No."

IDEAS AND ORGANIZATION	Yes!	No
I can brainstorm an engaging idea.	☐	☐
I can include and develop important people in my narrative.	☐	☐
I can describe a setting.	☐	☐
I can organize the events of my narrative.	☐	☐
I can write an introduction and conclusion.	☐	☐
CRAFT		
I can include specific facts and details.	☐	☐
I can use descriptive language.	☐	☐
I can write dialogue between people.	☐	☐
I can use transitions to show time order.	☐	☐
I can add, delete, rearrange, and combine ideas for clarity and sense.	☐	☐
CONVENTIONS		
I can include adjectives and adverbs to add detail.	☐	☐
I can use indefinite pronouns correctly.	☐	☐
I can edit for subject-verb agreement.	☐	☐

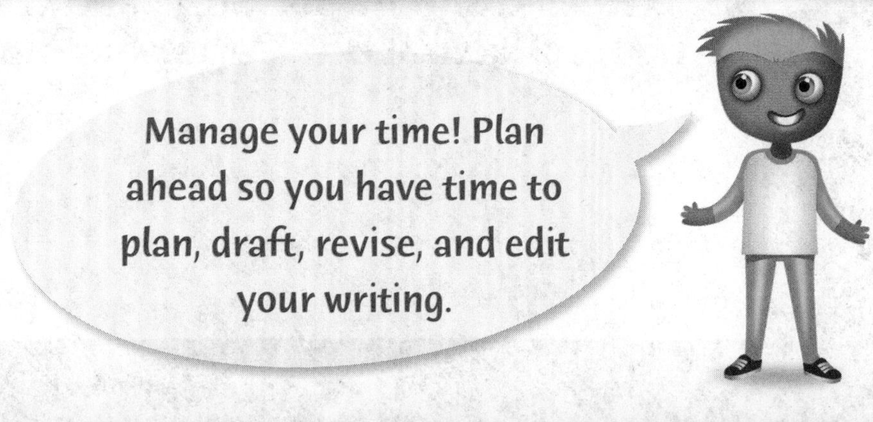
Manage your time! Plan ahead so you have time to plan, draft, revise, and edit your writing.

UNIT THEME

Journeys

TURN and TALK **CONNECT TO THEME** In this unit, you learned many new words to talk about *Journeys*. With a partner, go back to each selection and find a sentence that best illustrates the meaning of an academic vocabulary word. Explain why that word fits that quotation.

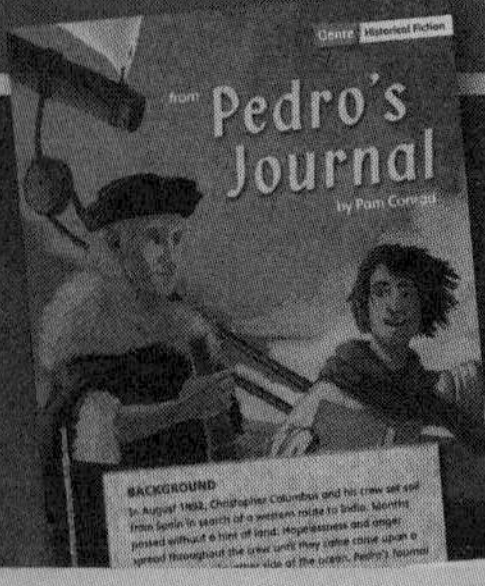

WEEK 3

from **Pedro's Journal**

WEEK 2

from **Life on Earth—and Beyond**

BOOK CLUB

BOOK CLUB

WEEK 1

"The Path to Paper Son" and **"Louie Share Kim, Paper Son"**

BOOK CLUB

WEEK 4

Poetry Collection

BOOK CLUB

WEEK 5

Picturesque Journeys

Essential Question

My TURN
In your notebook, answer the Essential Question: How do journeys change us?

BOOK CLUB

Project

WEEK 6

Now it is time to apply what you learned about Exploration in your **WEEK 6 PROJECT: Hit the Road!**

HiT the ROAD!

RESEARCH

Activity

Choose a country you would like to visit. Research the culture, language, holidays, food, currency, transportation, and other characteristics that make this country an exciting travel destination. Write a travel guide to convince others that it is the best country to visit. Include a map and facts about your chosen country.

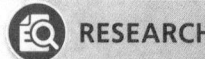

Research Articles

With your partner, read "Culture Shock" to generate questions you have about the topic. Make a research plan for writing your travel guide. A research plan involves generating questions, stating a claim, researching, writing, revising, editing, and presenting. Share responsibilities with your partner.

1. **Culture Shock**
2. **All Aboard!**
3. **Ellis Island: The Immigrant Journey**

Generate Questions

COLLABORATE Read "Culture Shock," and generate three questions you have about the article. Discuss your questions with a partner. Answer any you can before sharing them with the class.

1. ______________________________

2. ______________________________

3. ______________________________

Use Academic Words

COLLABORATE In this unit, you learned many words related to the theme of *Journeys*. Work with your partner to add more academic vocabulary words to each category. If appropriate, use this vocabulary when you write your travel guide.

Academic Vocabulary	Word Forms	Synonyms	Antonyms
insight	insightful insightfully uninsightful	understanding perception intuition	density dullness obtuseness
wandered	wander wandering wanderer	strayed roamed rambled	stayed remained settled
passage	passageway passenger passaging	pathway route road	block barrier obstacle
adventure	adventurer adventuring adventurous	trip experience exploit	bore safety inaction
curious	curiously curiousness curiosity	interested inquisitive questioning	uninterested indifferent incurious

Make a Statement

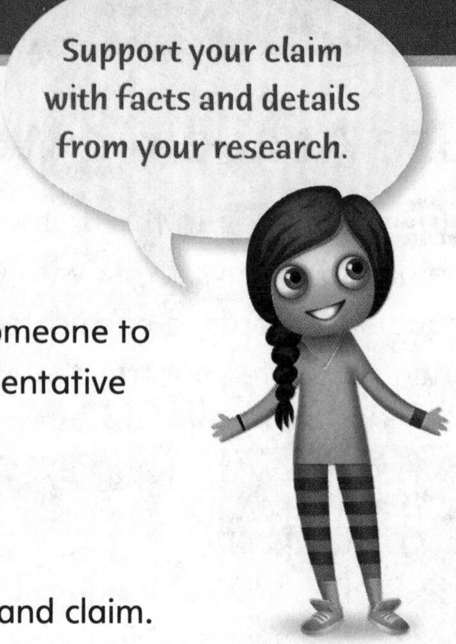

Support your claim
with facts and details
from your research.

People write argumentative texts to persuade someone to think or act a certain way. When reading argumentative texts, recognize and identify

- the claim,
- reasons that support the claim, and
- evidence, such as facts, to support the reasons and claim.

RESEARCH

COLLABORATE With your partner, read "All Aboard!" Then answer the questions about the text.

1. What is the author's claim, or opinion?

2. What reasons does the author include to convince readers?

3. What facts or details does the author use to support each reason?

Plan Your Research

COLLABORATE Follow your research plan's steps in order. Use the activity to help you write a claim and research evidence for your argumentative brochure.

Definition	Examples
CLAIM A claim is a statement that tries to persuade or convince a reader to agree with an opinion. A claim • defines a goal • is specific • is supported with evidence Read the examples in the right column. Then, with your partner, write a claim that persuades others to visit the country you chose.	One statement is an effective claim, and one is not. • You should visit the state of Ohio. No • You should visit Ohio for its beautiful lakes and forests as well as its thrilling amusement parks. Yes! My claim:
EVIDENCE You can support your claim with evidence, such as • facts • statistics • quotations • examples	**Fact:** One of the most popular treats in Ohio is buckeye candy. **Statistic:** Ohio's population is about 11.6 million people. **Quote:** "Ohio has just one national park," wrote Ann Smith. **Example:** Ohio is known for its attractions, such as the Rock and Roll Hall of Fame in Cleveland.

With your partner, list some possible options for researching evidence for your brochure about another country.

EXPLORE the Sites

A **navigation toolbar** is a feature of many Web sites used to identify and gather relevant information. A **site map** is a page that lists all the pages on a Web site. Using information from a variety of sources helps make your research complete, interesting, and accurate.

EXAMPLE Arya's family is planning a trip. She searches online for information. She visits Ohio's state government Web site. How can she find pages that will answer her research questions?

Visit Ohio

Dining   Tourism & Recreation

- Activities & Attractions
- Parks & Preserves
- Boating & Waterways
- Maps

The blue navigation toolbar at the top of the home page provides menus of links to popular topics, such as "Tourism and Recreation." Clicking on the menus will allow you to choose a topic, such as "Activities & Attractions."

Activities & Attractions

There is so much to see and do in Ohio. Stroll through historic neighborhoods, enjoy world-class exhibits at awe-inspiring museums, soar through emerald forests on a thrilling zipline adventure. Exploring the links on this page can help you plan a great visit!

Historic sites
Museums
Scenic rivers
Bike trails
State Parks
Forests
Hiking trails
Zipline adventures

A smaller navigation toolbar on the right side of the home page provides links for tourists, such as "State Parks."

Home | News | Features | Forms | Site Map | Contact Us

The "Site Map" link at the bottom of the page will take you to a list of the pages on the Web site. It is organized in a user-friendly way.

COLLABORATE With your partner, go online to research the country you chose. Share responsibilities. Use the navigation toolbar and the site map to find a variety of sources. Take notes on your research, and review the notes together to make sure you understand what you have read.

Evaluate your information. Make sure it is not only relevant but credible. Is the author an expert? Is the information current, accurate, and from reputable sources? If not, you need to keep searching.

Web site:

How I navigated this Web site:

How I evaluated the credibility of the information:

Web site:

How I navigated this Web site:

How I evaluated the credibility of the information:

Were you able to find current, accurate, and credible information? Explain the credibility of your sources to your partner.

Appeal to Your Audience

People write argumentative texts to convince others to think or do something based on a claim. Your travel guide should make a claim about the country you chose. It should include supporting evidence to convince others to visit the country.

Before you begin writing, decide on the audience for your travel guide. The audience you chose will determine the way in which you write your guide. Will it appeal to

- students?
- adults?
- families with children?
- senior citizens?
- experienced travelers?
- people new to traveling?

COLLABORATE Read the Student Model. Work with your partner to recognize the characteristics of argumentative writing.

Now You Try It!

Discuss the checklist with your partner. Work together to follow the steps as you write your persuasive travel guide.

Make sure your argumentative guide

- [ ] states a specific claim, or opinion.
- [ ] supports that claim with specific reasons.
- [ ] supports each reason with facts from your sources.
- [ ] organizes information in a logical way.
- [ ] appeals to the audience or reader you chose.

Student Model

Visit Ohio!

If you are looking for a fun state to visit with your parents, Ohio is your best bet. It has beautiful forests, exciting cities, thrilling amusement parks, and many activities that appeal to students. There is something for everyone! Once you visit this state, you will understand its tourism motto: "Ohio. Find It Here."

Underline the writer's claim, or opinion.

Highlight a reason for the claim.

Check out each section for more about Ohio:

- National Monuments and Parks (Cuyahoga Valley)
- State Parks (Hocking Hills State Park)
- Sports and Recreation (Ohio State Football)
- Arts, History, and Culture (Cleveland Museum of Art, Rock & Roll Hall of Fame)
- Family Activities (Columbus Zoo and Aquarium, Cedar Point Amusement Park)
- Restaurants and Shops (2nd Street Market, Dayton)

Underline one fact or detail that supports the reason you highlighted. Tell your partner how it supports the writer's argument.

Highlight a detail that reveals the intended audience.

*** FUN FACT ***

One of the most popular treats in Ohio is the buckeye, a candy modeled after the nuts that fall from buckeye trees.

In Your Own Words!

When you write, you must avoid plagiarizing your sources, or copying and using an author's words as if they are your own. To avoid plagiarism, quote or paraphrase your sources in ways that maintain meaning and logical order, and include citations.

Quoting is using an author's exact words. Include quotation marks around the words. Cite the author's name to give him or her credit.

> "Ohio has just one national park," wrote Elena Vargas. "Cuyahoga Valley National Park, near Cleveland, winds along the Cuyahoga River."

Quoting

Paraphrasing is putting information into your own words.

> Ohio's only national park, Cuyahoga Valley National Park, is located in the Cleveland area. The Cuyahoga River runs through the park.

Paraphrasing

RESEARCH

COLLABORATE Read "Ellis Island: The Immigrant Journey." Identify a fact from the article. Show how you would quote and paraphrase this fact.

Fact from article	
Quote the fact	
Paraphrase the fact	

COLLABORATE Read the paragraph and answer the questions.

Ohio's State Parks: A Big Draw for Tourists

by Suzanne Phelps

Ohio is a state with abundant natural beauty. Visitors will find a variety of state parks from which to choose. Central Ohio boasts Buckeye Lake State Park, where people can hike, boat, and camp. Northeast Ohio has Headlands Beach State Park, located on the shores of Lake Erie. Visitors can swim, build sandcastles, fish from the breakwall, or picnic on the sand. Southwest Ohio has Caesar Creek State Park. Visitors there can enjoy the mountain bike and bridle trails and try their hand at archery.

1. Quote a sentence from the paragraph and cite the author.

2. Paraphrase, or restate, the sentence that you quoted. Do not plagiarize by using the author's own words.

3. Is this an example of plagiarism, quoting, or paraphrasing? Explain.

"Central Ohio boasts Buckeye Lake State Park, where people can hike, boat, and camp."

Write a Business Letter

One way to research a topic is to ask an expert for information. You can interview the expert in person, or you can write an email or a letter like the one below, asking for formal answers to your questions.

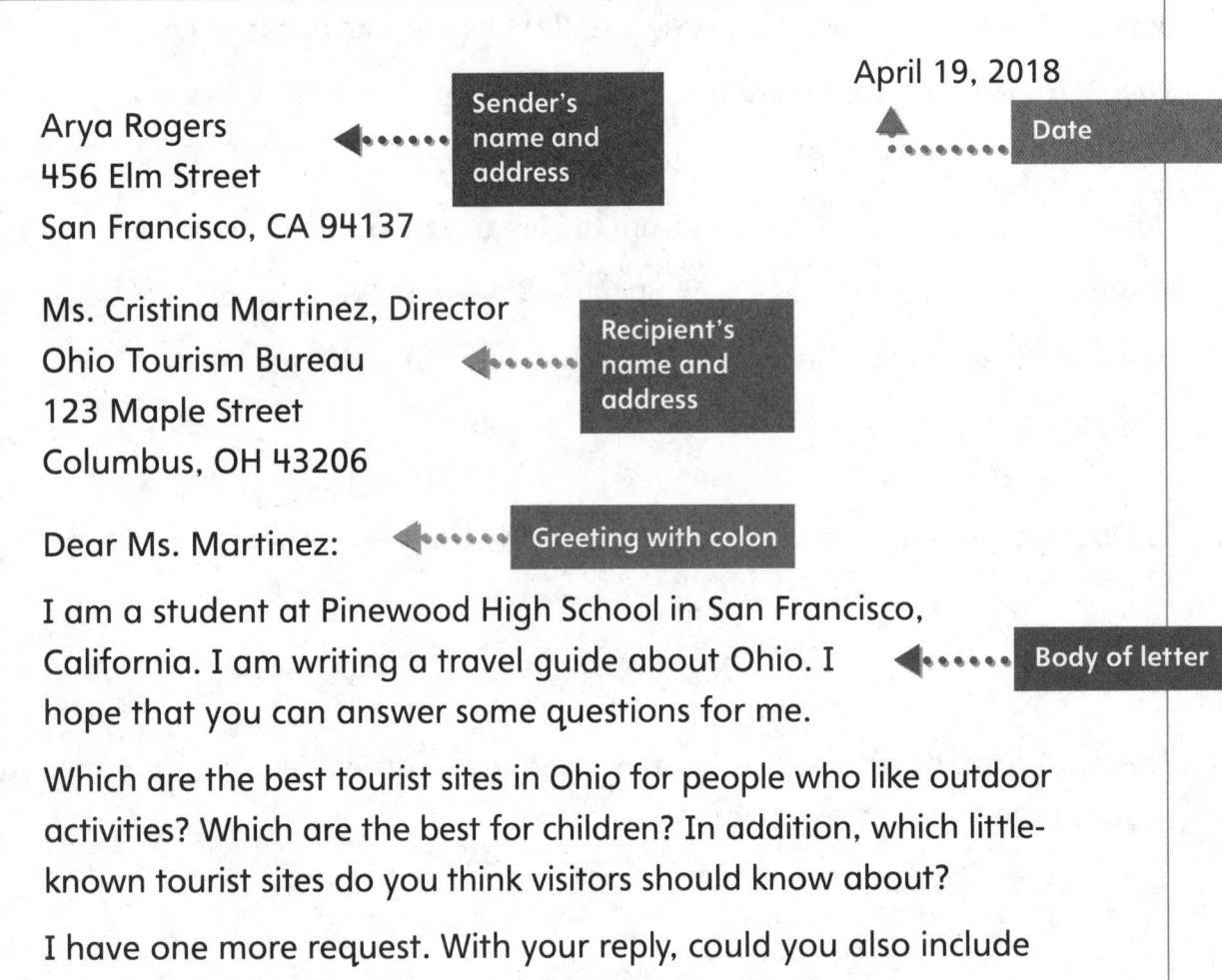

April 19, 2018 ← Date

Arya Rogers
456 Elm Street
San Francisco, CA 94137
← Sender's name and address

Ms. Cristina Martinez, Director
Ohio Tourism Bureau
123 Maple Street
Columbus, OH 43206
← Recipient's name and address

Dear Ms. Martinez: ← Greeting with colon

I am a student at Pinewood High School in San Francisco, California. I am writing a travel guide about Ohio. I hope that you can answer some questions for me. ← Body of letter

Which are the best tourist sites in Ohio for people who like outdoor activities? Which are the best for children? In addition, which little-known tourist sites do you think visitors should know about?

I have one more request. With your reply, could you also include some materials about Ohio tourist sites? I really appreciate your help with my project.

Closing → Sincerely,

Space for signature →

Sender's typed name → Arya Rogers

COLLABORATE With your partner, go online to find the email or postal address of the tourism bureau for the country you have chosen. Then use the outline below to compose a business letter to the director of the tourism bureau. Use the bureau's response to help you write your argumentative travel guide.

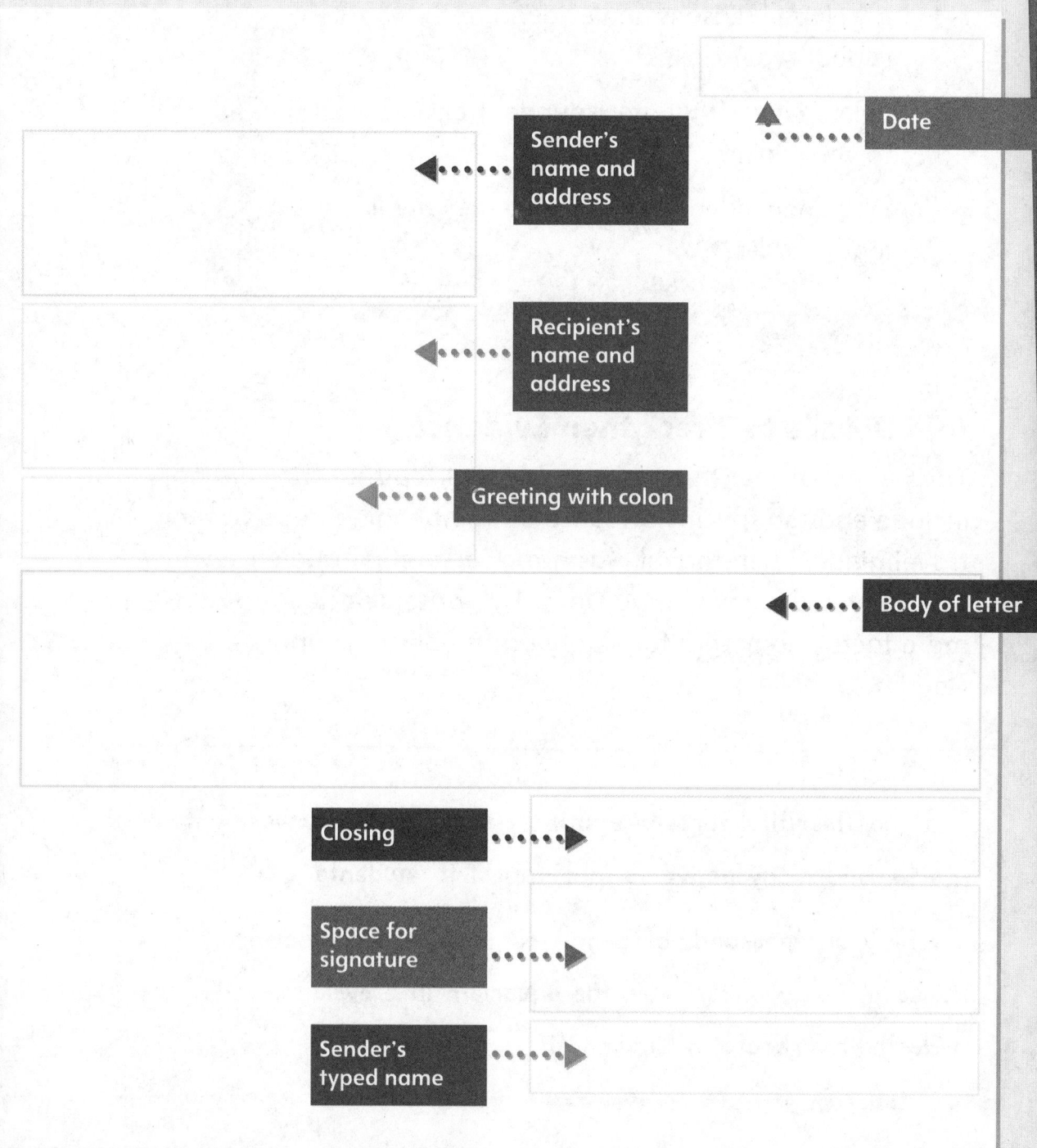

Date

Sender's name and address

Recipient's name and address

Greeting with colon

Body of letter

Closing

Space for signature

Sender's typed name

Revise

Revise for Clarity Reread your travel guide with your partner. Have you

- [ ] clearly stated your claim?
- [ ] developed reasons and evidence to fully support your claim?
- [ ] deleted ideas that are redundant or unrelated to your claim?
- [ ] rearranged ideas as needed so they are in logical order?

Add Details to Strengthen Evidence

The writers of the Ohio travel guide realized that they did not include enough specific evidence on the opening page of their travel guide. Therefore, it was not clear to their audience why people would enjoy visiting Ohio. The writers decided to add more facts and details for clarity and to better support their claim.

It has beautiful forests, exciting cities, thrilling amusement parks, and many activities that appeal to students.

Every year, thousands of people come to visit the science museum in Columbus, view the aquarium in Cleveland, and ride the riverboats in Cincinnati.

Edit

Conventions Read your travel guide again.
Have you used correct conventions?

- ☐ spelling
- ☐ punctuation
- ☐ commas in compound and complex sentences
- ☐ capitalization of proper nouns
- ☐ agreement with collective nouns

Peer Review

COLLABORATE Exchange travel guides with another group. As you read, try to recognize characteristics of argumentative texts. Look for the claim, reasons, supporting facts and details, organizational structure, and the intended audience. Then identify which supporting fact was the most convincing. Tell the authors why that supporting fact made you want to visit the country.

Time to Celebrate!

COLLABORATE Present your travel guide to another group. As you present, remember to make eye contact and to speak clearly at a natural rate and volume. Then listen actively to the group's questions. How did they react to your travel guide? Write some of their reactions.

Reflect on Your Project

My TURN Think about the argumentative travel guide you published and presented. Which parts of your travel guide do you think are the strongest? Which areas might you improve next time? Write your thoughts here.

Strengths

Areas of Improvement

Reflect on Your Goals

SCALE	1	2	3	4	5
	NOT AT ALL WELL	NOT VERY WELL	SOMEWHAT WELL	VERY WELL	EXTREMELY WELL

Look back at your unit goals.
Use a different color to rate yourself again.

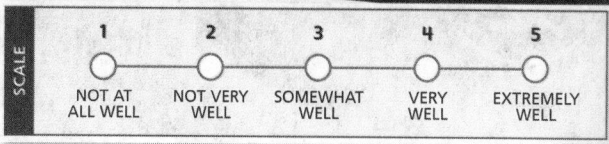

Reflect on Your Reading

Which three texts that you read for this unit most changed the way that you see the world? Explain.

Reflect on Your Writing

What was the most challenging aspect of writing a personal narrative for this unit? Explain.

UNIT 2

Observations

Essential Question

How do we learn through our observations?

Watch

"Observations and the Scientific Process"

TURN and TALK

In which situations would you make and use observations?

SAVVAS realize™

Go ONLINE for all lessons.

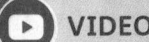

- VIDEO
- AUDIO
- INTERACTIVITY
- GAME
- ANNOTATE
- BOOK
- RESEARCH

Spotlight on Informational Text

READING WORKSHOP

Infographic: How Scientists Study Ocean Life

from *Far from Shore* .... **Informational Text**
by Sophie Webb

Map: Protecting Habitats

A Place for Frogs .... **Informational Text**
by Melissa Stewart

Poem: Perfect Inspiration

from *Hatchet* .... **Realistic Fiction**
by Gary Paulsen

Primary Sources: In the Words of Theodore Roosevelt

"Tracking Monsters" .... **Informational Text**
by Mary Kay Carson

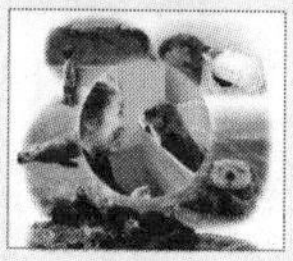

Video: Saving Natural Habitats

Let Wild Animals Be Wild* and *Don't Release Animals Back to the Wild .... **Argumentative Texts**
by David Bowles | by René Saldaña Jr.

READING-WRITING BRIDGE

- Academic Vocabulary • Word Study
- **Read Like a Writer • Write for a Reader**
- Spelling • Language and Conventions

WRITING WORKSHOP

- Introduce and Immerse • Develop Elements
- Develop Structure • Writer's Craft
- Publish, Celebrate, and Assess

Informational Article

PROJECT-BASED INQUIRY

- Inquire • Research • Collaborate

Independent Reading

When you establish a purpose for reading you improve your reading skills. In this unit, you will read informational texts. One purpose for reading informational texts is to gain new information. Keep this in mind as you select titles for independent reading.

Follow these steps to select a book to read on your own.

Step 1 Decide what you want to gain from the book. Ask yourself:

- Am I reading about a topic I find interesting?
- Do I want to learn something new?
- Do I want to read more from a series of texts I know about?

Step 2 Set a goal for your independent reading. Here are some examples. You can choose one of these or create your own.

- I want to read an informational text similar to a book I have already read in school.
- I want to read a book that helps me build my vocabulary.
- I want to read with accuracy and with good comprehension.

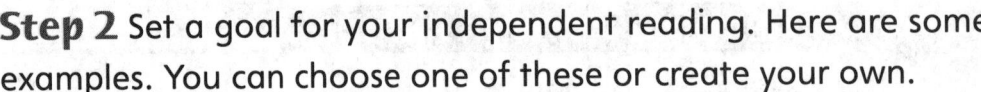

My goal for independent reading is ______________________

____

____

Independent Reading Log

Date	Book	Genre	Pages Read	Minutes Read	My Ratings
					☆☆☆☆☆

Unit Goals

Shade in the circle to rate how well you meet each goal now.

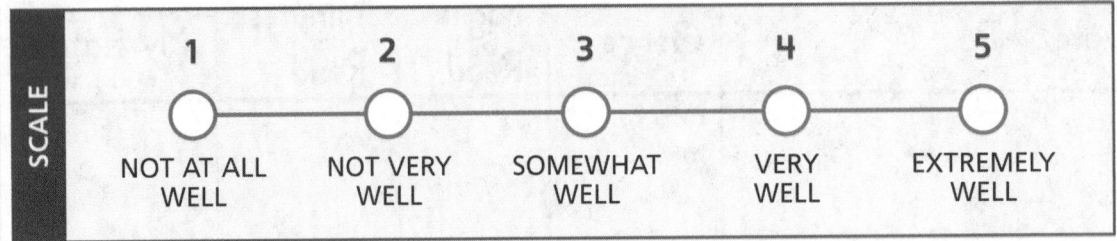

SCALE				
1	2	3	4	5
NOT AT ALL WELL	NOT VERY WELL	SOMEWHAT WELL	VERY WELL	EXTREMELY WELL

Reading Workshop	1	2	3	4	5
I know about different types of informational text and understand their structures and features.	○	○	○	○	○

Reading-Writing Bridge	1	2	3	4	5
I can use language to make connections between reading and writing informational texts.	○	○	○	○	○

Writing Workshop	1	2	3	4	5
I can use elements of informational writing to write an informational article.	○	○	○	○	○

Theme	1	2	3	4	5
I can collaborate with others to explore how we learn through observations.	○	○	○	○	○

Academic Vocabulary

Use these words to talk about this unit's theme, *Observations*: *expert*, *focus*, *visible*, *relate*, and *detect*.

TURN and TALK Read the words and definitions. Identify at least two places where each word might be used. Write a sample sentence to show how the word might be used in that context.

Academic Vocabulary	Definition	How it's used . . .	
		in school	at home
expert	one who shows special skill or knowledge gained from training	My teachers are academic experts.	My mom is an expert at building forts for us to play in.
focus	direct attention to something		
visible	easily seen		
relate	to tell; to show a relationship between two things		
detect	to discover the truth about something		

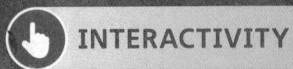

INTERACTIVITY

How Scientists Study OCEAN LIFE

The majority of Earth's surface is covered in water. Less than five percent of the ocean has been explored.

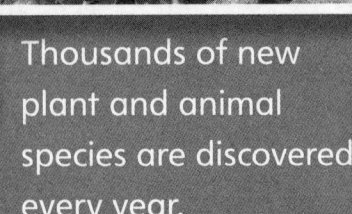

Thousands of new plant and animal species are discovered every year.

Up to one-quarter of all marine life calls a coral reef its home. Coral reefs have more biodiversity than any other biome.

Life forms as big as four feet tall and as small as a single cell have been found on the ocean floor. They live in or near cracks in the planet's surface known as hydrothermal vents.

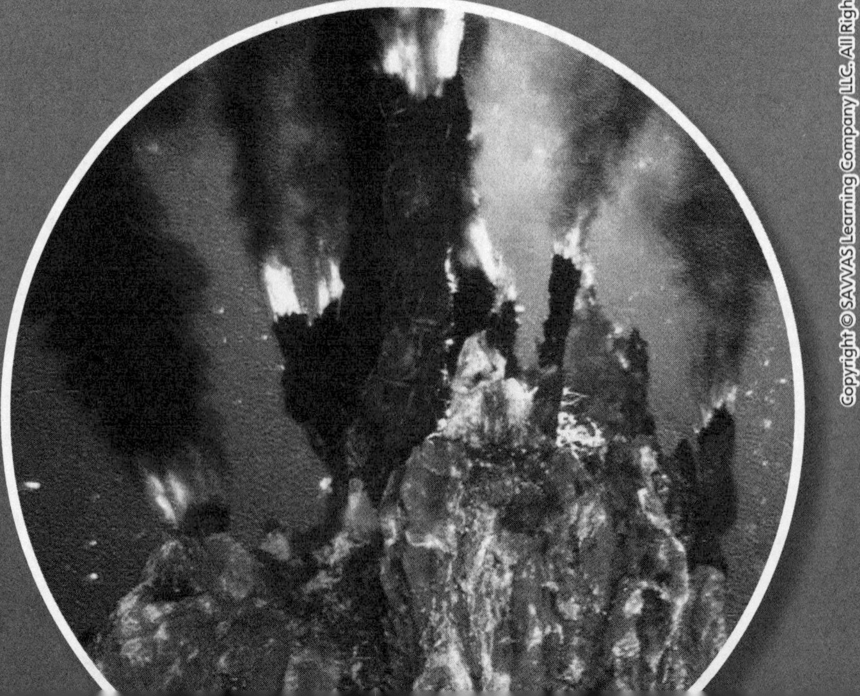

There are 47 different species of seahorse. Fourteen of those were discovered within the last two decades.

WEEK 1

Weekly Question

Why do scientists explore and study oceans?

TURN and TALK Summarize the information presented in the infographic. What parts of the ocean would you like to explore or know more about? Why? Discuss with a partner.

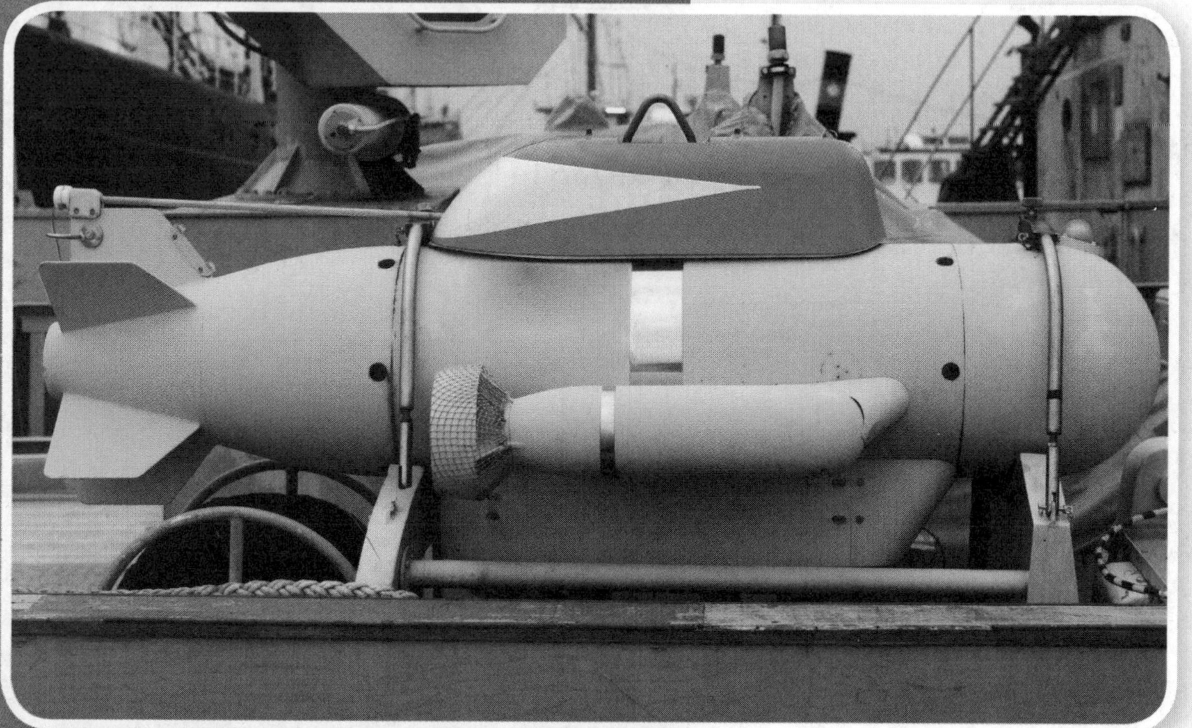

ROVs, or Remotely Operated Vehicles, can dive deeper than human observers can. Scientists control the underwater explorer and its sensors, lights, cameras, recording equipment, and sample collectors.

Learning Goal

I can learn about informational text by analyzing an author's purpose.

Spotlight on Genre

Informational Text

An **informational text** gives factual information about a topic, or the person, event, or idea that a text is about. It includes

- **Main ideas,** which are the most important ideas about the topic
- **Details,** such as facts and other information that support the main ideas
- **Text features,** including a title, headings, insets, bold words, and images, which provide clues about the main ideas

Look for text features and words that connect facts, ideas, and events.

TURN and TALK Identify the topic and main ideas of an informational text you have read. Use the anchor chart to help you describe the text's characteristics. Take notes on your discussion.

My NOTES

Informational Text Anchor Chart

Purpose

To give information about a topic or explain a concept

Elements

- Main ideas are the topic's most important ideas
- Details support or tell more about main ideas
- Text features offer clues to main ideas

Text Structure and Signal Words

Cause and Effect	because, as a result
Problem and Solution	required, improved
Chronological, or time order	first, second, then
Description	includes, makes up

Meet the Author

Sophie Webb has always loved to draw birds and mammals. As an ornithologist, a scientist who studies birds, she participates in research trips that take her to places around the world where she studies and draws. Other books by Webb include *My Season with Penguins* and *Looking for Seabirds.*

from

Far from Shore

Preview Vocabulary

As you read *Far from Shore*, pay attention to these vocabulary words. Notice how they relate to important ideas in the text.

marine **ecosystem** **flying bridge**
chlorophyll **nautical**

Read

Before you begin, establish a purpose for reading. Readers use these strategies when they read **informational texts** for the first time.

First Read

Notice how drawings, diagrams, and captions help you understand the topic.

Generate Questions about what the author wants you to learn and understand.

Connect ideas in the text to what you know about the world.

Respond by marking parts you find confusing or surprising.

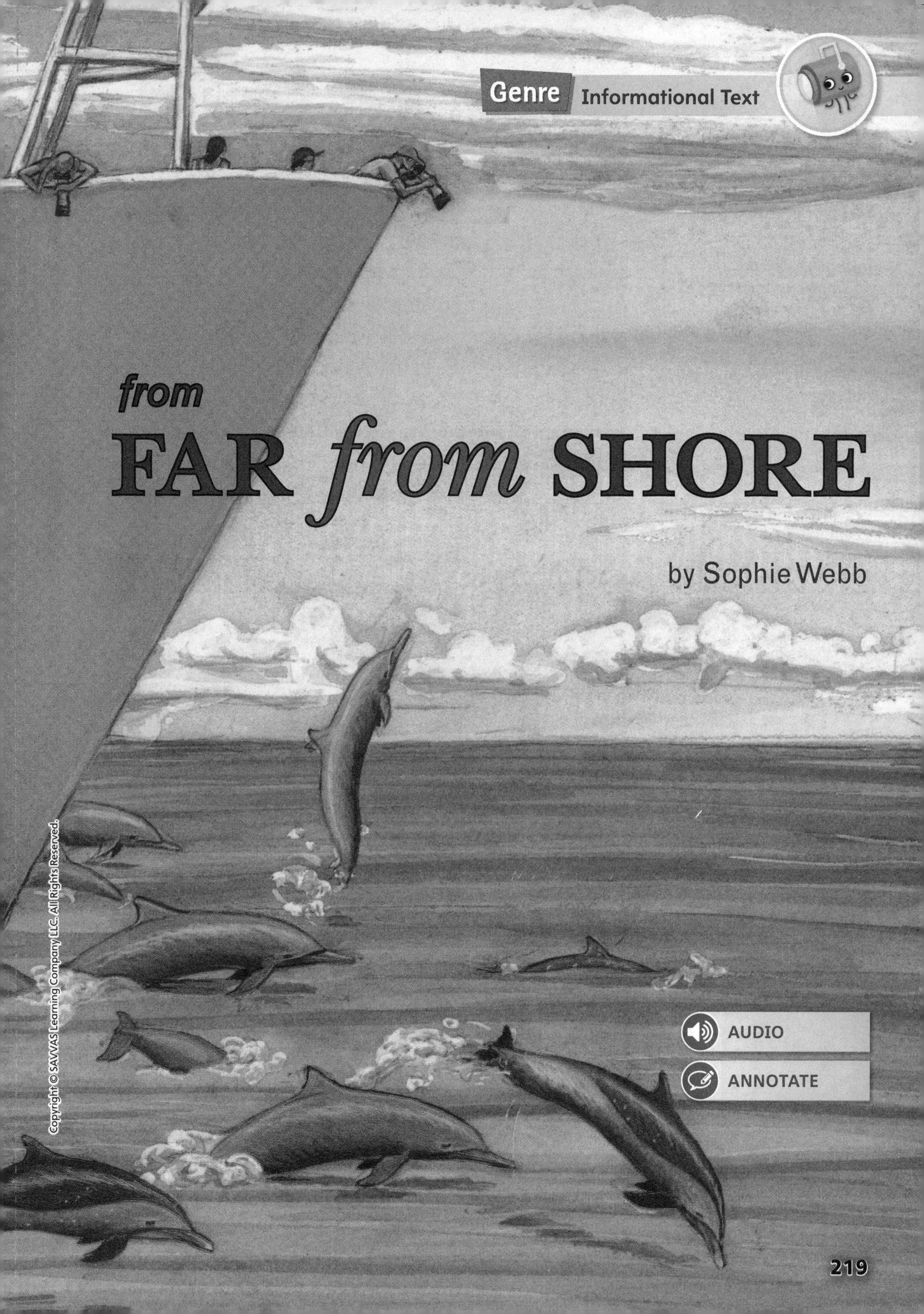

from

FAR *from* SHORE

by Sophie Webb

AUDIO

ANNOTATE

Explain Author's Purpose

Underline a sentence that gives you a clue about the author's purpose for writing this text.

marine of or relating to the ocean

1 My name is Sophie. I work as a field biologist and naturalist specializing in birds. Tomorrow I am going on a four-month journey to the Eastern Tropical Pacific Ocean (ETP) to study seabirds and marine mammals. I work for the Southwest Fisheries Science Center, a research laboratory run by the National Oceanic and Atmospheric Administration (NOAA) in California. The cruise's main goal is to discover what has happened to dolphin populations that have been affected by the tuna purse-seine fishery. However, we will also observe and count all other marine mammals that we encounter, count the seabirds (my main job), make oceanographic measurements, and study flying fish and squid. As scientists we want to understand the ecosystem as a whole, not only one part. The ETP, where we will work, is a huge portion of the Pacific, the world's largest ocean. It extends south from California to Peru and west to Hawaii, an area of 7.7 million square miles, larger than the continent of Africa.

ecosystem a community of living things and the environment it inhabits

2 The open ocean, far from land, can seem lonely and empty, yet there are areas in the ETP that are full of amazing wildlife. Because it is so difficult to study these deep-sea animals far from shore, little is known about their natural history and ecology. My shipmates and I are about to embark on an incredible opportunity to explore this complex and exciting ecosystem.

July—San Diego, California

32°73′ North Latitude, 117°17′ West Longitude

3 I drive south from my home in central California to San Diego. There I spend several days helping load scientific equipment aboard the NOAA ship *McArthur II* and setting up our work areas. Over the flying bridge, the highest deck on the ship, the ship's crew has strung a canvas canopy to provide shade. We will be grateful for the shade as we head south into the sunny tropics.

4 We've installed four sets of "big eyes," which will be key to our observations. We use these enormous mounted binoculars with a twenty-five-power magnification to scan to the horizon for marine mammals or count distant bird flocks. Three computer stations with chairs are also set up. Two stations, one per side, are where we birders sit to collect our bird data. The third one in the middle is where the marine mammal data recorder sits.

A bird's-eye view of the flying bridge shows the location of our stations and the big eyes.

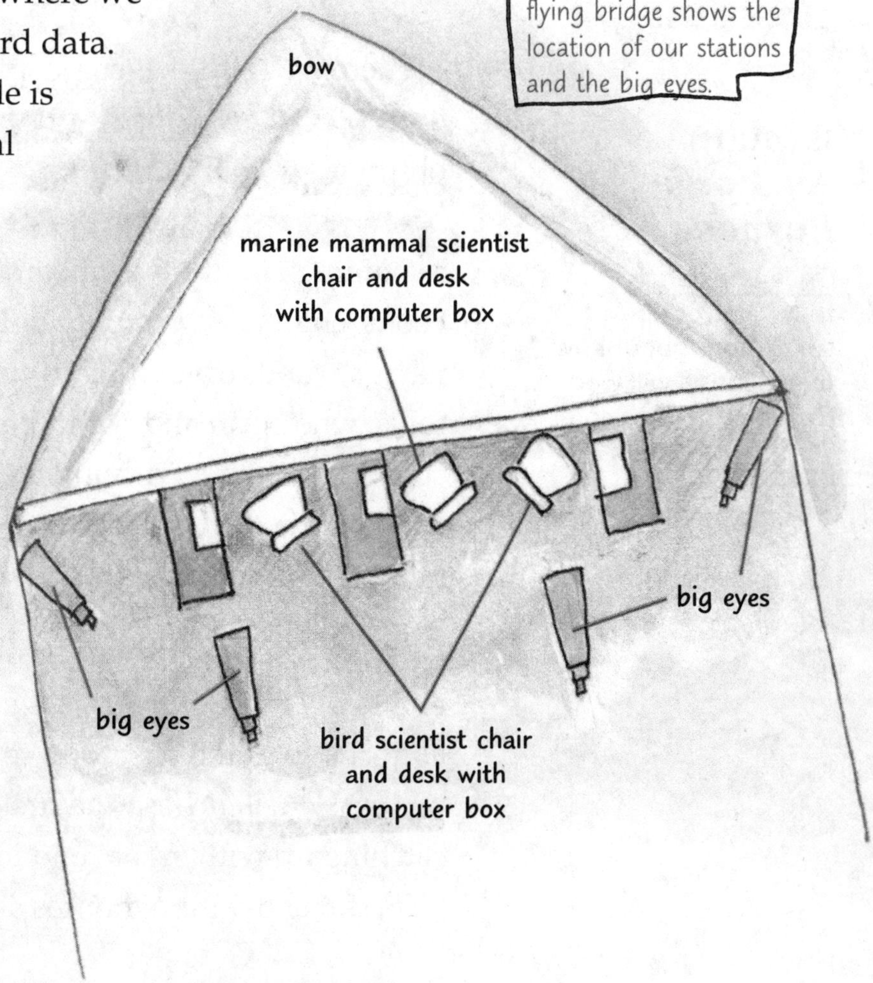

CLOSE READ

Evaluate Details

Highlight details in the text that help you understand why the author included a diagram of the flying bridge.

flying bridge the highest place on a ship from which it can be steered

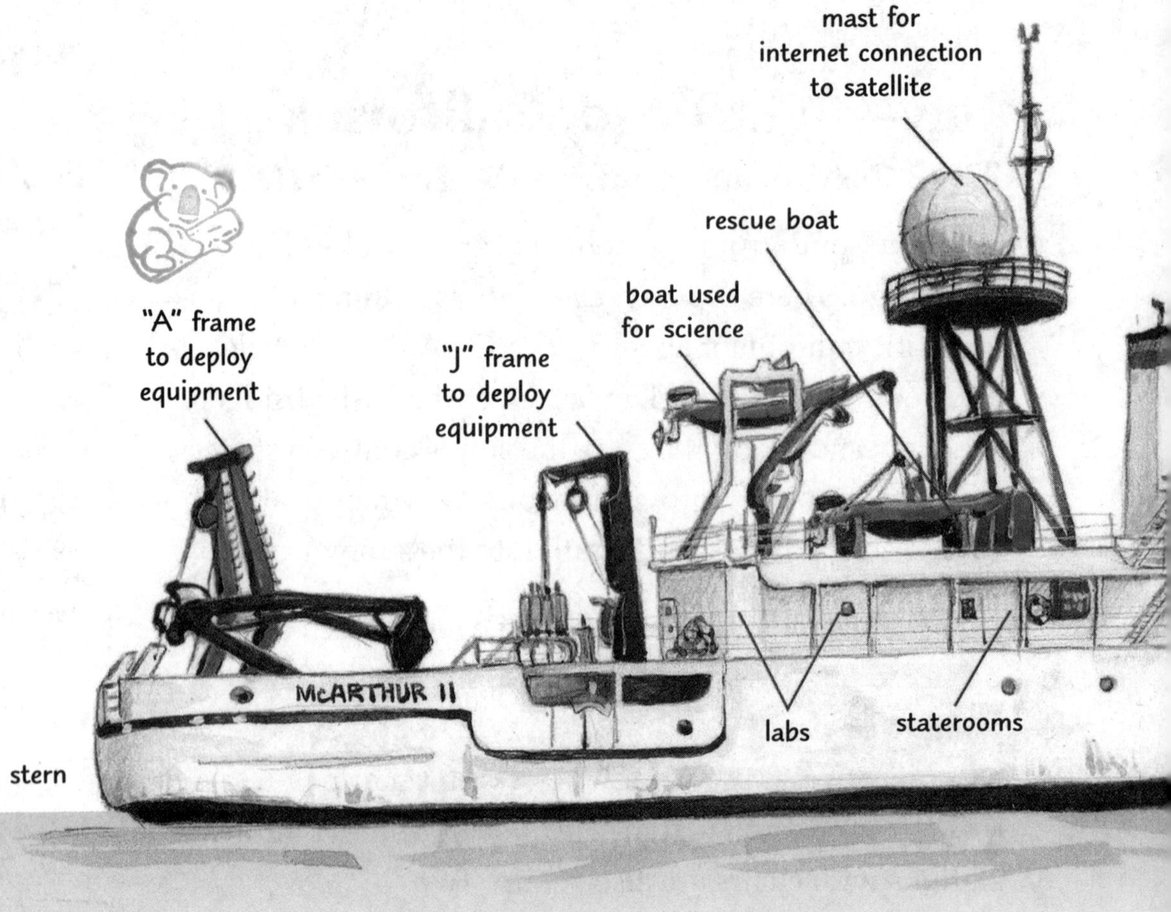

CLOSE READ

Explain Author's Purpose

Underline details that help you draw conclusions about how the scientists will work together on the ship.

5 There are thirty-seven people on the ship. Fifteen are scientists: one chief scientist, six marine mammal observers, two birders (one of them is me), two oceanographers, and four visiting scientists. The remaining twenty-two aboard include the captain, cooks, engineers, a variety of NOAA officers, who navigate and drive the ship, and the deck department folks, who clean and paint the ship and help us collect our data by driving the small boats and running the cranes and winches for casting nets and other equipment.

6 I have worked with many of the scientists before and know most of the ship's crew well. I've spent almost two of the past four years living and working on the *McArthur II*, so the first few days are always fun, catching up with others and learning what they have been doing over the months since the last trip.

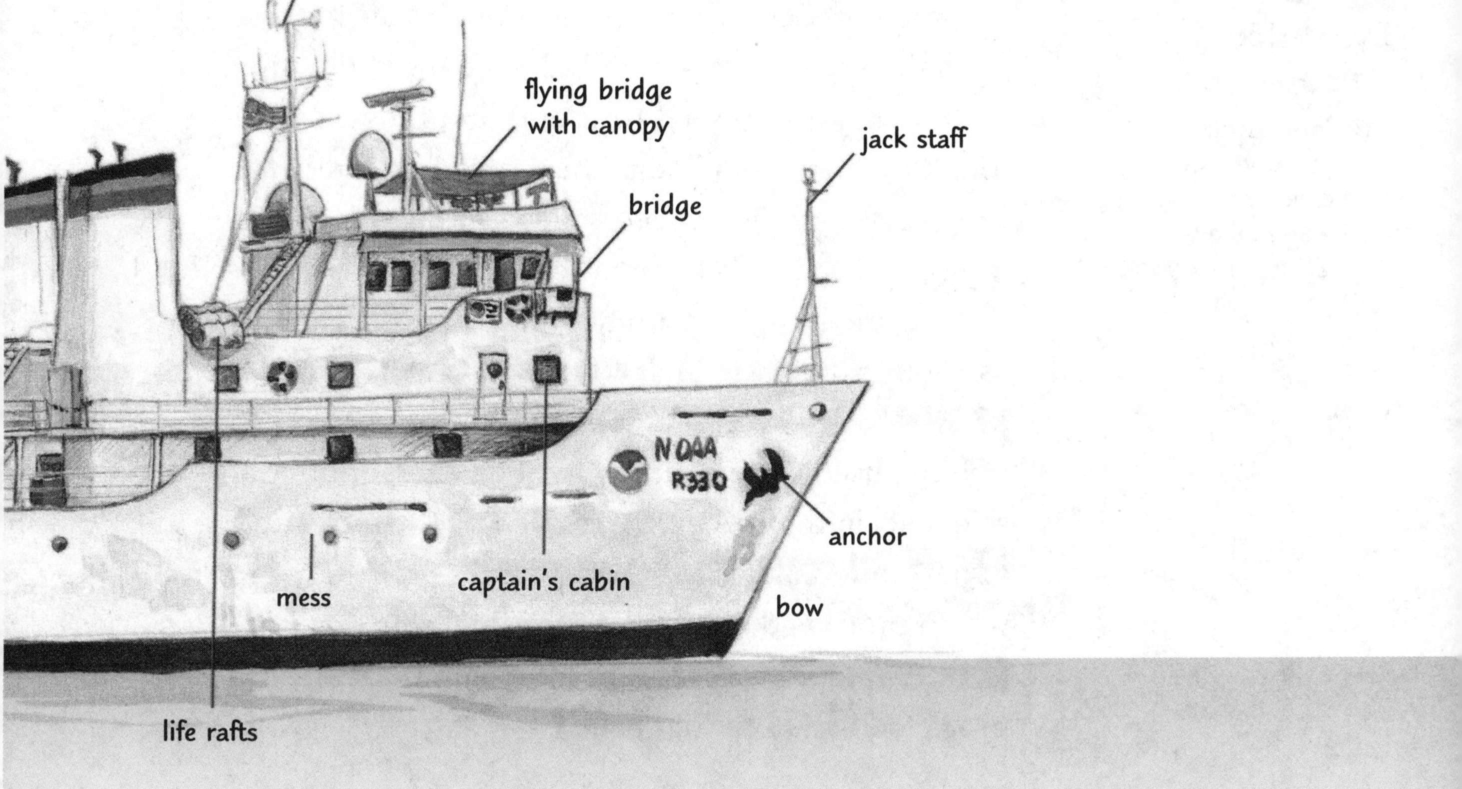

7 Although over the next months we will collect data on many aspects of the marine ecosystem, the primary focus of the trip is to find out what is happening to the populations of spotted and spinner dolphins.

The dry lab where the computers are located. There is a wet lab as well, with two large sinks, one with fresh water, the other with salt water, where the samples from net tows and other scientific activities are processed.

CLOSE READ

Evaluate Details

Highlight details that help you understand why this research trip is important.

Evaluate Details

Highlight details that help you understand how ocean scientists' work can make a difference in the world.

8 Why do we want to know about spotted and spinner dolphin numbers? There are several threats to these animals. The primary one used to be the yellowfin tuna fishery. In the ETP, tuna and dolphins are often found in large schools together. Tuna frequently are caught by a method called purse seining. A net is dragged to surround a tuna school, then drawn closed. If there are dolphins with the tuna, they are caught as well. In the past, tens of thousands of dolphins drowned each year in purse seines. This needless loss of life caused a great outcry by the general public and scientists in the 1970s. The result was the formation of the United States Marine Mammal Protection Act, which protects dolphins and other marine mammals in U.S. waters. Now most marine mammals are also protected by international law.

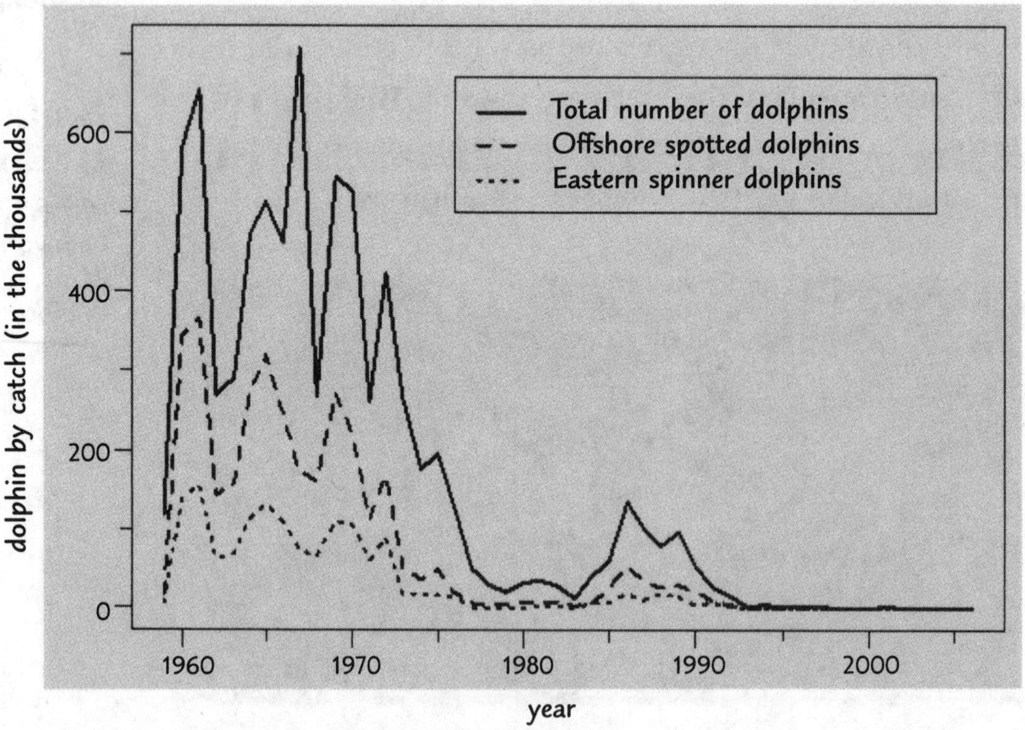

A graph showing how the numbers of dolphins killed in the yellowfin tuna purse-seine fishery has declined. Courtesy NOAA SWFSC.

9 Currently, scientists closely monitor the tuna fishery. Now most tuna fishermen allow the dolphins to escape before they drown, sometimes with a swimmer in the net to help the dolphins escape. But dolphin populations are not recovering as quickly as predicted, and scientists don't know why. Does capture cause stress that lowers their survival? Or perhaps overfishing and pollution combined with shifts in climate may be affecting the balance of the ocean ecosystem. With long-term monitoring, combined with ecosystem studies, we hope to understand why these populations aren't recovering at a faster rate.

CLOSE READ

Explain Author's Purpose

Underline details that help you understand the goals of these ocean scientists.

A tuna purse seiner hauls in its net. The yellow skiffs round up the tuna and dolphins into the net. As the net is drawn closed, the tuna dive down and the dolphins swim out. A helicopter and a manned crow's nest, a lookout platform at the top of a tall mast, are used to spot distant tuna schools. Bird flocks are often a clue that the fishermen look for.

Evaluate Details

Highlight details on both pages that the drawing of a bongo net and the caption explain.

10 Finally we are ready to leave San Diego. Before each long journey there is always a sense of anticipation. What will we see this time? There is, however, a downside to every long trip. I know I will miss my home, family, and friends.

Heading South

15°47′ N, 120°52′ W

11 Over the next days we move off shore and head south to warm tropical water. Our route takes us south of the Hawaiian Islands. In a few weeks, after a month at sea, we will turn and head north to Hawaii to resupply and fuel the ship. The ocean color has changed since we left San Diego; it is a beautiful clear blue. I look down through the water and it seems as though I can see for miles. Here the water can be much more than a mile deep. It looks nothing like the ocean near shore off California, which often has a murky green or brownish cast to it caused by lots of plankton and algae. The tropical ocean is clear because it has much less of these.

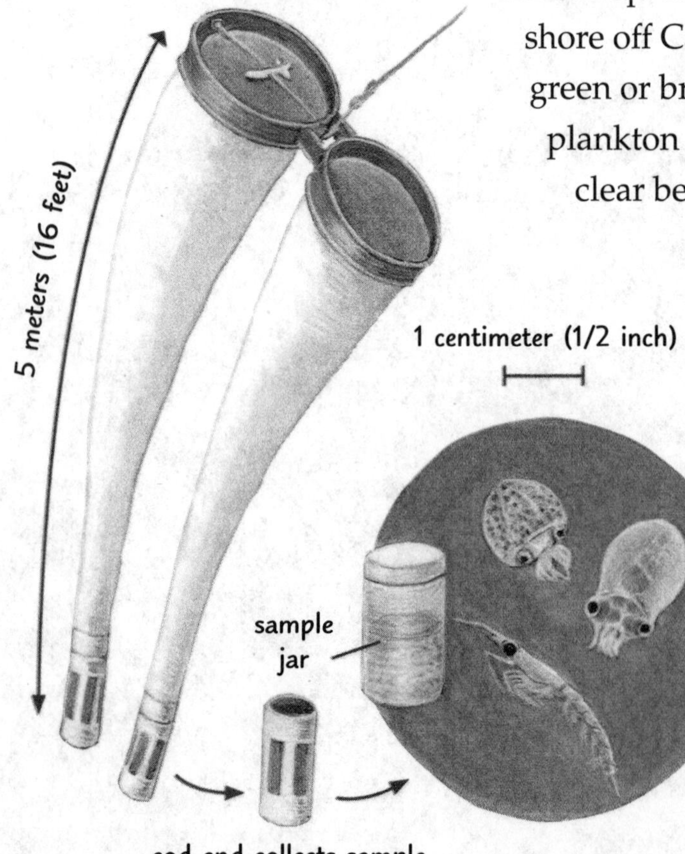

This net, called a bongo because it looks like the drum, is used for catching small fish and plankton. Some creatures frequently caught in a bongo tow are pictured here clockwise: a spotted larval squid, a semi-clear larval octopus, and a krill. Krill are small relatives of shrimp and are an important food for whales and birds.

12 Where there is food, there are animals. In the tropical ocean animals tend to be found in patches where there is more plankton and algae. Small fish and krill eat the plankton and algae, larger fish and squid eat them, and so on up the food chain to tuna and dolphins. One of the things we want to understand is what causes this patchiness. We combine our marine mammal and seabird observations with measurements of water, plankton, and algae. Every morning an hour before sunrise and every evening an hour after sunset we collect water samples from the surface down to 1,000 meters to look at the water's nutrients and chlorophyll. These nutrients are the building blocks of the ocean food chain. In the evening we also deploy nets to determine the amount and types of plankton at different depths. We use dip nets to catch flying fish and squid. All this information helps us have a more complete picture of the ecosystem of the tropical ocean.

CLOSE READE

Vocabulary in Context

Context clues are words and phrases in and around a sentence that help you understand the meaning of an unfamiliar word.

Underline the context clues that help you determine the meaning of *nutrients*.

chlorophyll a green substance found in plants that allows them to make food

A graph of a water sample showing measurements of oxygen, temperature, and salinity (salt) in the water from the surface to 1,000 meters (3,000 feet). As one follows the graph from 1,000 meters to the surface, note the drastic changes at a depth of about 100 meters: oxygen and temperature increase sharply as the salinity decreases. This is where two different water masses meet and is called the *thermocline.* A thermocline that is strong and close to the surface (50 to 100 meters) can indicate a highly productive area where we might find not only a large amount of algae and plankton but also animals much higher in the food chain such as tuna and dolphins. Courtesy NOAA SWFSC

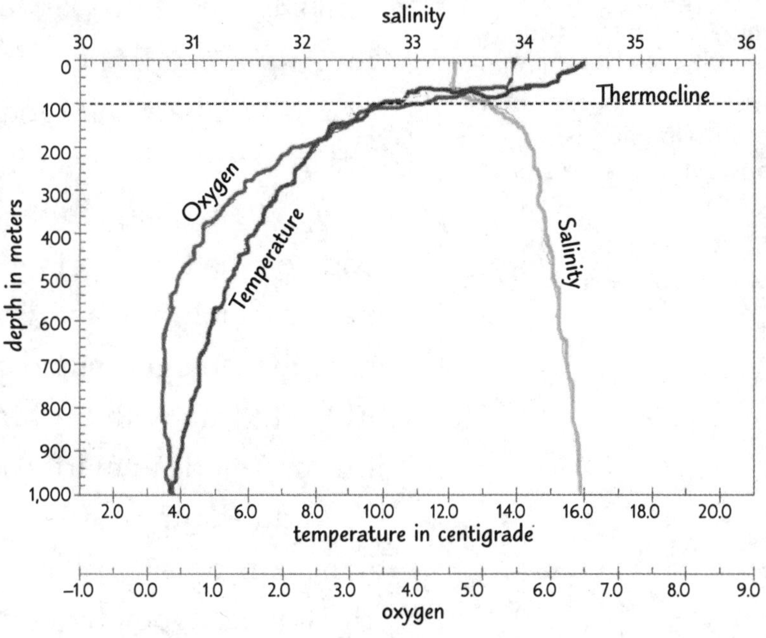

At Beaufort 0, the ocean is glassy calm. One can see for miles. The pink and violet sunrise reflects on the still water.

CLOSE READ

Evaluate Details

Highlight details that describe the ocean and weather conditions that best help scientists observe the ecosystem.

nautical related to ships or navigation

A Day Offshore

13°13′ N, 122°47′ W

13 The day dawns clear and calm, absolutely beautiful. The seas are glassy: Beaufort 0 (a nautical scale that assigns numbers based on wind speed and waves). Observations start just after dawn, when there is enough light to see out to the horizon. Everyone is ready on the flying bridge. Cornelia, a German marine mammal biologist, and Ernesto, a Mexican marine mammal biologist, stand on each side of the flying bridge to scan with the big eyes for marine mammals. Jim, an American marine mammal biologist, sits in the middle at the data computer. I sit with hand-held binoculars on either the port (left) or the starboard (right) side, depending on where I can avoid the sun's glare to scan for birds.

14 It's time to start looking for critters. It is ten minutes past sunrise and the light is good. We start to travel along a set course, what scientists call a transect. Soon after we start, Cornelia yells, "Dolphins!" All scanning stops and everyone focuses on Cornelia's sighting.

15 She swings the big eyes in the direction of the dolphins.

16 Using her hand-held radio, Cornelia calls the captain on the bridge deck below us, where the ship's steering controls are located. "Bridge, flying bridge—we have dolphins," she says. "Please turn twenty degrees to the left. Over." The ship turns.

CLOSE READ

Explain Author's Purpose

How do the scientists use the big eyes? View the images and underline details in the diagram that help you understand.

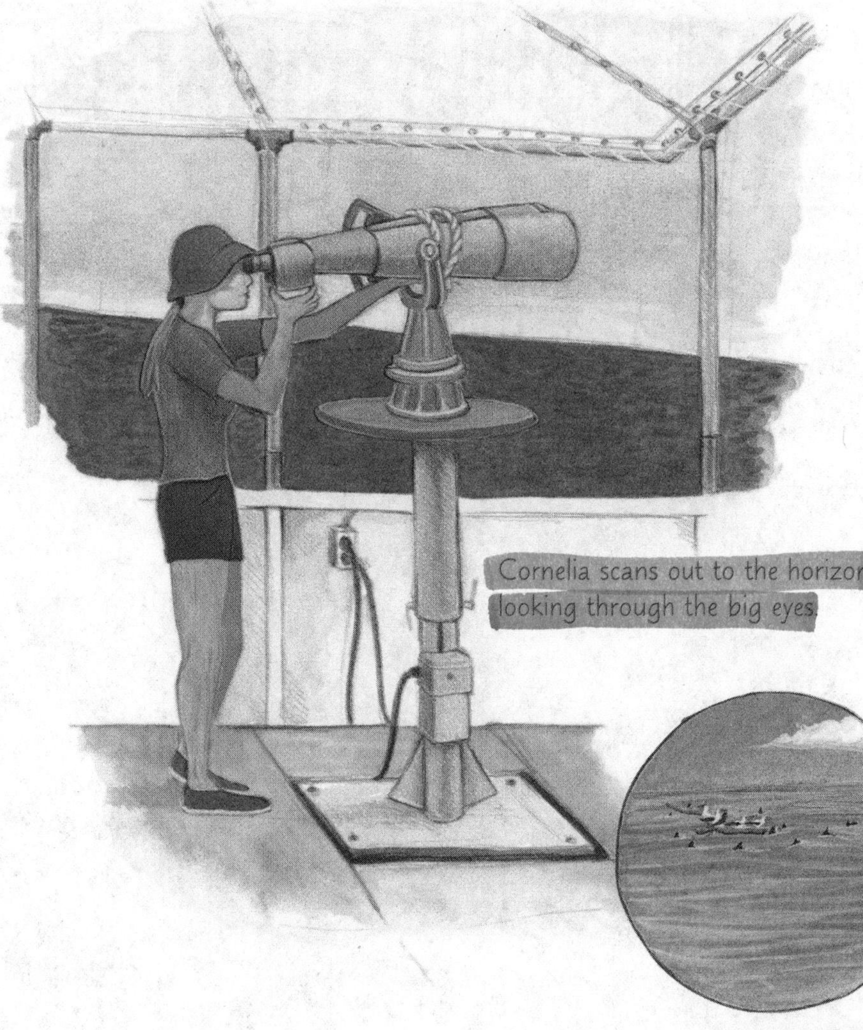

Cornelia scans out to the horizon, looking through the big eyes.

What Cornelia sees through the big eyes.

CLOSE READ

Explain Author's Purpose

Underline details in the text that the author clarifies in the drawing.

17 At first, all we see are several dorsal fins around the log. We approach the dolphins slowly.

One brown booby and four Nazca boobies rest on a log surrounded by dolphins. Boobies are often seen far out at sea, resting on any available floating object, including ships and sea turtles.

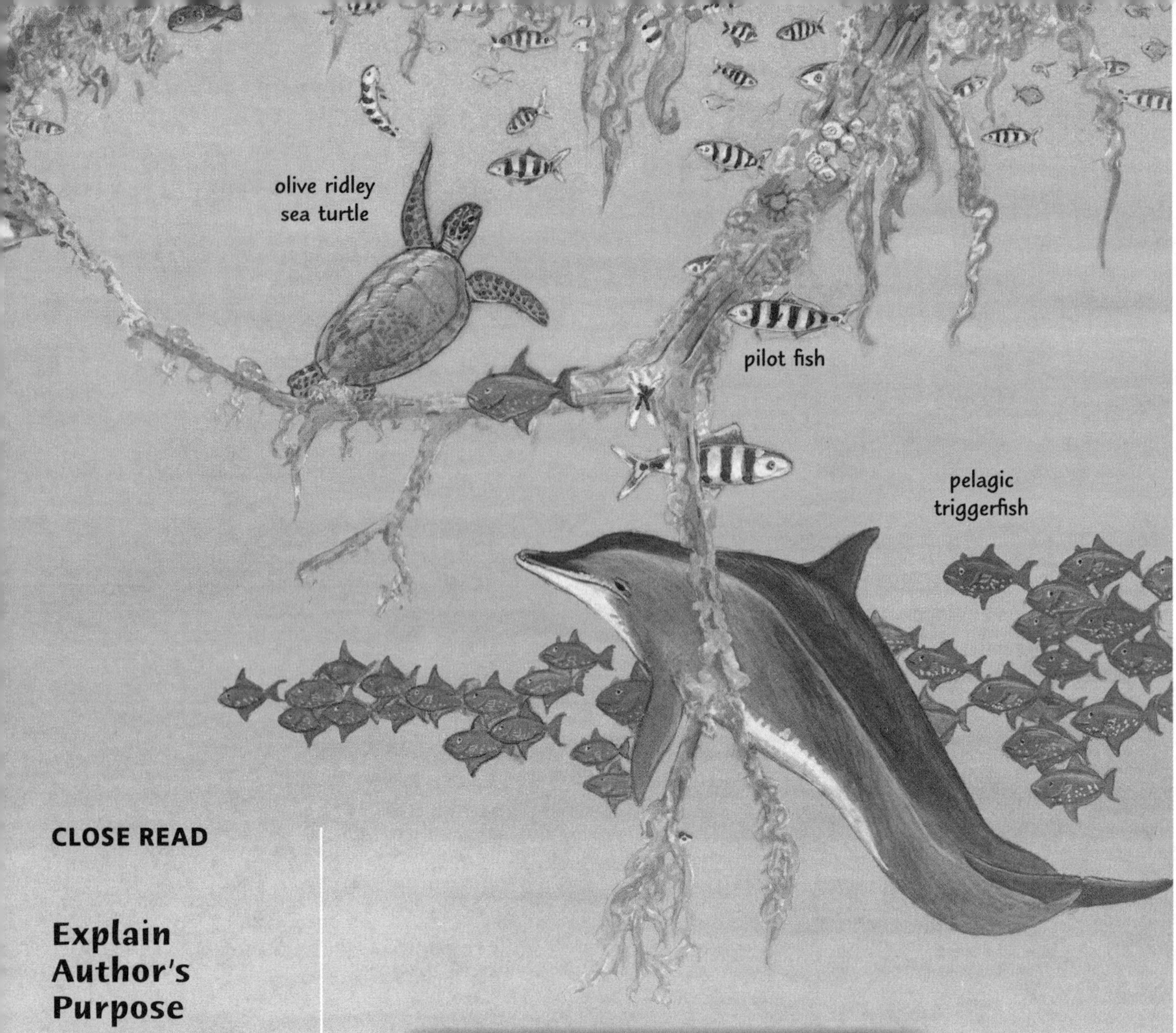

CLOSE READ

Explain Author's Purpose

Underline text in the caption that helps you understand how the author uses her knowledge of the ocean ecosystem to create informative drawings.

What I imagine it looks like below the log. Frequently, rough-toothed dolphins investigate logs, feeding on the fish that hide in the seaweed growing on the log. Many different animals are attracted to the habitat the log creates. Rough-toothed dolphins specialize in eating large fish such as the mahi-mahi.

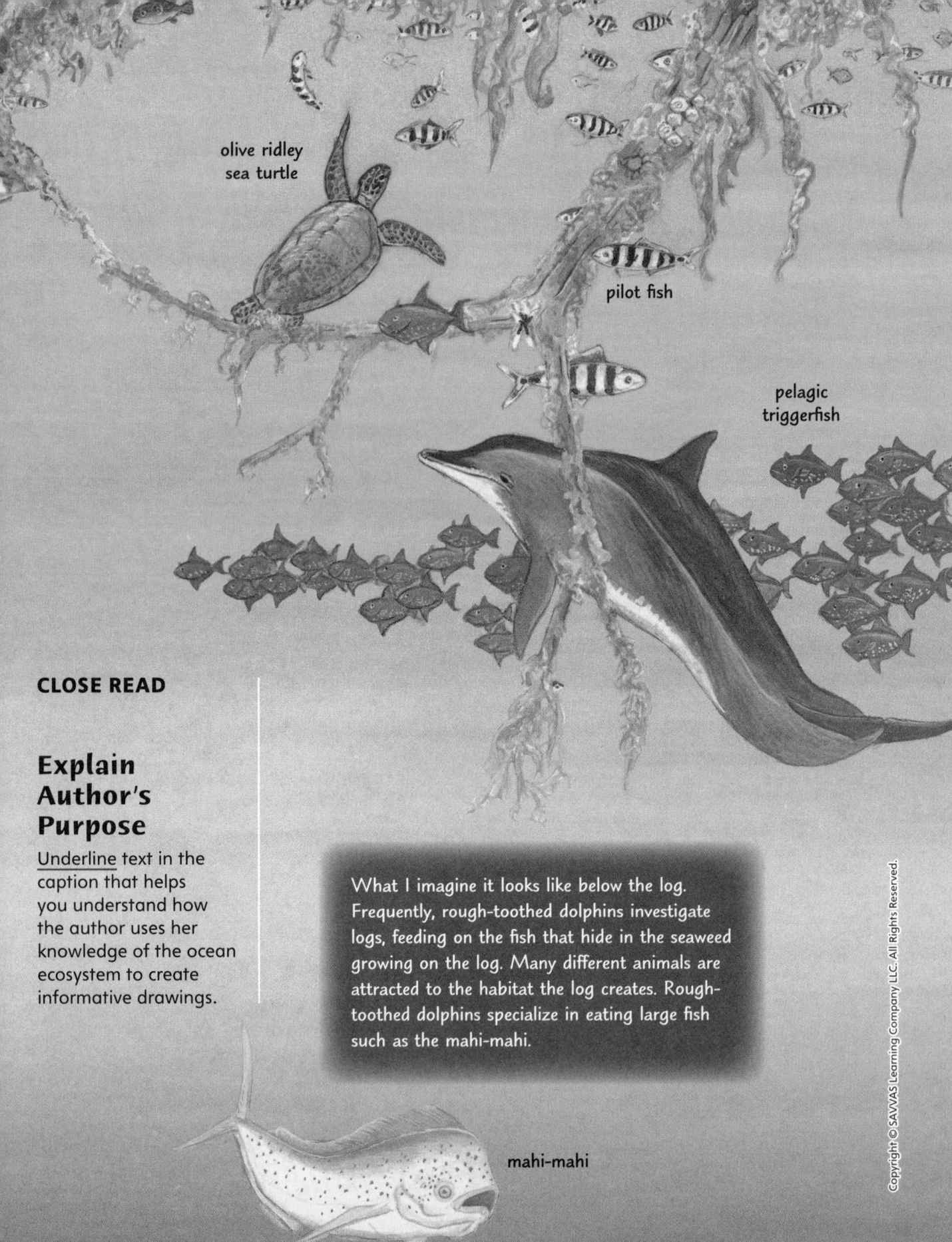

18 Finally we see odd sloped foreheads and long beaks: they are rough-toothed dolphins. This species is found in many oceans. Although relatively common, little is known of their natural history due to their deep ocean habitat. All creatures that inhabit the deep ocean are difficult to study.

19 The water is so clear, I see subtle markings on the dolphins as they swim by.

CLOSE READ

Vocabulary in Context

Underline a word in paragraph 18 that means "to live within." Then underline context clues that helped you identify the word.

CLOSE READ

Evaluate Details

Highlight details in the caption that help you understand the similarities between dolphins and whales.

All dolphins are *odontocetes* (toothed whales). Odontocetes also include porpoises, the little-known beaked whales, killer whales, and sperm whales. There is a great variation in size from the tiny harbor porpoise that measures 1.2 meters (4 feet) to the 18.5-meter (60-foot) male sperm whale.

Galápagos storm-petrels are found far out at sea feeding on small crustaceans, halobates (the only marine insect), fish, and jellyfish at the ocean's surface. They breed on the remote and protected Galápagos Islands, which have few predators. Their populations at the moment appear to be stable.

A Galápagos storm-petrel

20 We complete the rough-toothed dolphin count. There are twelve in the group and no calves (babies). Marine mammal biologists always note the presence or absence of calves and immature animals to gain clues about when and where the dolphins reproduce. We leave the dolphins by their log and continue on our course.

21 The day becomes progressively warmer. The air is still. Everyone is sleepy. The ship drones on along the transect line. We see no more marine mammals now, but birds occasionally fly by, such as the sparrow-size Galápagos storm-petrel. I record birds out to 300 meters (630 feet) on one side of the ship. Even when there are few birds, I have to stay focused and alert. I don't want to miss any of them in my count.

CLOSE READ

Explain Author's Purpose

Underline text that gives details about the purpose of the author's observations on the ship.

Develop Vocabulary

In informational texts, authors use domain-specific words, or words that are specific to the topic. These words can help the reader determine the relationship between ideas.

My TURN Read the topic of *Far from Shore*. Then complete the activity. Explain how each newly acquired term relates to the topic.

Topic

Studying ocean life on a scientific voyage

The word *marine* relates because

____.

The word *ecosystem* relates because

____.

The phrase *flying bridge* relates because

____.

The word *nautical* relates because

____.

Check for Understanding

MyTURN Look back at the text to answer the questions.

1. What examples from the text help you determine that *Far from Shore* is an informational text?

Some examples are the topic, studying marine life, Scientific facts, and data.

2. Authors use diagrams to present information clearly. How does the diagram of the tuna purse seiner help you understand this fishing process?

It helps me understand the fishing process because it shows how the dolphins can escape and the fish still get caught.

3. How do scientists build "a more complete picture of the ecosystem of the tropical ocean"?

Scientist help people better understand ocean life. Each scientist studies a different part of the subject. Together these clues provide a more complete picture of the ecosystem.

4. Analyze the methods for studying the ocean that you read about in the infographic at the beginning of the week. Then compare it to the methods described in *Far from Shore*.

They both study ocean life and provide pictures to help us understand.

Explain Author's Purpose

An **author's purpose**, or reason for writing, may be to inform, entertain, persuade, or express ideas and feelings. Authors often have more than one purpose for writing. The author's purpose determines what details and features the author includes in a text.

1. **My TURN** Go to the Close Read notes in *Far from Shore*. Underline the parts that help you explain the author's main purpose for writing.

2. **Text Evidence** Use the parts you underlined to complete the chart.

Author's Purpose	to inform readers about the dissappearance of dolphins.
Fact or Detail	"tens of thousands of dolphins drown each year"
Fact or Detail	"We hope to understand why the dolphin populations aren't recovering at a faster rate."

Explain how knowing the author's purpose helps you better understand the text.

Knowing the author's purpose is to inform helps me better understand the story because I know everything in the story is true.

Evaluate Details

Readers **evaluate details** to determine which key ideas are most important and to better understand the text. In informational text, an author often includes details in images as well as in words. The most important details clarify complex information or give clues about the author's purpose or message. A message is what the author wants you to learn or do.

1. **My TURN** Go back to the Close Read notes and highlight text evidence that helps you evaluate the author's use of details.

2. **Text Evidence** Record important details you highlighted. Then evaluate how each detail connects to the author's purpose and message.

Author's Purpose and Message

to inform reder about how Scientests Observe and Collect data about the Ocean.

Detail "The Primary ~~trip~~ foocus of the trip is to find out what is happening to the PouPutatiwas of Spotted and Spiner dolPhins!!

Connection to purpose/message
Tells us wht then making the trip

Detail " we combinde our mammal and bird observainas with the measorements of water Planeton and algae"

Connection to purpose/message
tells us how the author obseves ocean and ancmal

Image The image Shows the Ideal wether

Connection to purpose/message
Shows the best conditions for obseruing the Ocean.

Reflect and Share

Talk About It The scientists on the *McArthur II* worked together to better understand the ocean. Consider all the texts you have read this week. What can you infer about the importance of teamwork? Determine and discuss the most important ideas and supporting details that point you to the meaning of the text and to the author's purpose for writing.

Make Thoughtful Comments When discussing, it is important to make comments that are related to the topic.

- Share ideas that are on topic.
- Discuss specific ideas in the text.
- Build on others' comments.

Use these sentence starters to guide your comments:

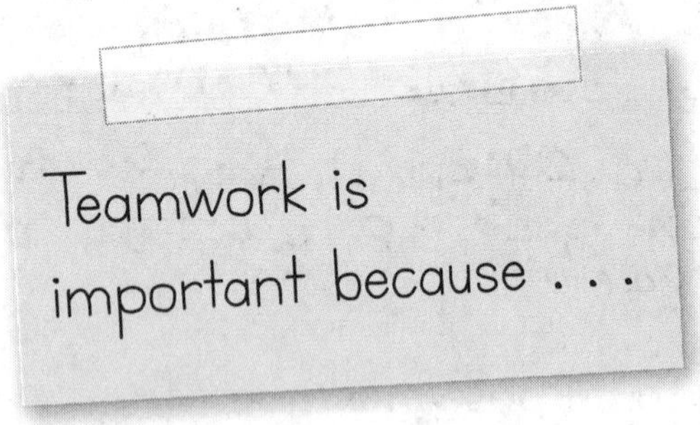
Teamwork is important because . . .

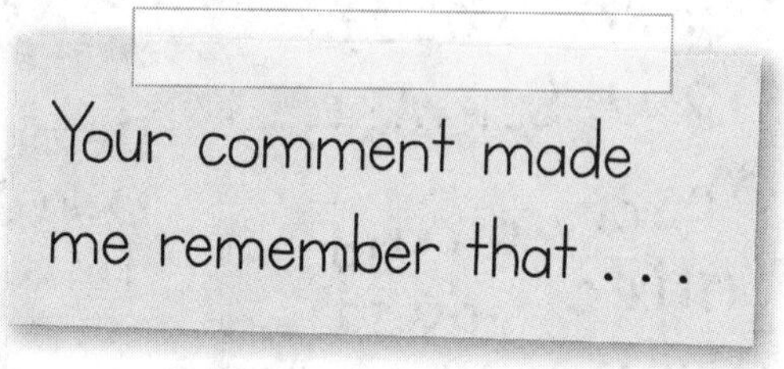
Your comment made me remember that . . .

Weekly Question

Why do scientists explore and study oceans?

Academic Vocabulary

Learning Goal

I can develop knowledge about language to make connections between reading and writing.

Related words may share roots or word parts. These words can have different meanings depending on how the word is used, such as *preserve*, *preserving*, and *preservation*.

My TURN For each word,

1. **Use** print or digital resources, such as a dictionary or thesaurus, to find related words.
2. **Add** a related word to the box.
3. **Choose** the correct form of the word to complete the sentence.

Word	Related Words	Fill in the Correct Form of the Word
expert	experts expertise __________	She consulted several __________ before she bought the painting.
focus	focused unfocused __________	Her mind was __________ as she thought about the game instead of studying.
relate	related relative __________	Tran's closest __________ lives three towns away from him.
detect	detecting detective __________	The __________ solved the crime in a matter of months.

Open and Closed Syllables V/CV and VC/V

An **open syllable (V/CV)** ends in a vowel and has a long vowel sound, such as the first syllable of *even*. A **closed syllable (VC/V)** ends in a consonant. The vowel in a closed syllable has a short sound, such as the first syllable in *frigid*.

The first syllable of the word *remaining* in paragraph 5 of *Far from Shore* is an open syllable because it ends in a vowel: re/main/ing. It has a long vowel sound. The first syllable of the word *finish* is a closed syllable because it ends in a consonant: fin/ish. It has a short vowel sound.

My TURN Read the words, and correctly divide each word into syllables. Then determine if the first syllable of each word is open or closed. If needed, check a print or digital dictionary.

Word	Syllables	Open or closed?
recording	re/cord/ing	open
living		
nature		
limitless		

Read Like a Writer

Authors of informational texts use graphic features such as photographs, diagrams, and other images to present information in a way that is easy to understand. Graphic features are usually paired with text features, such as headings, labels, or captions.

Model! Review the diagram and caption near paragraph 4 of *Far from Shore.*

1. **Identify** Sophie Webb uses a labeled image to present information in the text.
2. **Question** How does the graphic feature help me understand the concept?
3. **Conclude** The caption identifies what the picture shows, and the labels give details about how the scientists work together.

Reread paragraph 9 of the text, view the diagram on the same page, and read the caption.

My TURN Follow the steps to analyze the author's use of print and graphic features to clarify the concept she explains.

1. **Identify** Sophie Webb uses ______________________________

   ______________________________.
2. **Question** How do the graphic features help me understand the concept?
3. **Conclude** The graphic features ______________________________

   ____

   ______________________________.

Write for a Reader

Images can focus attention or clarify concepts.

Writers include specific text features and visuals in informational texts to engage readers and explain concepts.

My TURN Think about how Sophie Webb's use of graphic features in *Far from Shore* affects your understanding of the text. Now identify how you can use graphic features to clarify information and engage your own readers.

1. If you were trying to inform a reader about your favorite animal, what graphic features might you include?

2. Describe a graphic feature you would add to an informational report about scientific observations of the ocean. Tell why you would use that feature.

Spell Words with Open and Closed Syllables

An **open syllable (V/CV)** ends in a vowel. A **closed syllable (VC/V)** ends with a consonant.

My TURN Read the words. Spell and sort each word by its first syllable: V/CV or VC/V. After sorting, add a slash between each syllable of each word.

SPELLING WORDS

recent	rotate	energetic	malice
topical	musical	solar	recommend
honest	element	vacation	apex
lavish	minimum	register	enemy
vital	donut	slogan	agent

Open Syllables V/CV	Closed Syllables VC/V

Subject-Verb Agreement

The **subject** of a sentence tells what the sentence is about. The **verb** tells what the subject is or does. A subject and verb agree when they are both singular or both plural. The first and third sentences below are written incorrectly.

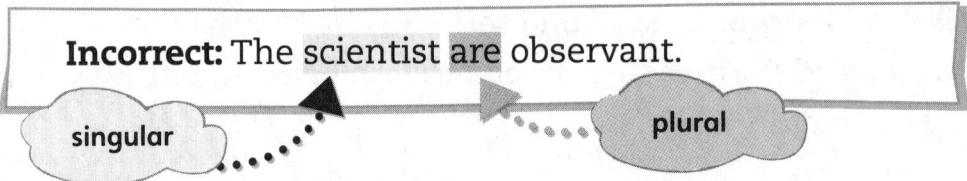

Incorrect: The scientist are observant.

singular plural

The author corrected the sentence by making the singular subject and verb agree.

Correct: The scientist is observant.

Incorrect: The concert for the girls are at noon.

singular plural

The author corrected the sentence by making the subject and verb agree.

Correct: The concert for the girls is at noon.

MyTURN Edit this draft by correcting any errors in subject-verb agreement.

Scientists and crew members both wears rubber boots on the boat. The lead researcher on the team follow all safety procedures. As they observe the dolphins and birds, the scientists takes some samples. One team collects living organisms, and another team classify them.

Analyze an Informational Article

Learning Goal

I can use elements of informational writing to write an informational article.

An **informational article** is a text that gives facts and details about who, what, where, when, and why important events happen. An informational article often gives the most important information first, followed by supporting details.

My TURN Use an informational article you have read to complete the chart. Write information readers need most at the top. Then add details.

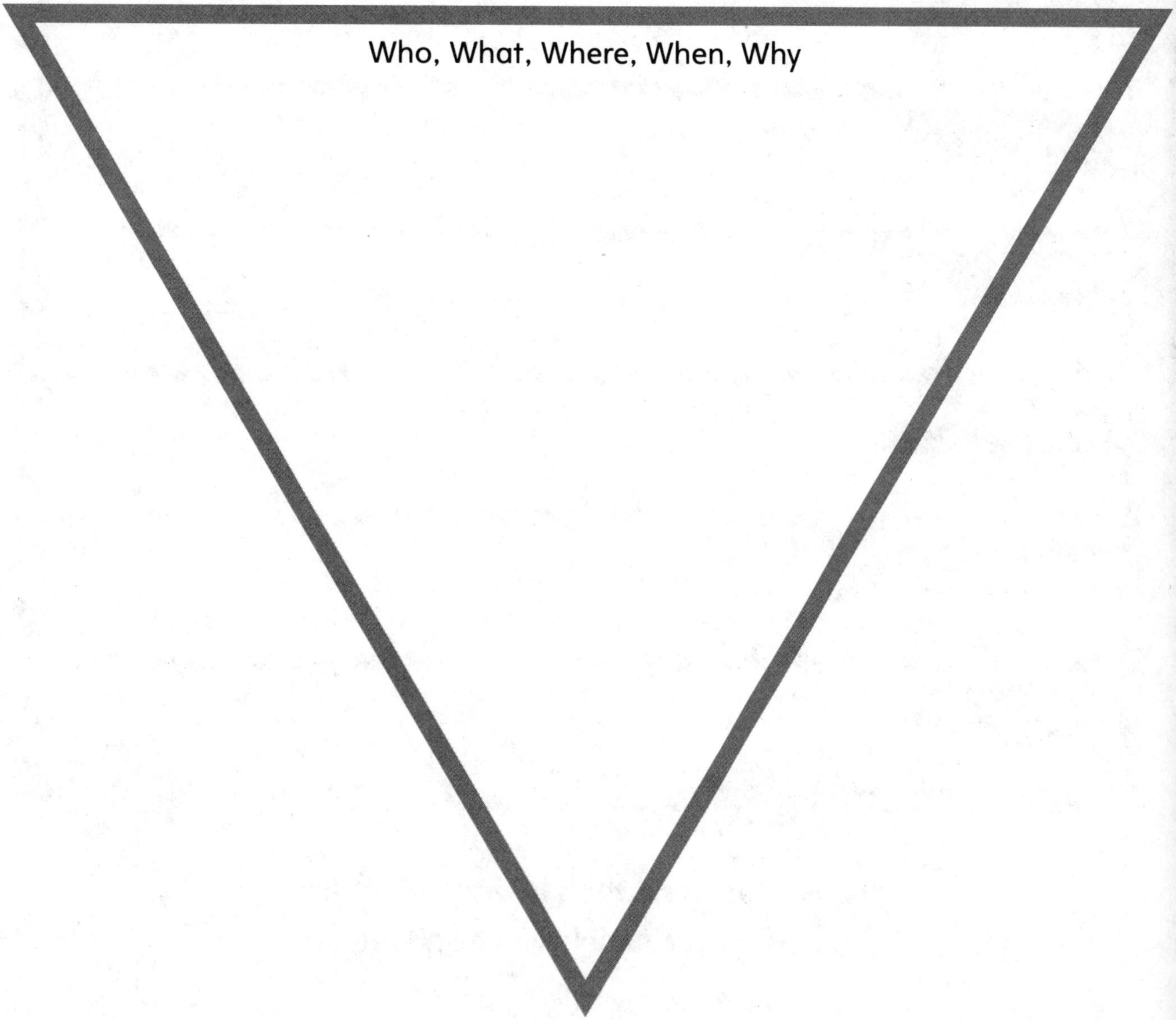

Analyze a Lead Paragraph

A lead, or first, paragraph in an informational article answers important questions about the topic: *Who? What? Where? When? Why?* and *How?*

My TURN Reread an informational article in your classroom library. Complete the chart as you analyze the lead paragraph.

Title	
Who?	
What?	
Where?	
When?	
Why?	
How?	

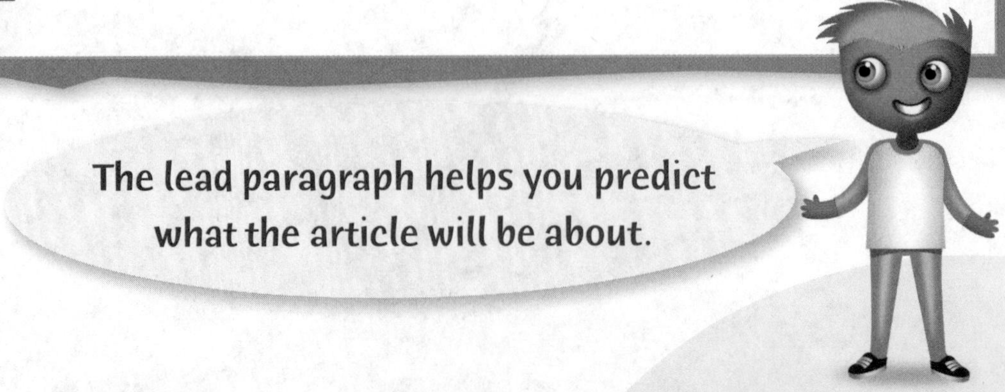

The lead paragraph helps you predict what the article will be about.

Identify Details in Photographs

Writers carefully choose the photographs that accompany informational articles. Photographs

- show important or meaningful events that are mentioned in the text.
- may provide additional details and add interest.
- help a reader better understand the text.

My TURN Read an informational article from your classroom library. Complete the chart to show what you learn from an image in the text.

Title
What is the article about?
Who or what does the picture show?
What details does the picture show that the text does not mention?
Why did the author include the photograph?

Set a Purpose

Before a writer begins, he or she considers the task, purpose, and audience.

My TURN Answer the questions as you plan your informational article.

The **task** is what you are assigned to do.
What are you being asked to do?

The **audience** is who will read your writing.
Who will read my article? What do my readers need to know about the topic?

The **purpose** is why you are writing.
Are you writing to entertain, persuade, or inform your readers? How will you achieve your purpose?

WRITE FOR YOUR AUDIENCE:

- ☐ I will give facts and details about a topic.
- ☐ I believe my audience will be interested in learning about this topic.
- ☐ I will use language that helps my readers understand the most important details.

Use this checklist to choose a topic for your informational article.

Plan Your Informational Article

Writers sometimes **map** to generate ideas for an article.

BEFORE YOU BEGIN

- Think of a topic to write about.
- Build a web diagram that looks like this with that topic written in the center circle.

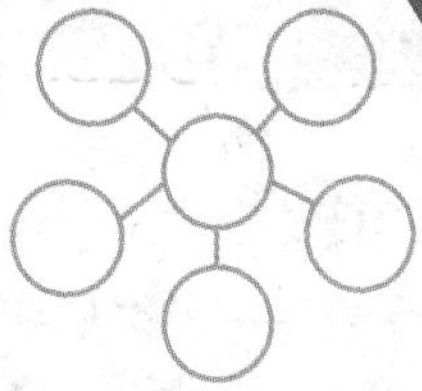

START PLANNING

- Brainstorm details about the topic.
- Write each detail in a circle that extends from the center.
- For each detail, consider supporting details or facts.
- Write the supporting information next to the detail it supports.

REVIEW YOUR MAP

- Reread the main idea and details you wrote.
- Highlight the details that are most important for your readers.
- Use those details as you continue to outline, research, and write.

DISCUSS YOUR PLAN

- Ask and answer relevant questions about each map in your Writing Club.
- Talk to your partners about how mapping your ideas helped to organize your thinking.

MY TURN Follow the steps to map ideas for your informational article.

INTERACTIVITY

Protecting HABITATS

A natural habitat is a place where environmental conditions allow certain plants and animals to thrive. When environmental conditions change, plants and animals may struggle to survive. When people protect natural habitats, they also protect the species that live in those habitats.

North America

South America

POLAR BEAR Polar bears are built for cold climates. They spend most of their time on sea ice in the Arctic Ocean. Warmer temperatures can melt away the ice a polar bear needs to survive. Arctic communities and governments have created incentives and plans to keep the polar bear safe from extinction.

THE AMAZON The Amazon is the world's largest tropical rain forest. It is home to 40,000 plant species, 1,300 bird species, 3,000 types of fish, 430 types of mammals, and 2.5 million different kinds of insects! Rain forests around the world are threatened by deforestation, the act of cutting down trees. Securing forest habitats as national parks is one effort that protects the Amazon and its inhabitants.

Weekly Question

What can people do to protect species from a changing environment?

MOUNTAIN GORILLA Mountain gorillas live in a small range in eastern and central Africa. Changes in climate and human activity, such as commercial development, threaten gorilla populations. Sanctuaries, ecotourism, and nature preserves help protect mountain gorillas and their habitat.

Freewrite Think of ways in which you can help protect plant and animal species in your environment. Quickly write your ideas.

Learning Goal

I can learn about informational text by analyzing text structure.

Spotlight on Genre

Informational Text

In **informational text**, the author's main purpose is to inform or explain. The author uses a text structure, or way of organizing the information, to clarify relationships between ideas in the text. Authors use text structure to

- compare and contrast ideas
- organize ideas by cause and effect
- show the order in which events happened
- describe details in depth
- state a problem and offer one or more solutions

Establish a Purpose The **purpose** for reading informational texts is often to learn something new. You also read informational texts to better understand a concept or process.

To identify text structure, look for descriptions, comparisons, causes, or problems that need solving.

TURN and TALK With a partner, discuss different purposes for reading *A Place for Frogs*. For example, you may want to learn about different types of frogs. Set your purpose for reading this text.

My PURPOSE ____________________

____

____

____

____

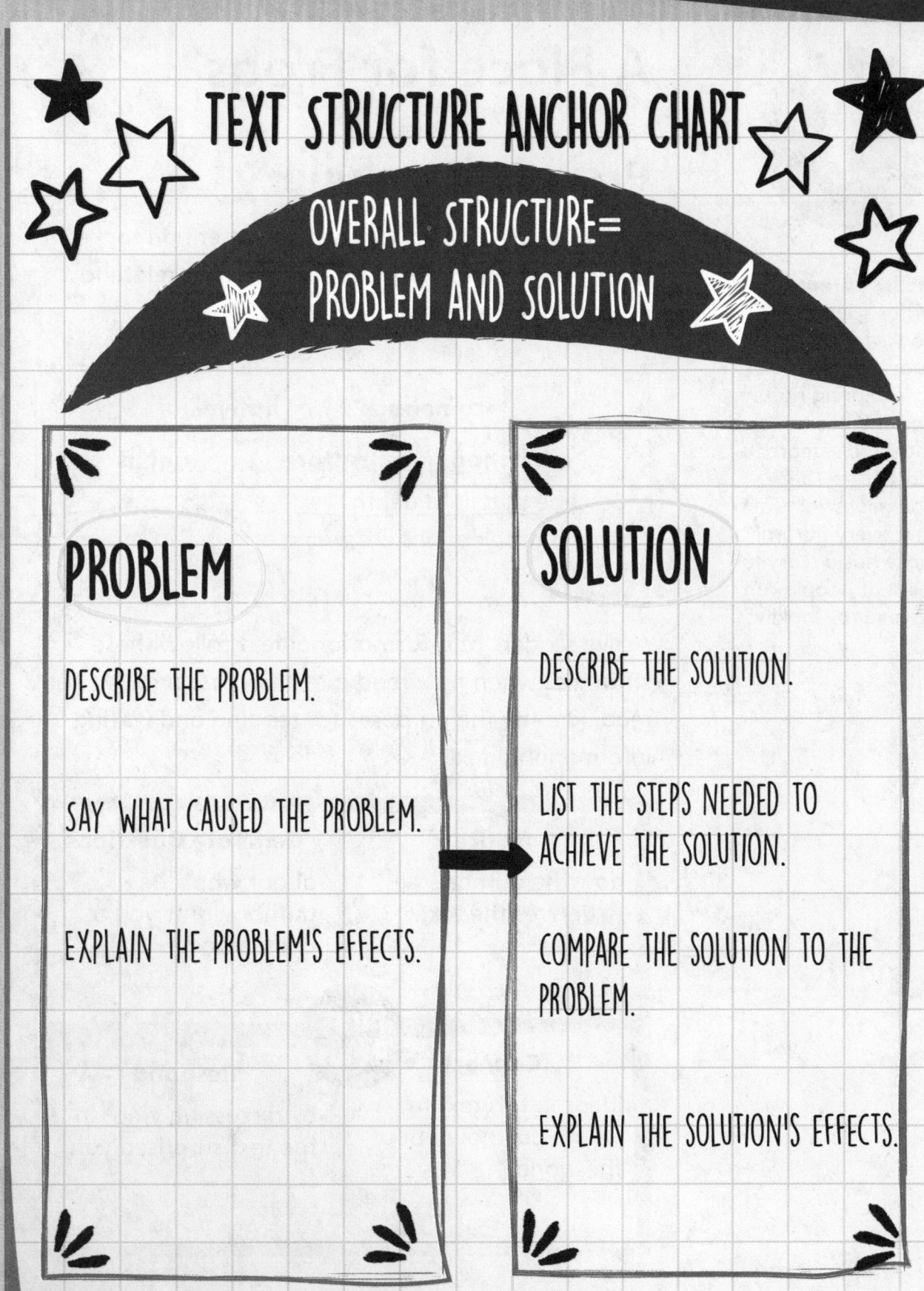

TEXT STRUCTURE ANCHOR CHART

OVERALL STRUCTURE= PROBLEM AND SOLUTION

PROBLEM	SOLUTION
DESCRIBE THE PROBLEM.	DESCRIBE THE SOLUTION.
SAY WHAT CAUSED THE PROBLEM.	LIST THE STEPS NEEDED TO ACHIEVE THE SOLUTION.
EXPLAIN THE PROBLEM'S EFFECTS.	COMPARE THE SOLUTION TO THE PROBLEM.
	EXPLAIN THE SOLUTION'S EFFECTS.

Meet *the* Author

Melissa Stewart writes science books for young people. She grew up exploring nature, and she has traveled widely to research more than 150 books. Stewart says that every natural place has a story to tell that people can discover by looking.

A Place for Frogs

Preview Vocabulary

As you read *A Place for Frogs*, pay attention to these vocabulary words. Notice how they relate to key ideas in the text.

comeback **native**
migrating **restore** **fungus**

Read

Active readers of **informational text** follow these strategies when they read a text the first time. As you read, identify the purposes for reading and writing an informational text.

First Read

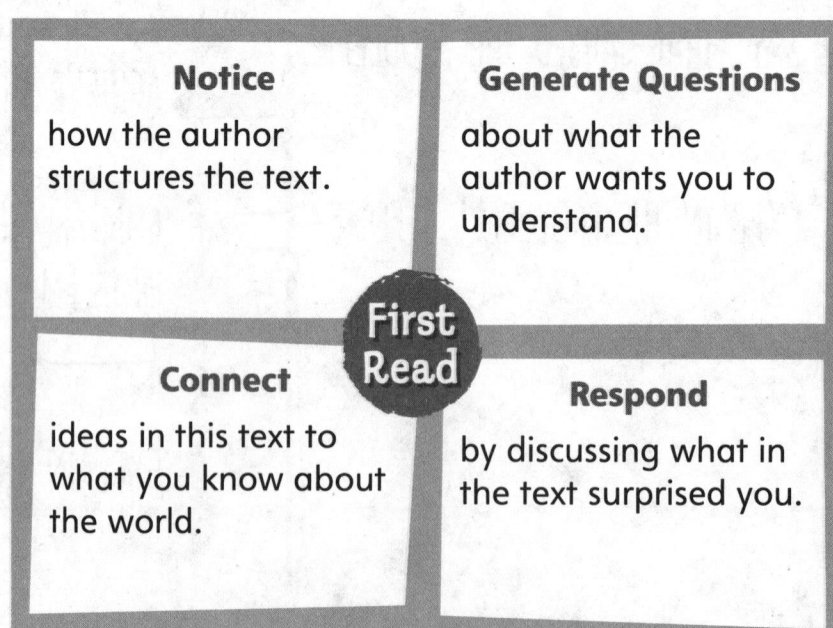

Notice how the author structures the text.

Generate Questions about what the author wants you to understand.

Connect ideas in this text to what you know about the world.

Respond by discussing what in the text surprised you.

Genre | Informational Text

A Place for FROGS

by Melissa Stewart | illustrated by Higgins Bond

AUDIO

ANNOTATE

CLOSE READE

Monitor Comprehension

Annotating a text can help you break it down and better understand it.

Highlight a detail that helps you identify the problem the author will describe in the text.

1 Frogs make our world a better place. But sometimes people do things that make it hard for them to live and grow.

2 If we work together to help these special creatures, there will always be a place for frogs.

A Frog's Life

As frogs grow, they go through four life stages. After mating, a female frog lays eggs in a wet place. When a tiny tadpole breaks out of its egg, it spends most of its time eating and growing. Soon the tadpole begins to develop legs. Its tail shrinks, and it starts breathing air. The froglet hops onto land. It grows quickly and loses its tail. When it becomes a full-grown frog, it is ready to find a mate.

3 For frogs to survive, they need to stay safe and healthy. Some frogs are harmed by poisons used to kill insects.

4 When people stop spraying these dangerous chemicals, frogs can live and grow.

California Red-Legged Frog

Because frogs have thin skin, they are very sensitive to human-made chemicals. When people in Northern California sprayed poisons to kill insects that harm crops, many California red-legged frogs died too. In 2006, the Center for Biological Diversity forced people to stop using the chemicals that harm frogs. Now scientists are hoping the frogs can make a comeback.

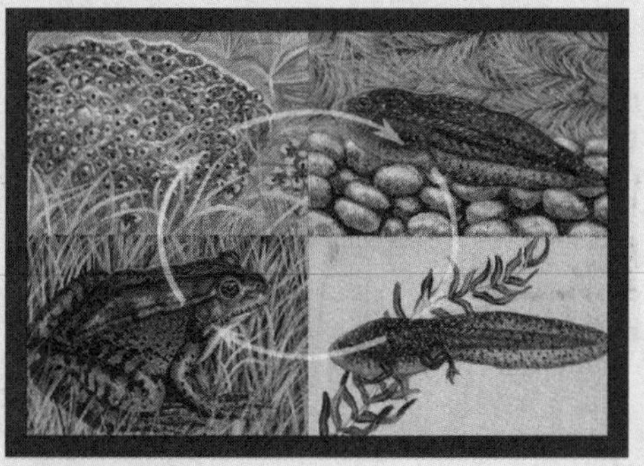

CLOSE READ

Analyze Text Structure

Underline the problem and solution presented on this page.

comeback a return to a healthy state

CLOSE READ

Monitor Comprehension

Reread the text to identify problems and solutions.

Highlight details that help you understand what caused the frogs' legs to be deformed.

5 Some tadpoles are harmed by chemicals farmers use to make crops grow bigger and stronger.

6 When farmers and scientists find new ways to improve their crops, frogs can live and grow.

Northern Leopard Frog

In 1995, students in Henderson, Minnesota, found frogs with deformed legs at a local pond. It took scientists many years to figure out what was wrong.

When fertilizers from fields drained into the pond, the population of tiny flatworms exploded. The worms burrowed into the tadpoles' bodies and their legs couldn't develop normally. Now that scientists understand the problem, they are searching for a solution.

7 Some frogs lay their eggs in shallow ponds. The eggs can be damaged by too much sunlight.

8 When people find ways to block some of the sun's harmful rays, frogs can live and grow.

Western Toad

In the 1960s, people began using chemicals called CFCs in refrigerators and air conditioners. As the CFCs rose into the sky, they destroyed the part of Earth's atmosphere that blocks the sun's harmful rays. Super-strong sunlight killed many developing western toad tadpoles before they hatched. In 1995, CFCs were banned. By 2003, Earth's atmosphere had begun to block more sunlight. Scientists hope that it is not too late to save western toads.

CLOSE READ

Analyze Text Structure

Underline a possible solution to the problem that strong sun damages western toad eggs.

CLOSE READ

Analyze Text Structure

Underline the problem and the solution presented on this page.

native belonging naturally to a specific place

9 Some frogs have trouble surviving when people introduce new plants to a natural habitat.

10 When people grow native plants to feed their horses and cattle, frogs can live and grow.

Oregon Spotted Frog

As Americans moved westward in the 1800s, some of them planted reed canary grass to feed their animals. It grew so thick that Oregon spotted frogs had trouble finding places to lay their eggs.

Soon, the frogs were almost gone. Now that scientists know why Oregon spotted frogs are disappearing, they can remove the reed canary grass and replace it with native plants.

11 Some tadpoles have trouble surviving when people add fish to lakes and ponds.

12 When people take out the fish, frogs can live and grow.

Sierra Nevada Yellow-Legged Frog

Because the lakes high in the Sierra Nevada Mountains are so beautiful, people thought it would be fun to go fishing there. They added tons of trout to the lakes. It didn't take long for the fish to devour most of the yellow-legged tadpoles. When scientists noticed the problem, they convinced people to remove the trout. Then the frog population began to recover.

CLOSE READ

Analyze Text Structure

Underline the solution that helped to rebuild the frog population.

CLOSE READ

Monitor Comprehension

Reread the text and text feature on this page.

Highlight text clues that show a possible solution to a problem.

13 Frogs have trouble surviving when their natural homes are destroyed. Many frogs lay their eggs in wetlands that dry up in the summer.

14 When people protect these part-time ponds, frogs can live and grow.

Houston Toad

In the 1960s, people started building homes, businesses, and parking lots on the land where Houston toads lived. As workers filled in temporary ponds, Houston toads began to disappear. But now scientists realize how important the pools are. They have asked people to build fences around the pools so Houston toads have a place to lay their eggs. If people protect enough ponds, the toads can make a comeback.

15 Frogs that lay eggs in part-time ponds live in nearby forests. They travel to the pools each spring to mate and lay eggs. Sometimes they are killed when they try to cross busy roads.

16 When people make the trip safer, frogs can live and grow.

Wood Frog

Frogs don't know that roads are dangerous, and drivers can't always stop in time. In some towns, people watch for wood frogs on warm, rainy nights in early spring. When they see migrating frogs, the caring citizens stop traffic while the frogs hop across the road.

CLOSE READ

Analyze Text Structure

Underline the problem and solution described on this page.

migrating moving from one habitat to another with the seasons

CLOSE READ

Monitor Comprehension

How can fires have a positive effect on frog habitats? Discuss with a partner.

Highlight details that help you understand this solution.

restore return to original condition

17 Some frogs can only survive in sunny, open woodlands.

18 When people work to restore these wild places, frogs can live and grow.

Gopher Frog

At one time, natural wildfires regularly burned back plants in areas where gopher frogs live. But when people settled in the area, they put out the fires. Some plants grew large, crowding out the smaller plants gopher tadpoles depend on for food and shelter. In spring, the big plants sucked up wetland water before tadpoles could develop into frogs. When scientists noticed the problem, they began to carefully burn some forest areas so gopher frogs can survive.

19 Other frogs depend on wetlands surrounded by thick, low shrubs.

20 When people work to save these watery worlds, frogs can live and grow.

Pine Barrens Tree Frog

In the late 1950s, the members of a county planning board in New Jersey proposed cutting down a pineland forest and building an airport. The project would have destroyed dozens of ponds where Pine Barrens tree frogs live. Fortunately, scientists and citizens worked together to stop the project and protect the land forever. Thanks to their efforts, Pine Barrens tree frogs will always have a place to live.

CLOSE READ

Vocabulary in Context

A **context clue** is a word or phrase that surrounds an unfamiliar word. Context clues help readers determine the meaning of unfamiliar words in a text.

Underline context clues that support your definition of *board*.

CLOSE READ

Analyze Text Structure

Underline details that show a solution to the problem of pollution in caves.

21 Some frogs can only live in cool, dark, rocky places.

22 When people clean up and protect these natural areas, frogs can live and grow.

Puerto Rico Rock Frog

The Puerto Rico rock frog lives in small caves in the southeastern part of Puerto Rico, an island in the Caribbean Sea. For many years, local people dumped their garbage in the caves. But now the dumping has stopped and citizens are cleaning up the caves. A healthy habitat will help the frogs survive.

23 Many frogs are dying of a terrible disease caused by a fungus. Scientists think the fungus is growing and spreading quickly because Earth is warming up.

24 When people use less oil, coal, and natural gas to heat their homes and power their cars, it helps slow down global warming. Then frogs can live and grow.

Harlequin Frog

More than a hundred kinds of harlequin frogs used to live in the rainforests of Central America. But now more than half of them are extinct. As we burn fossil fuels, Earth's atmosphere heats up and more clouds form over rainforests. That makes days cooler and nights warmer. These are perfect conditions for the fungus that is killing the frogs. If we can slow global warming soon, we may be able to save harlequin frogs.

CLOSE READ

Monitor Comprehension

Reread the text and talk to a partner.

Highlight evidence that helps you understand how humans can keep frogs alive.

fungus an organism that gets nutrition from decaying matter

CLOSE READ

Analyze Text Structure

Underline details that discuss why it is important to solve the main problem discussed in the text.

25 When too many frogs die, other living things may also have trouble surviving.

26 That's why it's so important to protect frogs and the places where they live.

27 Frogs have lived on Earth for about 200 million years.

We Need Frogs

Frogs help us survive. By eating insects, frogs protect farmers' crops and help us stay healthy. Frogs are very sensitive to changes in the environment. When we see problems in our frogs, it warns us of dangers that might affect other plants and animals too. Then we can look for ways to fix the problems.

Other Animals Need Frogs

Frogs are an important part of the food chain. Eggs and tadpoles are good sources of food for fish, large water insects, and ducks. Adult frogs are eaten by fish, snakes, lizards, bats, otters, foxes, water shrews, and birds. Without frogs, many other creatures would go hungry.

28 Sometimes people do things that can harm frogs. But there are many ways you can help these special creatures live far into the future.

29 Join a group of people keeping track of frogs that live in your area.

30 Join a group of people working to protect or restore wetlands near your home.

31 Talk to teachers at your school about celebrating Save the Frogs Day.

Helping Frogs

- Do not catch and keep frogs. Let them live in their natural environment.
- Do not buy frogs at a pet store. Frogs are wild animals and should live in their natural homes.
- If someone gives you a frog, do not release it in a wild place. It could eat other frogs or make them sick.
- Do not eat frogs' legs. Ask local restaurants not to serve them.
- Do not spray chemicals that could harm frogs.

CLOSE READ

Monitor Comprehension

Highlight a problem that the author is addressing in this section.

Monitor Comprehension

Ask a partner about the results of the scientists' research.

Highlight details that support your understanding.

Fascinating Frog Facts

32 No one knows exactly how many kinds of frogs live on Earth. So far, scientists have discovered and named almost five thousand different species. But people keep on finding new kinds of frogs every year.

33 The microfrog is the smallest frog on Earth. It's about the size of your fingernail. The Goliath frog is the world's largest frog. It's as big as a rabbit.

34 About five hundred kinds of frogs belong to a family called the "true toads." They have dry, scaly skin and spend more time on land than other frogs. That means all toads are frogs, but not all frogs are toads.

35 A female western toad can lay up to 16,500 eggs at a time. But less than 1 percent of those eggs hatch and develop into adults. The lucky few western toads that do grow up may live more than thirty-five years.

36 Harlequin frog tadpoles can only eat one kind of food—extra eggs laid by their moms.

37 In winter, wood frogs bury themselves in leaves and freeze solid. In spring, the males attract mates with a call that sounds like a quacking duck.

CLOSE READ

Analyze Text Structure

Underline a problem for which the author does not provide a solution.

Develop Vocabulary

In informational texts, authors use precise words to describe important ideas about a topic. For example, in *A Place for Frogs*, author Melissa Stewart uses the specific phrases “chemicals called CFCs” and “reed canary grass” to describe items that people introduced to frogs’ habitats.

My TURN Read each pair of words from *A Place for Frogs*. Then write a sentence to explain how these words help you understand an idea from the text.

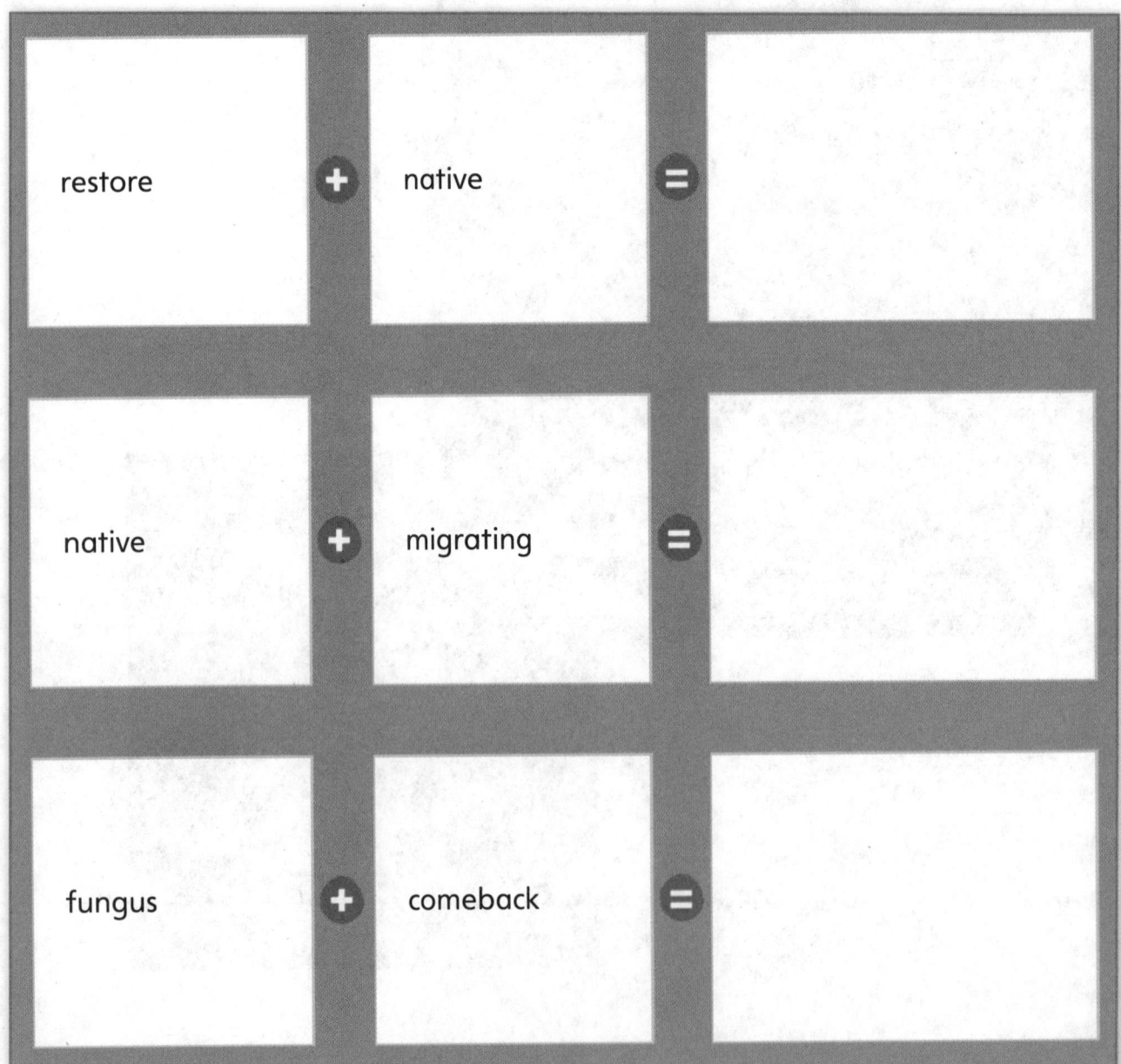

restore	+	native	=	
native	+	migrating	=	
fungus	+	comeback	=	

Monitor Comprehension

To ensure you understand what you read, monitor your comprehension of vocabulary, main ideas, and text structure. Make adjustments by rereading and asking questions when your understanding breaks down.

1. **My TURN** Go back to the Close Read notes and highlight text evidence that helps you understand the text.
2. **Text Evidence** Make adjustments to your understanding by annotating, rereading, and talking to a partner. Record your highlighted text in the graphic organizer.

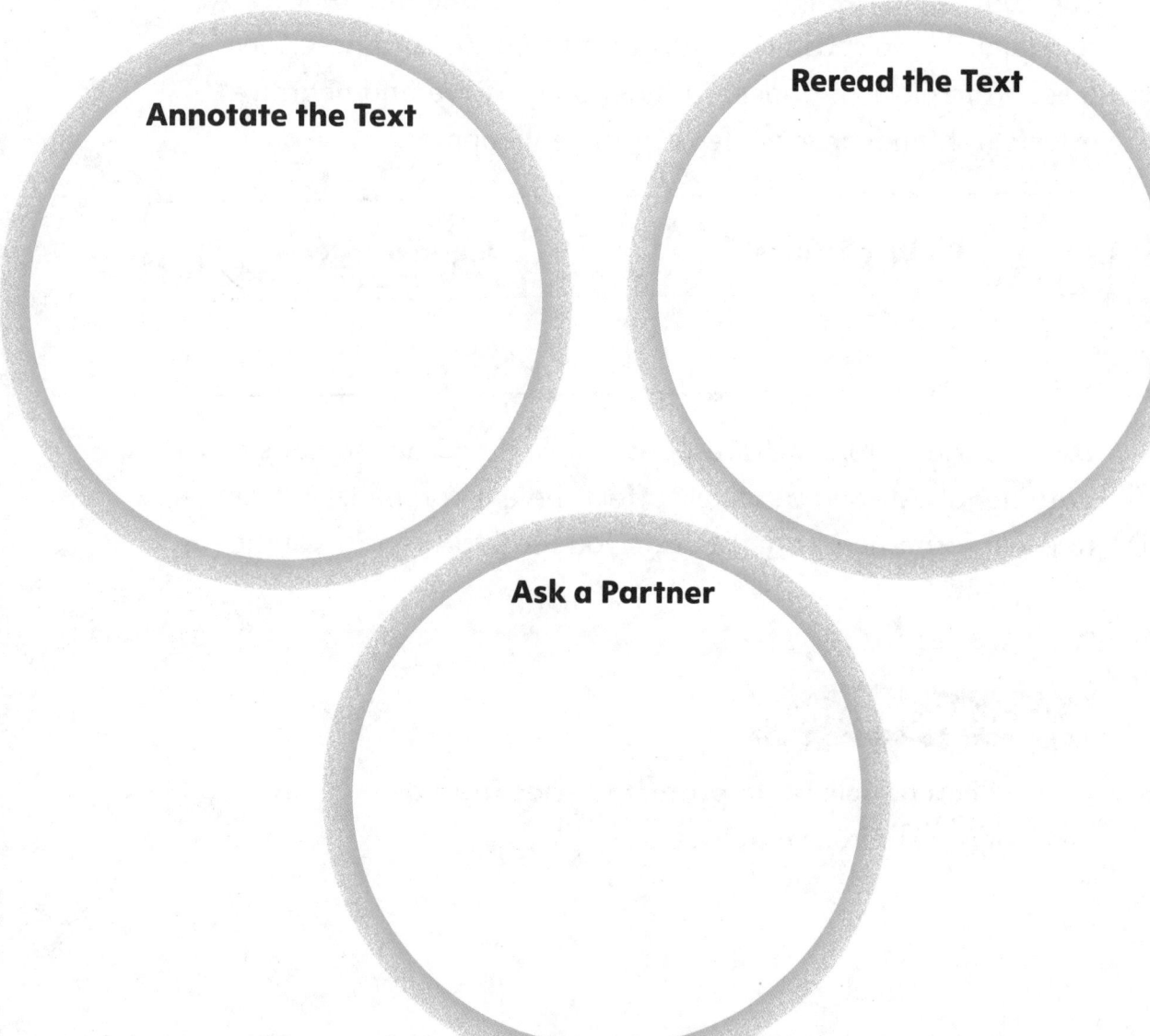

Annotate the Text

Reread the Text

Ask a Partner

Reflect and Share

Write to Sources *A Place for Frogs* includes several examples of human impact on frogs' habitats. Consider all the texts you have read this week. How have humans affected the environment in positive and negative ways? Use examples from the texts to write and support a response.

Compare and Contrast Writers use text evidence to compare and contrast ideas. They look at similarities and differences to explain a topic. Use the chart as a model to take notes on a separate piece of paper. Consider the positive and negative effects of human involvement on the environment.

Positive Effects	Negative Effects

Use your notes to write a response explaining how humans can both negatively and positively affect the environment. Remember to use information from the texts you read to support your ideas.

Weekly Question

What can people do to protect species from a changing environment?

Academic Vocabulary

Learning Goal

I can develop knowledge about language to make connections between reading and writing.

Synonyms, or words with similar meanings, and **antonyms**, words with opposite meanings, can help you better understand new words and express ideas.

MyTURN For each sample thesaurus entry,

1. **Read** each academic vocabulary entry word. Note that some words have more than one meaning.
2. **Choose** two synonyms and two antonyms.
3. **Confirm** your synonyms and antonyms in a print or online dictionary or thesaurus.

focus, *n.* **1** center of attention

Synonyms: main idea or topic, spotlight

Antonyms: edge, background

focus, *v.* to pay special attention to

Synonyms: ____________

Antonyms: ____________

relate, *v.* to tell a story or share detailed information

Synonyms: ____________

Antonyms: ____________

visible, *adj.* seen clearly

Synonyms: ____________

Antonyms: ____________

Final Stable Syllables *-le, -tion, -sion*

Final stable syllables always appear at the end of words. A final syllable ending in *-le* always has three letters: a consonant and *-le*. An example can be found in paragraph 9 of *A Place for Frogs*: the word *trou/ble.*

The final stable syllables *-tion* and *-sion* are both prounced *shun* or *zhun*. For example, the word *solution* in the "Northern Leopard Frog" text feature contains the final syllable *-tion: sol/u/tion.*

My TURN Read each word. Then rewrite each word using slashes to show the syllables. Check your syllabication in a print or digital dictionary if necessary.

terrible	decision
collision	comprehension
information	people
obstacle	article
population	question

ter/ri/ble

Read Like a Writer

An author's purpose is his or her reason for writing. Four common purposes for writing are to persuade, to inform, to entertain, and to express ideas and feelings. An author can have more than one purpose. For example, a text that informs readers about an issue may also persuade readers to take action.

Model! Read the text from *A Place for Frogs.*

> For frogs to survive, they need to stay safe and healthy. Some frogs are harmed by poisons used to kill insects.

1. **Identify** Melissa Stewart relates facts about the health of frogs.
2. **Question** What effect do her word choices have?
3. **Conclude** The reader is informed about frogs and persuaded to stop using poisons to kill insects.

Reread paragraph 23 of the text.

My TURN Follow the steps to analyze the passage. Explain the author's purpose for writing the text.

1. **Identify** The problem Melissa Stewart addresses is ______________________ ______________________. The author includes facts, such as ______________________ and the description ______________________.
2. **Question** What effect do the author's choices have on her purpose?
3. **Conclude** Her choices emphasize her purposes: to ______________________ and to ______________________.

Write for a Reader

Authors often have more than one purpose for writing. If an author's main purpose is to persuade, the author must support his or her opinion with reasons and evidence to make it convincing.

To persuade people, give them information that supports your point!

My TURN Think about why Melissa Stewart presents much of the information in *A Place for Frogs* in text features, such as sidebars. Now identify how you can present information to persuade readers to agree with your opinion.

1. Describe the purpose of Melissa Stewart's sidebars about different kinds of frogs.

2. Write a paragraph that begins with an opinion reflecting a concern about frogs. Support your opinion with details and facts that will help readers understand your concern. Develop a text feature that supports your opinion.

Spell Words with Final Stable Syllables *-le*, *-tion*, *-sion*

Final stable syllables always appear at the end of words.

My TURN Read the words. Spell and sort the words by their final stable syllable.

SPELLING WORDS

observation	article	observe	ripple
collide	declaration	situation	invasion
scuffle	invade	collision	occupation
extension	untangle	declare	extend
situate	assemble	occupy	particle

-le

______
______
______
______
______
______

-tion

______
______
______
______

-sion

______
______
______
______
______

Other

______
______
______
______
______
______
______

Principal Parts of Regular Verbs

Verb tense shows various times, sequences of events, states, and conditions. Verb tenses are formed from a verb's principal parts: the present, the present participle, the past, and the past participle.

The present tense tells what is happening now. The past tense tells what has already been or happened. Form participles by adding forms of *be* or *have*.

Principal Part	Add	Example
Present	singular subject: *-s* or *-es* plural subject: no change	He *walks.* The girls *walk.*
Present Participle	a form of *be* + *-ing*	She *is walking.* The boys *are walking.*
Past	*-ed*	The man *walked.* They *walked.*
Past Participle	a form of *be* or *have* + *-ed*	The dog *has walked.* I *have walked.*

My TURN Edit this draft by changing the verbs to past tense or the past participle.

People's actions affect frogs' environments. Some chemicals and fertilizers harm the animals. Humans move into frogs' habitats and increase dangers for frogs. Many groups form to save frogs.

Develop an Engaging Idea

Learning Goal

I can use elements of informational writing to write an informational article.

Develop ideas for an informational article by choosing a topic that you have thought deeply about. The article might also be about an issue on which you feel strongly. You will focus your writing by including specific facts and details that help your reader understand and take a similar interest in the topic.

MY TURN Read the About the Author features in articles from your classroom library. Use the chart to list details about where those authors got ideas.

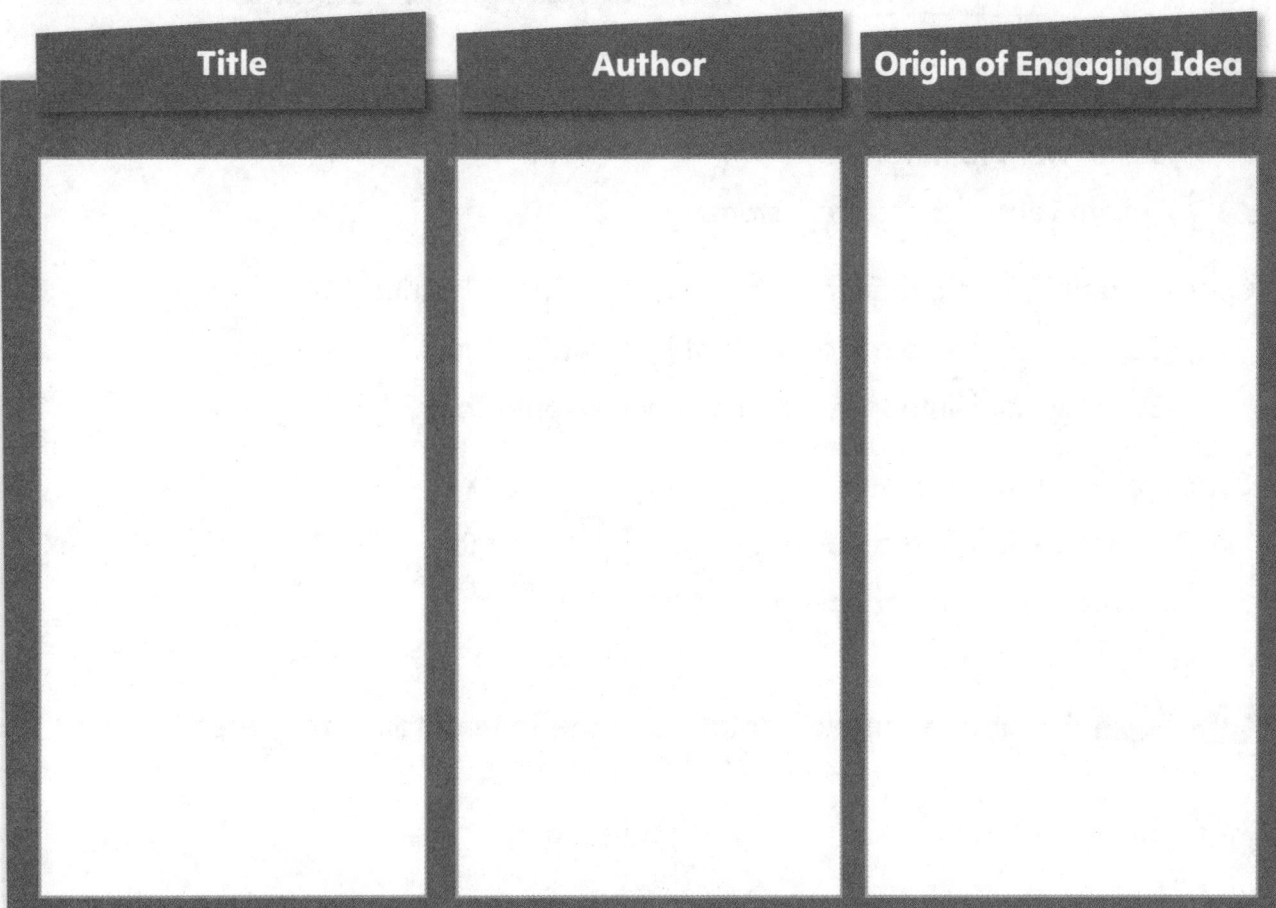

Title	Author	Origin of Engaging Idea

MY TURN In your writing notebook, develop several ideas for your own informational article. Choose the most engaging, and create a map or outline of specific facts and details to focus your writing.

Draft with Specific Facts and Concrete Details

Make your informational article more effective and trustworthy by including specific facts and concrete details. Facts are true statements that can be proven with research and evidence.

Lacey is five feet tall.	**Fact:** This can be proven by measuring Lacey's height.
Lacey works too hard.	**Not a Fact:** This is an opinion that cannot be proven with hard evidence.

Concrete details are specific instead of general.

Julian went to the store.

Julian went to the grocery store.

Concrete details help a reader visualize what a writer describes.

Susanna sank into the comfort of her favorite chair.

Susanna sank into the cushions of her favorite chair.

Concrete details are precise.

Lawrence left for school at the end of the summer.

Lawrence left for school on August 29.

My TURN For each example, replace an indefinite detail with a precise term.

At night ______________________ Meal ______________________

Softness ______________________ Niceness ______________________

My TURN In your writing notebook, draft an informational article using specific facts. Revise your draft to make general details more concrete.

Develop with Definitions and Quotations

A writer thinks about what his or her audience needs to know in order to understand the topic. Because informational texts often use terms that are specific to a particular subject, a writer may need to provide definitions to guide readers who are unfamiliar with that subject.

> , small animals similar to shrimp,
> Blue whales eat about four tons of krill ^ every day.

A writer may also include quotations from research or from firsthand accounts. Information from these sources makes an article more trustworthy or reliable.

Quotation from Research

The NOAA Web site about blue whales states that after the systematic hunting of whales ended in the 1900s, populations began to increase. However, it cautions, "Mortality and serious injury caused by ship strikes can be a threat to blue whales."

Quotation from Firsthand Account

John Richardson, a marine biologist, studies whales that have become confused by the sounds of modern ships and other underwater machinery. "Whales communicate with clicks and other noises," he says. "The sounds coming from ships can obscure those sounds and decrease the whales' ability to hear each other."

My TURN In your writing notebook, develop a draft of your informational article with definitions and quotations related to the topic. Conduct research as needed. Use correct punctuation for quotations.

Develop with Other Information and Examples

A writer helps readers relate information in an article to what they already know. The writer can do this by providing information and examples that help develop the topic.

> A narwhal has a long, spiraled tusk that grows from the animal's upper lip. While the tusk may look like a rhinoceros's horn, it is actually a tooth, **like an elephant's tusk.** ◀······ Example

My TURN Read a new text from your classroom library. Identify examples and other information the writer uses to describe the topic. An example may compare or contrast the topic with familiar topics.

Title

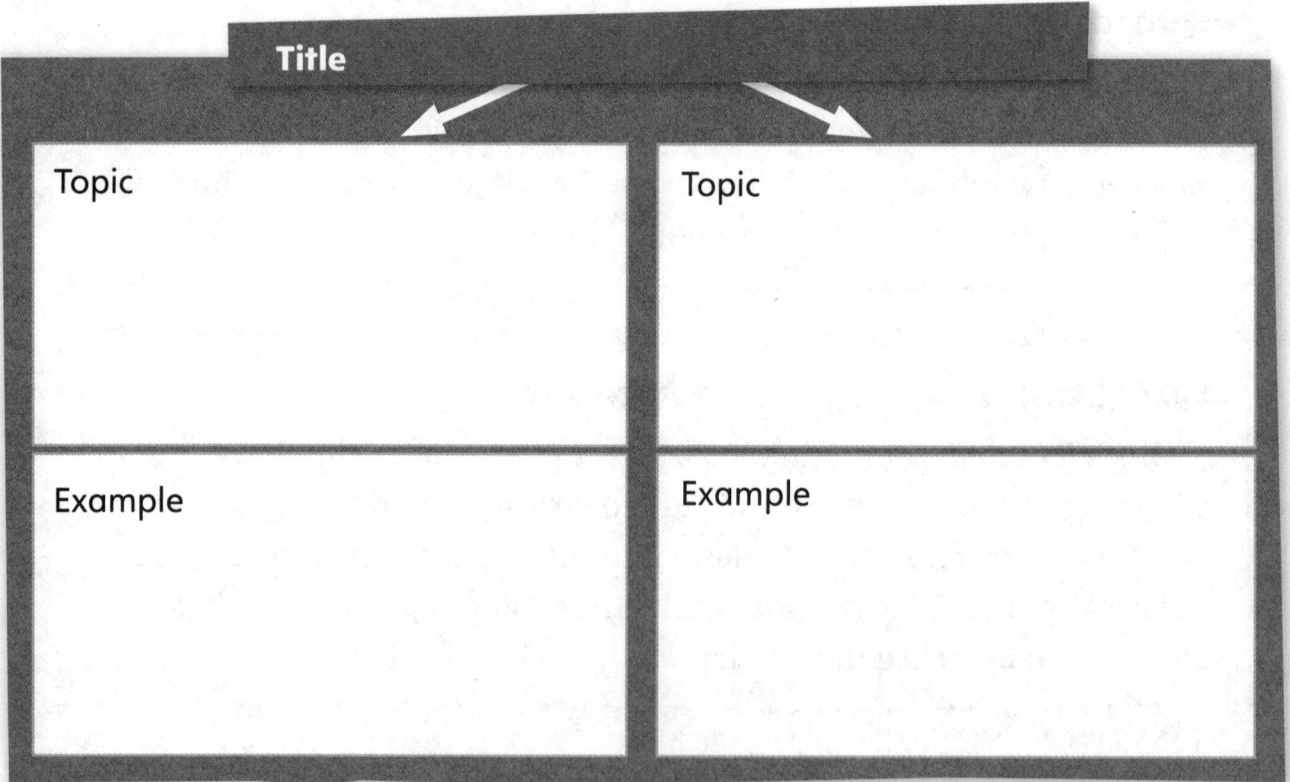

Topic	Topic
Example	Example

My TURN In your writing notebook, develop a draft of your informational article with examples and other information related to the topic.

Develop with Visuals and Multimedia

Writers use illustrations or photographs to tell about a topic. In a digital article, a writer may include videos, sound clips, or other multimedia to help readers visualize information.

The Komodo Dragon

It is easy to understand where the Komodo dragon got the name "dragon." Native to islands near Indonesia—including Komodo—the lizards have scaly skin, flat heads, long noses, and large, strong tails. These dragons can't breathe fire, but they can kill water buffalo with the bacteria in their saliva.

My TURN Use the paragraph and the photograph to answer the questions.

What does the image show that the text does not? What effect does this have?

My TURN Use the checklist to help you select visuals to include in your article. Share your ideas with your Writing Club. Listen actively.

VISUALS AND MULTIMEDIA SHOULD

- [ ] clearly relate to your topic.
- [ ] add something new to the text.
- [ ] help the reader understand the text.

INTERACTIVITY

PERFECT Inspiration

by Emil Martin

I'll be here a week.
The nights will be cool.
In the mornings I'll need
a combustible fuel—

Firewood, that is,
from the wood pile out back.
I split it two years ago,
built up the stack.

The wood is well seasoned;
it's cured, you could say,
now dry as a desert—
it burns best that way.

Weekly Question

How can careful observation help a person survive?

I center the kindling
and carefully light
wood shavings beneath it.
Soon embers glow bright.

A log or two added—
soon crackles and flames
capture my gaze
and whisper their names:

Red cedar, cottonwood,
aspen, and yew;
juniper, hemlock,
and spruce. All will do.

This toasty gold fire
which I feed to make burn
lets me snooze over words
on each page that I turn.

TURN and TALK With a partner, take turns reading stanzas of the poem aloud. Summarize the poem. Then describe a time when you noticed something that other people did not. How did this observation help you?

Learning Goal

I can learn more about the theme *Observations* by understanding point of view in realistic fiction.

Realistic Fiction

Realistic fiction includes events and characters that seem real—but are not. Look for

- A **purpose** of entertaining with a believable story
- **Characters and events** that are imaginary but believable
- The **plot,** or what happens in the story and could also happen in real life
- The **setting,** or the time and place of the story
- The **theme,** or the author's message

TURN and TALK Describe how realistic fiction is different from informational texts you have read. Use the chart to compare and contrast genres. Share your thoughts with a partner.

Be a Fluent Reader Fluent readers read with expression. Realistic fiction often contains dialogue between characters as well as internal monologue, which is one character's inner voice. Dialogue and internal monologue are perfect for practicing reading with expression.

When you read dialogue or internal monologue,

- Raise or lower the pitch of your voice to express the emotion of the character.
- Use inflection when you see a question mark at the end of a sentence.

Realistic Fiction Anchor Chart

PURPOSE:

- To entertain or tell a story

ELEMENTS:

- The setting is real or could be real.
- The characters act and change like real people.
- The plot events could happen in real life.

TEXT STRUCTURE:

- Chronological order

Meet the Author

Gary Paulsen is no stranger to adventure. He has lived in the woods, raced dogs in Alaska, and, like Brian in *Hatchet*, survived tough situations alone. He also goes to extremes with books. Paulsen says that he reads "like a wolf eats"—and wants you to read like that, too!

from

Hatchet

Preview Vocabulary

As you read the excerpt from *Hatchet*, pay attention to these vocabulary words. Notice how they relate to Brian's feelings or actions.

gingerly **ignite**

sputtered **painstaking** **gratified**

Read

Before you read, use what you know about **realistic fiction** to establish a purpose for reading. Follow these strategies as you read this text for the first time.

First Read

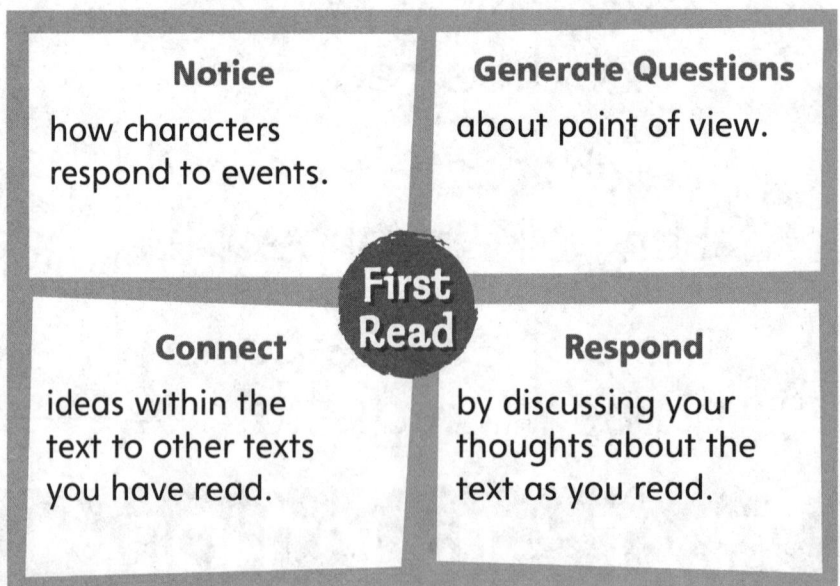

Notice
how characters respond to events.

Generate Questions
about point of view.

Connect
ideas within the text to other texts you have read.

Respond
by discussing your thoughts about the text as you read.

Genre Realistic Fiction

from Hatchet

by Gary Paulsen

AUDIO

ANNOTATE

BACKGROUND

When the pilot of a small plane has a heart attack, thirteen-year-old Brian Robeson, the only other passenger, crash-lands the plane deep in the wilderness. His only survival tool is a hatchet that his mother gave him. Forced to fend for himself, Brian makes a rough shelter and finds berries. After seeing a bear, Brian resolves to keep his hatchet close.

Analyze Point of View

Underline the words in paragraphs 1 through 7 that show that the narrator telling the story is not the main character.

1 At first he thought it was a growl. In the still darkness of the shelter in the middle of the night his eyes came open and he was awake and he thought there was a growl. But it was the wind, a medium wind in the pines had made some sound that brought him up, brought him awake. He sat up and was hit with the smell.

2 It terrified him. The smell was one of rot, some musty rot that made him think only of graves with cobwebs and dust and old death. His nostrils widened and he opened his eyes wider but he could see nothing. It was too dark, too hard dark with clouds covering even the small light from the stars, and he could not see. But the smell was alive, alive and full and in the shelter. He thought of the bear, thought of Bigfoot and every monster he had ever seen in every fright movie he had ever watched, and his heart hammered in his throat.

3 Then he heard the slithering. A brushing sound, a slithering brushing sound near his feet—and he kicked out as hard as he could, kicked out and threw the hatchet at the sound, a noise coming from his throat. But the hatchet missed, sailed into the wall where it hit the rocks with a shower of sparks, and his leg was instantly torn with pain, as if a hundred needles had been driven into it. “Unnnngh!”

4 Now he screamed, with the pain and fear, and skittered on his backside up into the corner of the shelter, breathing through his mouth, straining to see, to hear.

5 The slithering moved again, he thought toward him at first, and terror took him, stopping his breath. He felt he could see a low dark form, a bulk in the darkness, a shadow that lived, but now it moved away, slithering and scraping it moved away and he saw or thought he saw it go out of the door opening.

6 He lay on his side for a moment, then pulled a rasping breath in and held it, listening for the attacker to return. When it was apparent that the shadow wasn't coming back he felt the calf of his leg, where the pain was centered and spreading to fill the whole leg.

7 His fingers gingerly touched a group of needles that had been driven through his pants and into the fleshy part of his calf. They were stiff and very sharp on the ends that stuck out, and he knew then what the attacker had been. A porcupine had stumbled into his shelter and when he had kicked it the thing had slapped him with its tail of quills.

CLOSE READ

Generate Questions

Highlight something the narrator describes. What question do you have about the narrator's point of view?

Record your question on the chart.

gingerly cautiously; with great care

CLOSE READ

Analyze Point of View

Underline sentences that show that the narrator is revealing Brian's thoughts to the reader.

8 He touched each quill carefully. The pain made it seem as if dozens of them had been slammed into his leg, but there were only eight, pinning the cloth against his skin. He leaned back against the wall for a minute. He couldn't leave them in, they had to come out, but just touching them made the pain more intense.

9 So fast, he thought. So fast things change. When he'd gone to sleep he had satisfaction and in just a moment it was all different. He grasped one of the quills, held his breath, and jerked. It sent pain signals to his brain in tight waves, but he grabbed another, pulled it, then another quill. When he had pulled four of them he stopped for a moment. The pain had gone from being a pointed injury pain to spreading in a hot smear up his leg and it made him catch his breath.

10 Some of the quills were driven in deeper than others and they tore when they came out. He breathed deeply twice, let half of the breath out, and went back to work. Jerk, pause, jerk—and three more times before he lay back in darkness, done. The pain filled his leg now, and with it came new waves of self-pity. Sitting alone in the dark, his leg aching, some mosquitos finding him again, he started crying. It was all too much, just too much, and he couldn't take it. Not the way it was.

11 I can't take it this way, alone with no fire and in the dark, and next time it might be something worse, maybe a bear, and it wouldn't just be quills in the leg, it would be worse. I can't do this, he thought, again and again. I can't. Brian pulled himself up until he was sitting upright back in the corner of the cave. He put his head down on his arms across his knees, with stiffness taking his left leg, and cried until he was cried out.

12 He did not know how long it took, but later he looked back on this time of crying in the corner of the dark cave and thought of it as when he learned the most important rule of survival, which was that feeling sorry for yourself didn't work. It wasn't just that it was wrong to do, or that it was considered incorrect. It was more than that—it didn't work. When he sat alone in the darkness and cried and was done, was all done with it, nothing had changed. His leg still hurt, it was still dark, he was still alone and the self-pity had accomplished nothing.

CLOSE READ

Analyze Point of View

Underline sentences that show the narrator telling Brian's thoughts using the first-person point of view.

CLOSE READ

Generate Questions

Highlight details that show that the narrator is communicating what Brian sees and hears as he dreams.

Generate a question about the relationship between Brian and his father based on his dream. Record your question in the chart.

13 At last he slept again, but already his patterns were changing and the sleep was light, a resting doze more than a deep sleep, with small sounds awakening him twice in the rest of the night. In the last doze period before daylight, before he awakened finally with the morning light and the clouds of new mosquitos, he dreamed. This time it was not of his mother, not of the Secret, but of his father at first and then of his friend Terry.

14 In the initial segment of the dream his father was standing at the side of a living room looking at him and it was clear from his expression that he was trying to tell Brian something. His lips moved but there was no sound, not a whisper. He waved his hands at Brian, made gestures in front of his face as if he were scratching something, and he worked to make a word with his mouth but at first Brian could not see it. Then the lips made an *mmmmm* shape but no sound came. *Mmmmm—maaaa.* Brian could not hear it, could not understand it and he wanted to so badly; it was so important to understand his father, to know what he was saying. He was trying to help, trying so hard, and when Brian couldn't understand he looked cross, the way he did when Brian asked questions more than once, and he faded. Brian's father faded into a fog place Brian could not see and the dream was almost over, or seemed to be, when Terry came.

15 He was not gesturing to Brian but was sitting in the park at a bench looking at a barbecue pit and for a time nothing happened. Then he got up and poured some charcoal from a bag into the cooker, then some starter fluid, and he took a flick type of lighter and lit the fluid. When it was burning and the charcoal was at last getting hot he turned, noticing Brian for the first time in the dream. He turned and smiled and pointed to the fire as if to say, see, a fire.

16 But it meant nothing to Brian, except that he wished he had a fire. He saw a grocery sack on the table next to Terry. Brian thought it must contain hot dogs and chips and mustard and he could think only of the food. But Terry shook his head and pointed again to the fire, and twice more he pointed to the fire, made Brian see the flames, and Brian felt his frustration and anger rise and he thought all right, all right, I see the fire but so what? I don't have a fire. I know about fire; I know I need a fire.

17 I know that.

CLOSE READ

Generate Questions

Highlight words that tell you what is going on inside Brian's head.

What question would you ask the author about Brian? Record your question in the chart.

Analyze Point of View

Underline clues that show you that the narrator knows Brian's physical and emotional feelings.

18 His eyes opened and there was light in the cave, a gray dim light of morning. He wiped his mouth and tried to move his leg, which had stiffened like wood. There was thirst, and hunger, and he ate some raspberries from the jacket. They had spoiled a bit, seemed softer and mushier, but still had a rich sweetness. He crushed the berries against the roof of his mouth with his tongue and drank the sweet juice as it ran down his throat. A flash of metal caught his eye and he saw his hatchet in the sand where he had thrown it at the porcupine in the dark.

19 He scootched up, wincing a bit when he bent his stiff leg, and crawled to where the hatchet lay. He picked it up and examined it and saw a chip in the top of the head.

20 The nick wasn't too large, but the hatchet was important to him, was his only tool, and he should not have thrown it. He should keep it in his hand, and make a tool of some kind to help push an animal away. Make a staff, he thought, or a lance, and save the hatchet. Something came then, a thought as he held the hatchet, something about the dream and his father and Terry, but he couldn't pin it down.

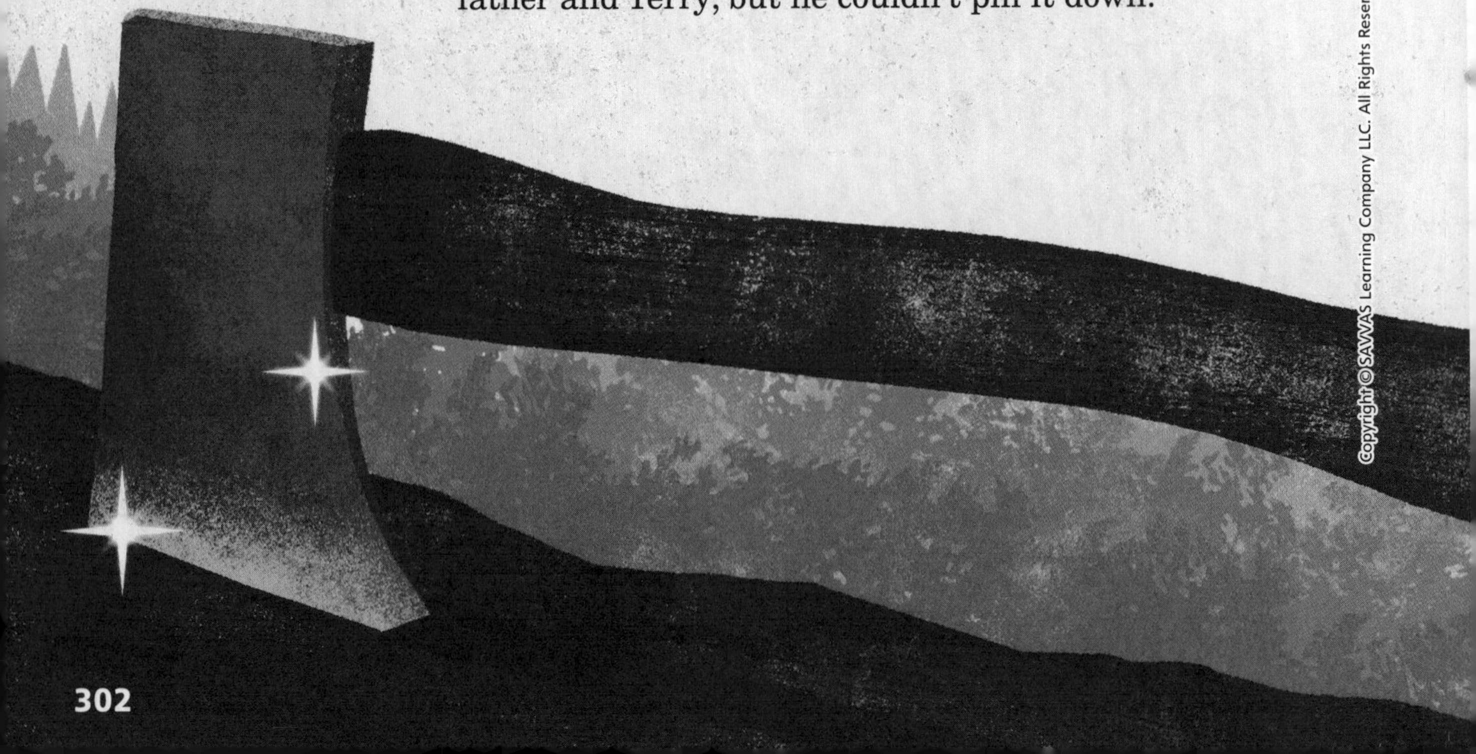

21 "Ahhh . . ." He scrambled out and stood in the morning sun and stretched his back muscles and his sore leg. The hatchet was still in his hand, and as he stretched and raised it over his head it caught the first rays of the morning sun. The first faint light hit the silver of the hatchet and it flashed a brilliant gold in the light. Like fire. That is it, he thought. What they were trying to tell me.

22 Fire. The hatchet was the key to it all. When he threw the hatchet at the porcupine in the cave and missed and hit the stone wall it had showered sparks, a golden shower of sparks in the dark, as golden with fire as the sun was now.

23 The hatchet was the answer. That's what his father and Terry had been trying to tell him. Somehow he could get fire from the hatchet. The sparks would make fire.

24 Brian went back into the shelter and studied the wall. It was some form of chalky granite, or a sandstone, but imbedded in it were large pieces of a darker stone, a harder and darker stone. It only took him a moment to find where the hatchet had struck. The steel had nicked into the edge of one of the darker stone pieces. Brian turned the head backward so he would strike with the flat rear of the hatchet and hit the black rock gently. Too gently, and nothing happened. He struck harder, a glancing blow, and two or three weak sparks skipped off the rock and died immediately.

CLOSE READ

Generate Questions

Highlight details that help you ask a question about the narrator's understanding of Brian's reasons for his actions.

Analyze Point of View

Underline descriptions that show that the narrator relates Brian's thoughts when Brian thinks them.

25 He swung harder, held the hatchet so it would hit a longer, sliding blow, and the black rock exploded in fire. Sparks flew so heavily that several of them skittered and jumped on the sand beneath the rock and he smiled and struck again and again.

26 There could be fire here, he thought. I will have a fire here, he thought, and struck again—I will have fire from the hatchet.

27 Brian found it was a long way from sparks to fire.

ignite catch fire

28 Clearly there had to be something for the sparks to ignite, some kind of tinder or kindling—but what? He brought some dried grass in, tapped sparks into it and watched them die. He tried small twigs, breaking them into little pieces, but that was worse than the grass. Then he tried a combination of the two, grass and twigs.

sputtered gave out popping sounds

29 Nothing. He had no trouble getting sparks, but the tiny bits of hot stone or metal—he couldn't tell which they were—just sputtered and died.

30 He needed something finer, something soft and fine and fluffy to catch the bits of fire.

31 Shredded paper would be nice, but he had no paper.

32 "So close," he said aloud, "so close . . ."

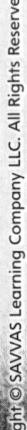

33 He put the hatchet back in his belt and went out of the shelter, limping on his sore leg. There had to be something, had to be. Man had made fire. There had been fire for thousands, millions of years. There had to be a way. He dug in his pockets and found the twenty-dollar bill in his wallet. Paper. Worthless paper out here. But if he could get a fire going . . .

34 He ripped the twenty into tiny pieces, made a pile of pieces, and hit sparks into them. Nothing happened. They just wouldn't take the sparks. But there had to be a way—some way to do it.

35 Not twenty feet to his right, leaning out over the water were birches and he stood looking at them for a full half-minute before they registered on his mind. They were a beautiful white with bark like clean, slightly speckled paper.

36 Paper.

37 He moved to the trees. Where the bark was peeling from the trunks it lifted in tiny tendrils, almost fluffs. Brian plucked some of them loose, rolled them in his fingers. They seemed flammable, dry and nearly powdery. He pulled and twisted bits off the trees, packing them in one hand while he picked them with the other, picking and gathering until he had a wad close to the size of a baseball.

CLOSE READ

Generate Questions

Highlight parts of the narrator's description that help you answer questions about how Brian sees the world changing.

Vocabulary in Context

Skilled readers use **context clues** to determine the meaning of unknown words.

Underline the context clues that help you define *tendrils*.

Analyze Point of View

Underline Brian's thoughts told from the narrator's point of view.

painstaking done with great care and attention

38 Then he went back into the shelter and arranged the ball of birchbark peelings at the base of the black rock. As an afterthought he threw in the remains of the twenty-dollar bill. He struck and a stream of sparks fell into the bark and quickly died. But this time one spark fell on one small hair of dry bark—almost a thread of bark—and seemed to glow a bit brighter before it died.

39 The material had to be finer. There had to be a soft and incredibly fine nest for the sparks.

40 I must make a home for the sparks, he thought. A perfect home or they won't stay, they won't make fire.

41 He started ripping the bark, using his fingernails at first, and when that didn't work he used the sharp edge of the hatchet, cutting the bark in thin slivers, hairs so fine they were almost not there. It was painstaking work, slow work, and he stayed with it for over two hours. Twice he stopped for a handful of berries and once to go to the lake for a drink. Then back to work, the sun on his back, until at last he had a ball of fluff as big as a grapefruit—dry birchbark fluff.

Analyze Point of View

Underline sentences in which the narrator relates Brian's thoughts.

42 He positioned his spark nest—as he thought of it—at the base of the rock, used his thumb to make a small depression in the middle, and slammed the back of the hatchet down across the black rock. A cloud of sparks rained down, most of them missing the nest, but some, perhaps thirty or so, hit in the depression and of those six or seven found fuel and grew, smoldered and caused the bark to take on the red glow.

43 Then they went out.

44 Close—he was close. He repositioned the nest, made a new and smaller dent with his thumb, and struck again.

45 More sparks, a slight glow, then nothing.

46 It's me, he thought. I'm doing something wrong. I do not know this—a cave dweller would have had a fire by now, a Cro-Magnon man would have a fire by now—but I don't know this. I don't know how to make a fire.

47 Maybe not enough sparks. He settled the nest in place once more and hit the rock with a series of blows, as fast as he could. The sparks poured like a golden waterfall. At first they seemed to take, there were several, many sparks that found life and took briefly, but they all died.

48 Starved.

49 He leaned back. They are like me. They are starving. It wasn't quantity, there were plenty of sparks, but they needed more.

50 I would kill, he thought suddenly, for a book of matches. Just one book. Just one match. I would kill.

51 What makes fire? He thought back to school. To all those science classes. Had he ever learned what made a fire? Did a teacher ever stand up there and say, "This is what makes a fire . . ."

52 He shook his head, tried to focus his thoughts. What did it take? You have to have fuel, he thought—and he had that. The bark was fuel. Oxygen—there had to be air.

53 He needed to add air. He had to fan on it, blow on it.

54 He made the nest ready again, held the hatchet backward, tensed, and struck four quick blows. Sparks came down and he leaned forward as fast as he could and blew.

55 Too hard. There was a bright, almost intense glow, then it was gone. He had blown it out.

56 Another set of strikes, more sparks. He leaned and blew, but gently this time, holding back and aiming the stream of air from his mouth to hit the brightest spot. Five or six sparks had fallen in a tight mass of bark hair and Brian centered his efforts there.

CLOSE READ

Analyze Point of View

Underline text evidence that shows the narrator has access to Brian's thoughts and memories.

CLOSE READ

Generate Questions

Highlight parts of the narrator's description that show Brian's actions. What question do you have about Brian's actions?

Record your question on the chart.

gratified felt great satisfaction

57 The sparks grew with his gentle breath. The red glow moved from the sparks themselves into the bark, moved and grew and became worms, glowing red worms that crawled up the bark hairs and caught other threads of bark and grew until there was a pocket of red as big as a quarter, a glowing red coal of heat.

58 And when he ran out of breath and paused to inhale, the red ball suddenly burst into flame.

59 "Fire!" He yelled. "I've got fire! I've got it, I've got it, I've got it . . ."

60 But the flames were thick and oily and burning fast, consuming the ball of bark as fast as if it were gasoline. He had to feed the flames, keep them going. Working as fast as he could he carefully placed the dried grass and wood pieces he had tried at first on top of the bark and was gratified to see them take.

61 But they would go fast. He needed more, and more. He could not let the flames go out.

62 He ran from the shelter to the pines and started breaking off the low, dead small limbs. These he threw in the shelter, went back for more, threw those in, and squatted to break and feed the hungry flames. When the small wood was going well he went out and found larger wood and did not relax until that was going. Then he leaned back against the wood brace of his door opening and smiled.

63 I have a friend, he thought—I have a friend now. A hungry friend, but a good one. I have a friend named fire.

64 "Hello, fire . . ."

65 The curve of the rock back made an almost perfect drawing flue that carried the smoke up through the cracks of the roof but held the heat. If he kept the fire small it would be perfect and would keep anything like the porcupine from coming through the door again.

66 A friend and a guard, he thought.

67 So much from a little spark. A friend and a guard from a tiny spark.

68 He looked around and wished he had somebody to tell this thing, to show this thing he had done. But there was nobody.

69 Nothing but the trees and the sun and the breeze and the lake.

70 Nobody.

CLOSE READ

Analyze Point of View

Underline words that show the narrator communicating Brian's loneliness.

Fluency

Read paragraphs 57–70 aloud with a partner to practice reading with expression. Pay attention to words in quotation marks.

Develop Vocabulary

In realistic fiction, words that describe actions and feelings help the reader understand the characters, the narrator, and the story's point of view.

My TURN Complete the web of vocabulary words. Write a sentence explaining how the author uses each word to describe feelings or actions. Notice how the words help show details about character and point of view in *Hatchet*.

BRIAN

gingerly

After a porcupine attack, Brian gingerly runs his hands over needles the animal left behind in Brian's calf.

ignite

painstaking

gratified

Generate Questions

Before, during, and after reading, readers **generate,** or come up with, questions about the text to deepen understanding. Readers use evidence from the text to answer these questions.

1. **My TURN** Go back to the Close Read notes and highlight parts that helped you generate questions while reading *Hatchet*.

2. **Text Evidence** Use your highlighted text to ask questions, and use evidence to support your understanding of the text. Complete the chart by asking and answering one more question now that you have finished reading.

When I Asked the Question	My Questions	Evidence in the Text
Before Reading		
During Reading		
After Reading		

Reflect and Share

Write to Sources In *Hatchet*, Brian uses natural resources around him to survive. What other survival stories have you read this week? Were these situations as dangerous as that of Brian? Use examples from the texts to compose and support a response.

Paraphrase Texts When writing a response, it is important to understand the texts you are writing about. Think about what you read this week and in this unit so far.

- Which texts helped you learn something new about survival?
- Which texts told risky stories of survival?

1. Choose two texts about survival.
2. Identify passages in each text that tell you about the dangers people faced and the solutions they found.
3. Next, paraphrase what happens in the text. As you use your own words to describe people, places, and events, be sure to maintain meaning and logical order.
4. Then ask questions such as *What did I learn about how people respond to unsafe situations?* Answer those questions and record any other thoughts that come to mind.
5. Finally, use what you paraphrased to compose a response.

Weekly Question

How can careful observation help a person survive?

Academic Vocabulary

Learning Goal

I can develop knowledge about language to make connections between reading and writing.

Context clues, or surrounding words and phrases, can be used to determine the meaning of words. Look for definitions of unfamiliar or multiple-meaning words within and beyond sentences. Also look for examples that help you determine relevant meanings.

My TURN For each sentence,

1. **Read** the underlined academic vocabulary word.
2. **Highlight** the context clue or clues.
3. **Write** a brief definition of the word based on the clues.

Dr. Garcia is a well-respected expert who gives lectures and speeches about wilderness survival.

Definition: a person who is Knowledgable about a topic.

The math team made sure to focus by studying hard and concentrating on the questions.

Definition: to have your attention on something.

Using dry wood and leaves, the camper built a big, bright fire that was clearly visible from several miles away.

Definition: able to be seen

As he looked for evidence in the woods, Mr. O'Hara tried to detect if any animals were hiding nearby.

Definition: to find something

N

r-Controlled Vowels

***r*-Controlled vowels** are vowels connected to the letter *r*. The sounds of vowels change when they are followed by the letter *r*. Many *r*-controlled vowels sound the same but are spelled differently. The *r*-controlled vowel sound you hear in the word *turn* can be spelled *er*, *ir*, *or*, or *ur*. The *r*-controlled vowel sound you hear in the word *store* can be spelled *or*, *ore*, or *oar*.

My TURN For each row, read each word with an *r*-controlled vowel. Then complete the chart by adding two words with an *r*-controlled vowel from *Hatchet* or from other texts you have read this week. Use a print or digital dictionary to check for correct pronunciation.

Sound	Spellings	Words	
ar	ar	sparks	
er	er ir or ur	perhaps thirteen worked turned	
or	or ore oar	morning tore roaring	

Read Like a Writer

In literature, readers experience story events through a narrator's or a character's eyes, thoughts, and voice. Authors use specific language, including word choice and descriptive details, when writing from a particular point of view.

Model! Read the text from *Hatchet*.

> He grasped one of the quills, held his breath, and jerked. It sent pain signals to his brain in tight waves, but he grabbed another, pulled it, then another quill.

descriptive language

1. **Identify** In *Hatchet*, the narrator uses descriptive language to describe what Brian does and how he feels.
2. **Question** How does the narrator's voice help me understand what Brian feels?
3. **Conclude** The descriptive details help me feel Brian's pain vividly and immediately, as if I were there.

Reread paragraph 63 from *Hatchet*.

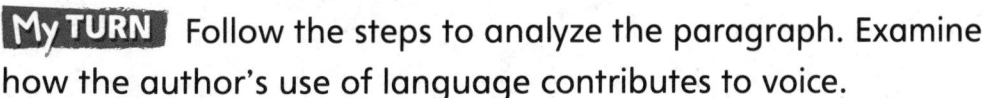

My TURN Follow the steps to analyze the paragraph. Examine how the author's use of language contributes to voice.

1. **Identify** The narrator uses the language ____________________

   ____________________.
2. **Question** How does the narrator's voice help me understand what Brian is thinking?
3. **Conclude** The descriptive details help me understand that Brian ____________________

   ____________________.

Write for a Reader

Use specific language to make your voice heard!

Authors use point of view and language to contribute to a narrator's or character's voice. They often use sensory details—about sights, sounds, and more—to help readers experience a character's thoughts and feelings.

My TURN Think about how the narrator's voice in *Hatchet* affects you as a reader. Now identify how you can use a character's voice to influence your own readers.

1. If you were trying to create a character with a specific voice, and that character was in a dangerous environment, what language would you use?

2. Write a passage describing your character's thoughts and actions. Choose a point of view that best expresses the character's voice. Use descriptive details to help your readers feel and "see" what the character is experiencing.

Develop and Compose an Introduction

Learning Goal

I can use elements of informational writing to write an informational article.

An **introduction** to an informational article creates a structure for the text. Many introductions use the following structure.

> After being domesticated, or tamed, 10,000 years ago, dogs soon became companions for humans. Today many dogs provide more than companionship for people—they provide lifesaving help. Many people assume that service dogs are a modern development, but a painting unearthed in the ancient Roman city of Herculaneum tells a different story.

General statement or observation about topic

Topic narrowed to what article will be about

Hooks reader's interest with interesting statement, fact, or question

My TURN In your writing notebook, use the graphic organizer as a model for the introduction to your informational article. Then develop a draft of your introduction.

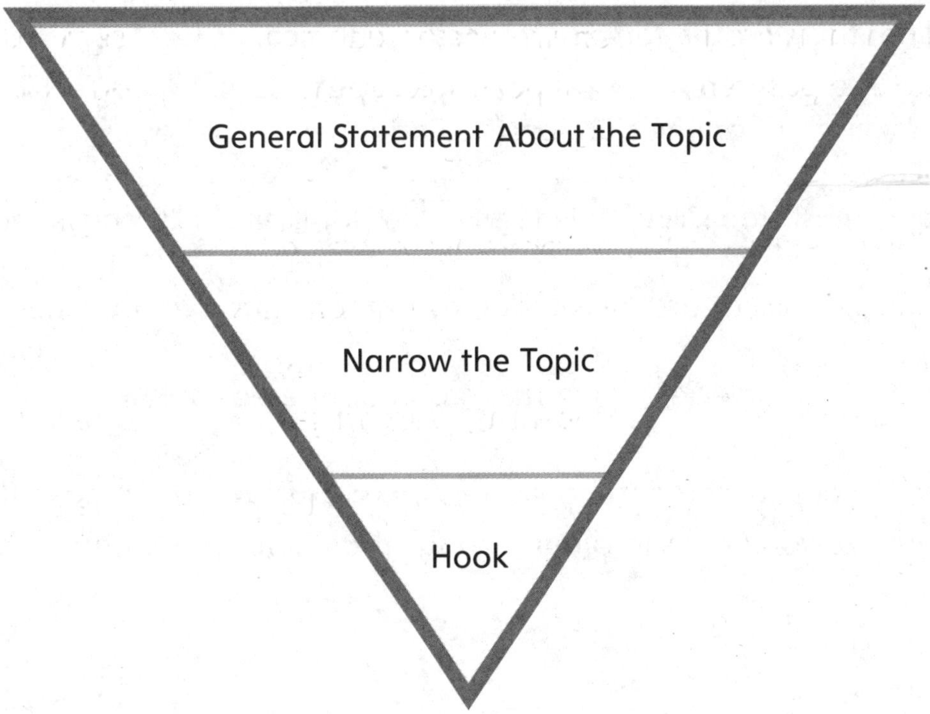

Develop with Related Information

Paragraphs and sections show how facts and details relate to each other. Each paragraph often has one topic sentence that explains its main idea. All paragraphs support the main idea of the entire text. A writer can organize paragraphs in different ways.

Specific to General

Amur tigers once roamed most of Asia.	→	All tigers that are endangered must be saved.

General to Specific

If we don't protect the planet, the human race may not have a future.	→	Preventing runoff from factories and farms can reduce pollution in our lakes.

My TURN Each sentence is the topic sentence of a paragraph in an informational text. Put the topic sentences in a logical order.

_____ Many kinds of animals are on the Endangered Species List.

_____ People must stop killing green sea turtles for their shells, eggs, and meat.

_____ Green sea turtles are threatened by humans and climate change.

_____ Almost every species of sea turtle is endangered.

My TURN In your writing notebook, develop a draft of your informational article. Organize your ideas into paragraphs that support your main idea.

Develop with Transitions

Writers use transitions and linking words to guide readers through a text. The transitional words, phrases, and clauses in an informational article provide structure by showing the logical relationships between details. Different text structures use different transitions. Depending on the writer's purpose, an informational article may follow one of these common text structures.

Structure	Transitions	Example
Cause and Effect	*because, as a result, then, since, for, cause, effect*	Jackie learned to be a great tennis player **because** she worked hard at tennis camp.
Time Order/ Chronology	*first, then, meanwhile, immediately, until, now, next, finally, soon*	**First**, she learned the basics. **Then** she began to practice her technique daily.
Comparison and Contrast	*similar, different, especially, as, yet, like, unlike, however, although, in contrast, but, at first*	Her playing style **at first** was clumsy, **but** soon she learned discipline and gained strength.
Problem and Solution	*as a result, problem, solution, challenge*	**As a result**, her playing improved rapidly.
Process	*after, since, during, when, while, first, second, third, next, finally, after that, then, last, meanwhile, in the end*	Now she tells other young players, "**First**, you need a goal. **Then** you have to practice all the time. **Meanwhile**, you have to believe in yourself. **In the end**, you will succeed."

My TURN In your writing notebook, develop a draft of your informational article. Use transitions to create structure.

Use Formatting

Formatting allows a writer to highlight important information and words within an informational article. Types of formatting include headings, bulleted lists, bold words, and italics.

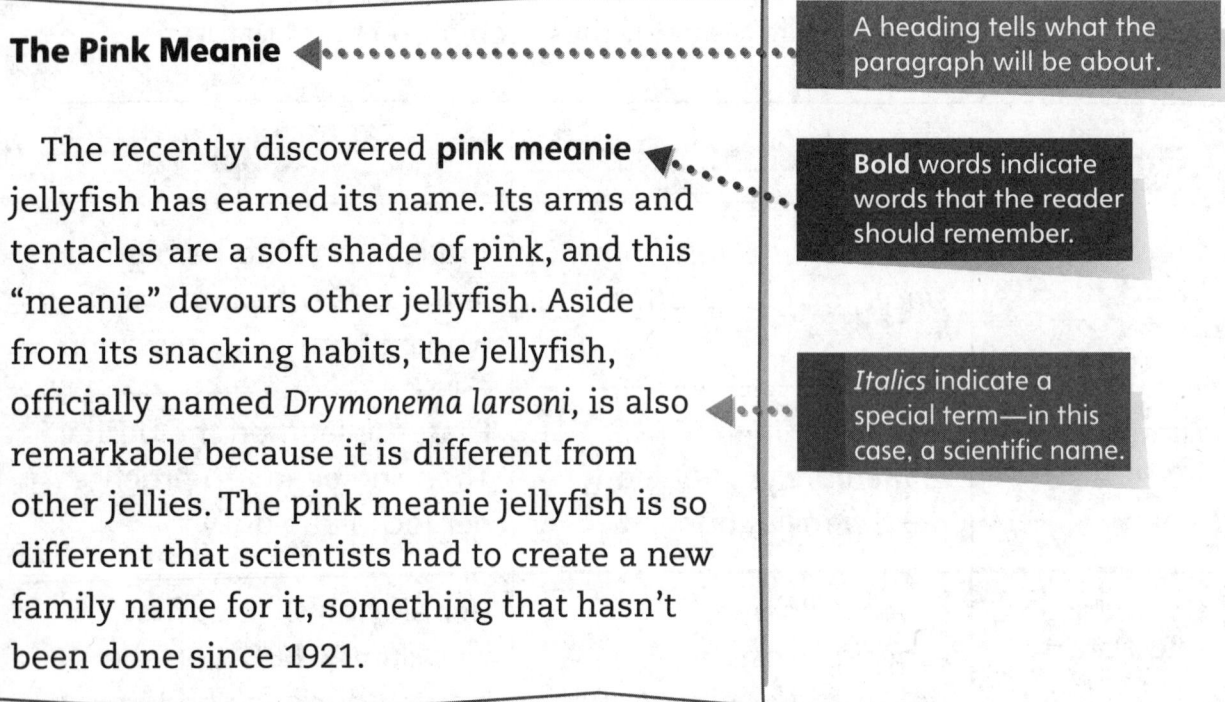

The Pink Meanie

The recently discovered **pink meanie** jellyfish has earned its name. Its arms and tentacles are a soft shade of pink, and this "meanie" devours other jellyfish. Aside from its snacking habits, the jellyfish, officially named *Drymonema larsoni*, is also remarkable because it is different from other jellies. The pink meanie jellyfish is so different that scientists had to create a new family name for it, something that hasn't been done since 1921.

A heading tells what the paragraph will be about.

Bold words indicate words that the reader should remember.

Italics indicate a special term—in this case, a scientific name.

MyTURN Create a bulleted list from the information in the paragraph. A writer can use a bulleted list when he or she wants a reader to quickly understand basic facts.

The Pink Meanie

- ______________________________
- ______________________________
- ______________________________
- ______________________________

MyTURN In your writing notebook, compose a draft of your informational article. Use formatting to help your readers understand what you write.

Develop and Compose a Conclusion

A writer sums up the events in an informational article with a concluding statement or section. The conclusion provides structure and helps readers understand how they can use the information in the article. For example, a writer may conclude an article with a suggestion about how the reader could learn more about the topic.

MY TURN Choose a topic and develop a draft. Focus your writing around a clear structure. Be sure to include a conclusion.

How can you sum up the topic of your article?

Why is the topic important for your readers to learn about?

What do you want your readers to do with the information in the article?

INTERACTIVITY

In the Words of THEODORE ROOSEVELT

Theodore Roosevelt served as president of the United States from 1901 to 1909. He did important work as a conservationist, someone who protects and preserves natural resources, such as plants and animals. During his terms, he protected around 230 million acres of land by declaring them national forests, parks, and monuments.

Read the following quotations from President Roosevelt about why it is important to protect land.

"Of all the questions which can come before this nation . . . there is none which compares in importance with the great central task of leaving this land even a better land for our descendants than it is for us."

"There can be nothing in the world more beautiful than the Yosemite, the groves of the giant sequoias and redwoods, the Canyon of the Colorado, the Canyon of the Yellowstone, the Three Tetons; and our people should see to it that they are preserved for their children and their children's children forever, with their majestic beauty all unmarred."

"It is not what we have that will make us a great nation; it is the way in which we use it."

Weekly Question

What can we learn from studying animals in their natural habitat?

Illustrate Think about a time you observed a natural landscape. What did it look like? What key characteristics did it have? Draw your landscape and describe it to a partner.

Learning Goal

I can learn more about informational text by explaining relationships between ideas.

Spotlight on Genre

Informational Text

Text features are an important part of informational text because they help readers find and use information. They explain relationships between topics, ideas, or events by presenting information in a specific way. Text features include

- titles, headings, and subheadings
- images, labels, and captions
- bulleted lists, sidebars, and time lines
- diagrams, charts, graphs, and maps
- special text styles, such as boldface, italics, and highlighting

Establish a Purpose The **purpose**, or reason, for reading informational texts is often to learn something new. Active readers of informational texts analyze text features and make predictions to help them understand new information.

If a text tells facts about real people, places, or things, it's informational text!

TURN and TALK Describe the text features used in one of the texts you read in this unit. Tell how the features helped you understand information. Take notes on your discussion.

TEXT FEATURES

ANCHOR CHART

PURPOSE: To help readers understand informational text

Title

[Tells you what the text is about]

PHOTOS GIVE A VISUAL REPRESENTATION.

[captions explain photos]

BULLETED LISTS

- call out
- important information
- for readers

SUBHEADINGS: tell you what sections of the text are about

BOLDFACED WORDS HIGHLIGHTED WORDS

CALL OUT KEYWORDS

Meet *the* Author

When author **Mary Kay Carson** was a child, she had a houseful of pets, including several possums. She wanted to become a scientist, but writing letters to family and friends inspired her love of writing. Today, Carson writes nonfiction books for children about scientific and historical topics.

Tracking Monsters

Preview Vocabulary

As you read "Tracking Monsters," pay attention to these weekly vocabulary words. Notice how they provide specific descriptions.

fragmented **transmitter**

nocturnal **burrows** **iconic**

Read

Before you read, **make predictions** about what you will learn based on the genre. Record your predictions in the chart after the selection. Then follow these strategies as you read this **informational text**.

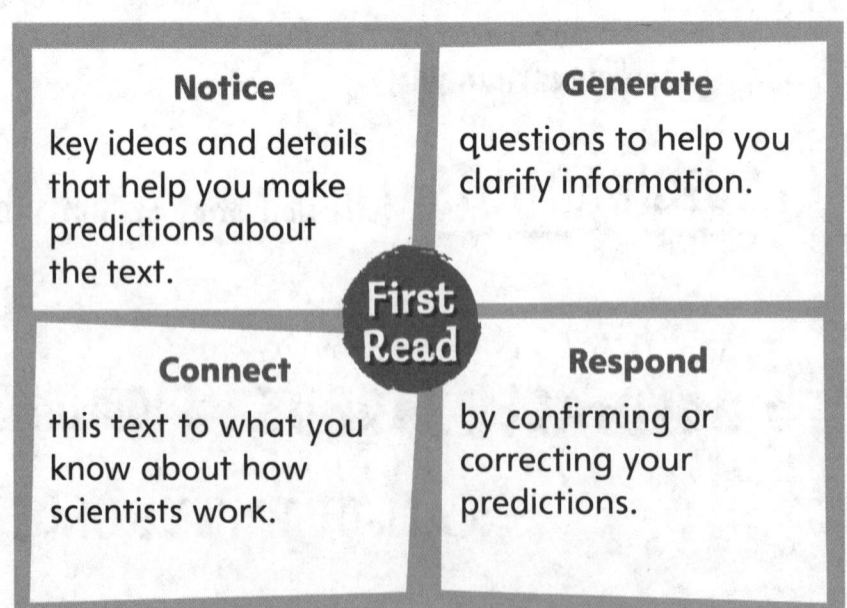

Notice key ideas and details that help you make predictions about the text.	**Generate** questions to help you clarify information.
Connect this text to what you know about how scientists work.	**Respond** by confirming or correcting your predictions.

First Read

Genre | Informational Text

Tracking Monsters

from *Park Scientists* • by Mary Kay Carson

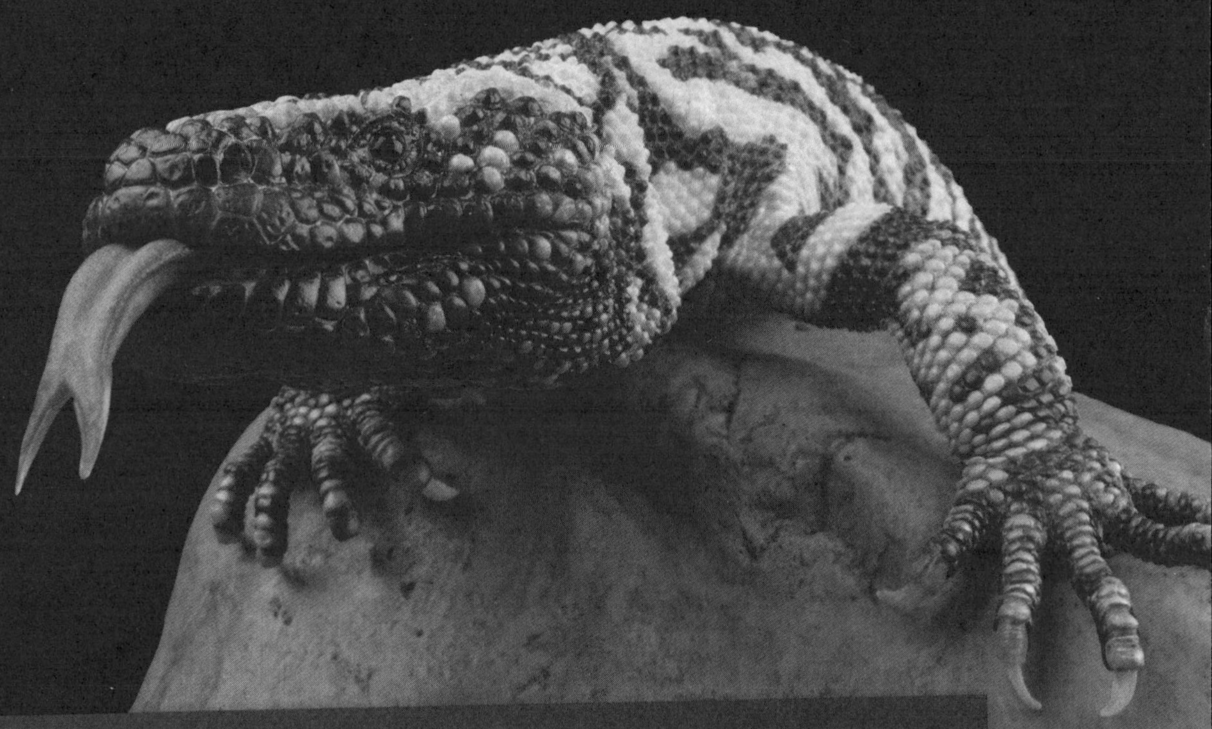

BACKGROUND

Park Scientists: Gila Monsters, Geysers, and Grizzly Bears in America's Own Backyard is about opportunities for scientific study in America's national parks. In this excerpt, the author joins researchers and citizen scientists in southern Arizona's Saguaro National Park to gather data about Gila monsters. These large lizards are notoriously difficult to study.

AUDIO

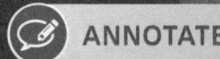

ANNOTATE

Explain Relationships Between Ideas

Underline the text feature that introduces the text's main idea.

Tracking Monsters

1 Saguaro National Park, in southern Arizona, looks like a giant cactus garden. Acres of evenly spaced cacti in every imaginable spiny, prickly shape grow out of pastel-colored gravel. The park's Sonoran Desert home is full of fierce plants adapted to living thirsty. Tough grasses, waxy-leafed bushes, and smooth-skinned trees fill the space between cacti with smells of cooking herbs, tar, and soap. Sounds are part of the desert, too. The background buzz of insects is broken by a hawk's call—and there's also a *beep . . . beep . . . beep* noise.

Researchers use radio telemetry to track Gila monsters in and around Saguaro National Park.

2 The beeping is coming from a small black box carried by a man wearing a wide-brimmed hat. Brian Park also holds up what looks like an old-fashioned TV antenna. The beeping box and antenna are radio telemetry instruments. Brian is using them to zero in on a critter with a radio transmitter inside of it. The beeps are getting louder. That means she's nearby, Brian tells the half dozen people hiking up a hill with him. Being careful to avoid the prickly pear and fishhook cacti, he sets down his gear near a hump of granite. The sun-hatted hikers circle the big rock and begin inspecting its crevices and cracks.

3 "She's visible, everybody!" Brian announces. He's stooped over and is using a small mirror to bounce strong desert sunlight underneath the rock. Everyone moves in for a look. "I can see her head in there," someone says. A crouching middle-aged woman puts a hand on the rock to steady herself. "I wouldn't put your fingers there," warns Brian. Why not? The animal stuffed underneath the rock can deliver a painful, venomous bite. It's a Gila (HEE-la) monster.

CLOSE READ

Explain Relationships Between Ideas

Underline details that help you understand the relationship between the "trackers" and the "monsters."

transmitter equipment that makes and sends electromagnetic waves that carry messages

The researcher Brian Park and volunteer citizen scientists zero in on a Gila monster using radio telemetry.

Explain Relationships Between Ideas

Underline details that develop a main idea presented earlier in the text.

iconic famous, popular, and representative of a place or time

nocturnal awake and active at night

burrows holes or tunnels dug by animals as places to live

Monstrous Lizards

4 Gila monsters are big lizards with powerful, clamping, venomous jaws. They're the largest lizards in the United States, growing up to two feet (61 cm) long and weighing up to three pounds (1.4 kg). "Gila monsters belong to a reptile group called Monstersauria," says Kevin Bonine. He's a scientist at the University of Arizona and heads up a Gila monster study. Monstersaurs roamed alongside *T. rexes* and other dinosaurs a hundred million years ago. Today, the only other remaining "monster lizard" species is the beaded lizard, who is also big and venomous.

5 Gila monsters make their homes in the deserts of the southwestern United States and northern Mexico. They're common in Arizona, and it's hard to mistake the large, slow-moving lizards. Gila monsters are chunky, low-to-the-ground lizards covered in pink, orange, and black skin studded with tiny pebbly bumps. "Gila monsters are an iconic species of the Sonoran Desert," says Kevin. But being famous hasn't gotten Gila monsters much scientific attention over the years. Gila monsters aren't easy to study. They're nocturnal much of the year and spend a lot of their time in underground burrows. Gila monsters don't need to be out constantly searching for food, like a bird or mouse does. A large adult lizard may eat only a few times a year. "Their favorite food is a nest full of baby bunnies or quail eggs," says Kevin. Gila monsters are expert nest raiders.

The Gila monster's name comes from the Gila River region of Arizona.

6 Kevin Bonine is a herpetologist, a scientist who studies amphibians and reptiles. He's hoping his research will solve some Gila monster mysteries. "We're not sure how many Gila monsters are out there, or exactly what they do all year," says Kevin. Scientists don't even know the time of year the lizards are born. Gila monster moms lay eggs in underground burrows in the late summer, and baby Gila hatchlings leave burrows the following spring. When exactly they hatch during those eight to ten months is their well-kept secret. Perhaps they hatch in autumn and the hatchlings spend the winter underground. "Or are they in the egg for a heck of a long time?" asks Kevin. The list of needed answers about Gila monsters in and around Saguaro National Park is long, says Kevin. How far do they travel in a year? Do they leave the park? How many burrows do they use? Do roads and housing developments affect them? "There's a whole lot of mystery," Kevin says.

CLOSE READ

Confirm or Correct Predictions

Highlight details in paragraph 6 that you can use to confirm a prediction you made about information in the text.

CLOSE READ

Explain Relationships Between Ideas

Underline details in the text that support the idea noted in the heading.

WARNING!

Armed and Armored

Gila monsters look ready for a fight. Their skin is covered in round bumps filled with bone, called osteoderms. This studded skin covers their head, tail, and body like armor. Long, powerful claws for digging and strong, powerful clamping jaws are their weapons—and so is their venom.

"They have venom glands in their lower jaw," explains Brian Park, a Gila monster researcher. Unlike a rattlesnake, a Gila monster can't inject venom. The venom simply mixes into its saliva, or spit, when they feel threatened. "When they bite you, they latch on," explains Brian, "and all that venom trickles into you." Sharp, grooved teeth help deliver it, as does chewing on the victim for a good long time. A Gila monster bite is intensely painful, but not fatal to humans. There's no antivenom treatment, and the bite can make a person sick for weeks. Medical scientists are interested in the venom that Gila monsters make. They've copied unique chemicals found in the lizard's saliva and are testing them as possible drugs for diabetes, attention deficit disorder, and memory loss.

While Gila monsters look tough, they aren't aggressive and don't go after people. If you see one, it's likely to be shuffling away from you. "If you don't ever stick a finger in front of one or pick it up, you should never have a problem," says Brian. "Most bites happen when harassing a Gila monster." If pain and suffering aren't reason enough to steer clear of Gila monsters, how about the law? As a protected species, harassing, handling, collecting, or killing them is illegal. Gila monsters were the first protected reptile in Arizona and in 1952 became the first protected venomous animal in the United States.

Female #291

7 The Gila monster that Brian Park has tracked down is providing some clues. Gila monster #291 has a radio inside her. Kevin's team has implanted tiny transmitters inside eight different Gilas. Now that Brian's telemetry receiver has found #291 under the big granite rock, Brian and his helpers get to work.

8 As she snoozes undisturbed in her burrow, they write down the lizard's GPS position, note the time of day, take air temperature and humidity measurements, and list the kinds of plants growing around her rock. All of this information will help scientists figure out how much Gila monsters travel about—and why. The study is finding that how much a Gila gets around depends on its age, sex, habitat, and the season. During spring and early summer, for example, when males are out looking for mates they will wander more than females generally. Female #291 may be on the move, too. She was down the hill in the picnic area near the road just two weeks ago, says Brian. Is #291 looking for a place to spend the winter?

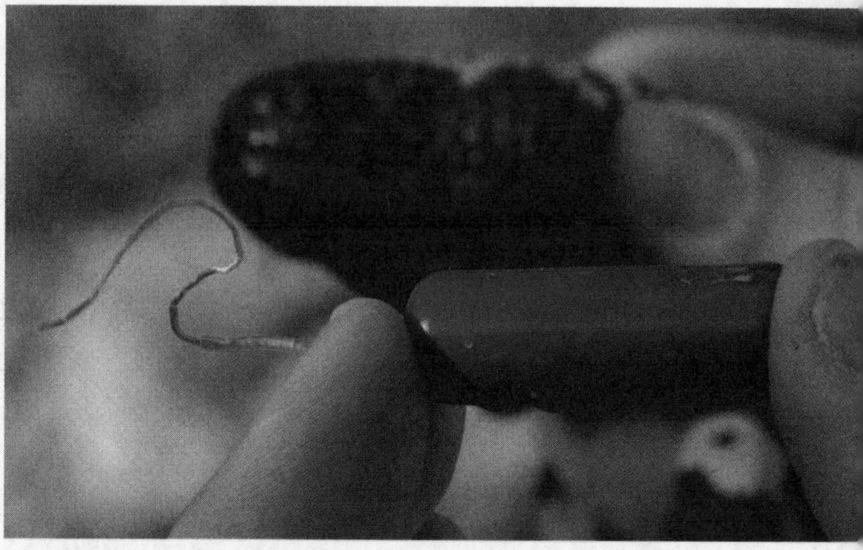

The radio transmitters like this one that scientists surgically implant into Gila monsters are about the size of an AA battery. A radio collar wouldn't work because it would get in a Gila monster's way as it squeezed under rocks or into holes.

CLOSE READ

Explain Relationships Between Ideas

Look at the photo. Underline details in the text that help you understand the concept shown in the image.

Confirm or Correct Predictions

How are the text features related to ideas in the paragraph? Make a prediction and highlight text that you can use to support it.

The herpetologist Kevin Bonine uses radio telemetry to track the wanderings of Gila monsters.

9 Gila monsters don't have permanent homes. An abandoned packrat burrow might be a good cool summer spot, while squeezing under a sunny rock can provide a cozy winter shelter. As with all reptiles, the body temperature of Gila monsters changes with their environment. The beeping radio inside the tracked Gila monster also estimates its body temperature. The warmer the body temperature, the faster the radio beeps. Researchers carefully record the body temperature of each lizard every time they track it. That way they know how much warmer or cooler the animal is in the various shelters it uses throughout the year. The rock that #291 is currently under gets a lot of sun on one side, says Brian. It might make a decent winter home.

BioBlitz and Microchips

10 Filling out #291's data sheet is taking a bit longer than usual. Everyone except Brian Park is new to Gila monster science. The hikers are volunteers taking part in BioBlitz, a twenty-four-hour scientific inventory of every species in Saguaro National Park. They are among the thousands of citizen scientists helping out during the event. So that lots of people can join in the activities and learn about biodiversity, BioBlitzes often take place in national parks near urban areas like Saguaro National Park. The city of Tucson, Arizona, fills the space between the park's two separate halves.

CLOSE READ

Confirm or Correct Predictions

Use text features to make a prediction about BioBlitz.

Highlight details on this page that confirm or correct your prediction.

11 "Citizen science is important for involving the community," says Kevin. It's a big part of the study that researchers at the University of Arizona, including Kevin Bonine and Brian Park, are doing in Saguaro. In fact, their Gila Monster Project depends on it. "We try to get the public to send us their sightings," explains Kevin. How? They've posted colorful signs at kiosks near trails and in visitor centers. The signs say HAVE YOU SEEN ME? above a plump pink Gila monster. Below the photo are instructions for documenting the sighting and sending in the information. Kevin says, "People out hiking and park staff can really help us out." The key is taking a photograph of the Gila monster that clearly shows its markings. "The pattern on each individual is like a fingerprint," says Kevin. Researchers use the color patterns to identify individual Gila monsters.

Brian Park and BioBlitz volunteers collect information about Gila monster #291 in Saguaro National Park.

CLOSE READ

Vocabulary in Context

Readers use **context clues**, or nearby words and phrases, to determine the meaning of unknown phrases.

Underline context clues that help you define the phrase *microchip tag*.

12 Sometimes the researchers receive a photo from a citizen scientist that matches a Gila monster they've tagged, "which is pretty exciting," says Kevin. The Gila Monster Project has been tagging the large lizards with microchips since 2009. Each tiny microchip tag looks like a metal grain of rice. It's the same kind of ID microchip tag that veterinarians use for dogs, cats, and other pets. Each tag has an identification number that a handheld scanner can read. "We've tagged more than one hundred and fifty Gila monsters," says Kevin. Every new Gila monster that the field biologists come across gets a tag.

By implanting a radio transmitter inside a Gila monster, researchers can track the lizard's movements over time with radio telemetry (above).

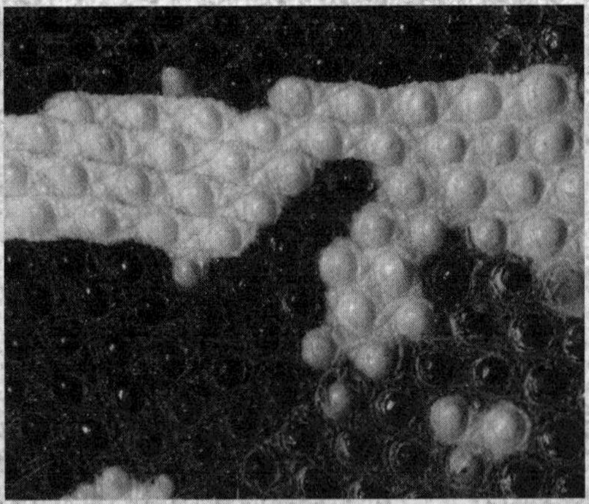

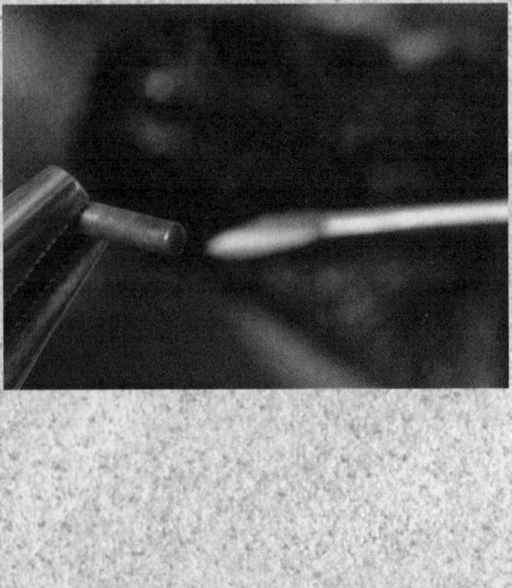

The skin bumps of Gila monsters have tiny bones in them called osteoderms (close-up top right). The patterns of color are unique to each animal. This Gila monster tag (bottom right) is a small metal pellet with an ID microchip in it.

Catching Monsters

13 The punishing desert sun is sinking toward the distant mountaintops, but it's still 85°F (29°C). The giant piled-up pink and beige boulders soak up heat like pizza stones. Kevin doesn't seem to break a sweat, however, even though he's got one hand firmly gripping a Gila monster. In his other hand is what looks like a small plastic toothbrush. Kevin puts the softer end of the plastic tool on the lizard's closed mouth—and gives it a nudge. How do you get a Gila monster to open wide? "You talk very nicely to him," jokes Kevin. Evidently it's true. The smoky-pink lizard takes the bait, giving the plastic prod a few chomps. It will leave behind enough mouth cells for a DNA sample.

CLOSE READ

Explain Relationships Between Ideas

Underline details that help you explain how researchers collect data about Gila monsters.

The white plastic probe collects mouth cells full of DNA when chewed on (above).

Kevin estimates how much fat is stored in this Gila monster's tail by measuring the volume of water it displaces when pushed into the graduated cylinder (left). Well-fed, healthy Gila monsters have fat tails.

Researchers measure each animal's head width using calipers (left). Body length is measured, as well as overall length from snout to tail tip (right).

CLOSE READ

Explain Relationships Between Ideas

Underline ideas that work together to explain how researchers collect data.

14 Gila Monster Project researchers such as Kevin and Brian hike and drive in Saguaro National Park regularly, tracking and checking in on the Gila monsters with radios and looking for new ones. When they come across a Gila monster, they catch it—very carefully. Foot-and-a-half-long medical tongs can help hold a squirmy one still. Each animal is measured, weighed, photographed, and injected with a microchip tag under the skin. Researchers also measure the volume of its fat-filled tail to find out how well fed it is. The plastic stick chewed on by the lizard is sent off to a DNA lab for analysis. "It gives us the ability to answer a whole range of questions," says Kevin—big-picture questions such as how similar Saguaro's Gila monsters are to those in California or Mexico, and how closely related the lizards in the park are to one another.

15 One of the goals of the Gila Monster Project is learning what these large, venomous lizards need to thrive, so they can be protected in the future. Are highways and fences separating Gila monsters and creating small, fragmented populations? DNA studies can tell if they are losing genetic diversity or inbreeding. Are new neighborhoods taking away needed habitat? Comparing the lives of Gila monsters not in the park with those inside it can help find out. "We want to learn a lot more about them both in the protected areas of the park as well as in the wildland-urban interface," says Kevin. "That's where they interact with roads and cars, people and dogs, and that sort of thing."

16 The Sonoran Desert is something special—fragile and harsh, dazzling and mysterious. "My life has always been tied to the desert," says Kevin of the Sonoran and its creatures. He hopes that the work of the Gila Monster Project will ensure that future generations have that connection, too. "We are hoping to get data that will be useful for decades to come," he says, "so we can learn a lot more about these magnificent lizards and help to protect them as well." If you're lucky enough to see a Gila monster in Saguaro National Park, take its picture and write down where you saw it. But keep your fingers to yourself.

CLOSE READ

Confirm or Correct Predictions

Use the text features to make a prediction about the Gila Monster Project.

Highlight text that confirms or corrects your prediction.

fragmented broken into pieces

Gila monsters live in the Mojave, Sonoran, and Chihuahuan Deserts of North America. They smell by picking up scent particles with their purplish forked tongues (top). Gila monsters have feet and claws made for digging burrows and uncovering prey nests (bottom).

Develop Vocabulary

In informational texts, domain-specific words give precise information about the topic and help develop concepts. Readers can use print or digital resources, such as glossaries, dictionaries, and educational Web sites about the topic, to confirm word meanings.

My TURN Complete the chart. First, identify a resource that could be used to confirm your understanding of each vocabulary word. Then, write the word's meaning. Finally, explain how the author of "Tracking Monsters" uses each word to give information about a scientific concept.

Word	Resource	Meaning	Scientific Concept
transmitter	dictionary	equipment that makes and sends messages	explains how scientists track Gila monsters
nocturnal			
burrows			
fragmented			

Check for Understanding

MyTURN Look back at the text to answer the questions.

1. How do you know that "Tracking Monsters" is an informational text?

2. What is the author's purpose and message? How does it affect your understanding of the text?

3. Summarize how, where, and why researchers study Gila monsters.

4. Are Gila monsters a greater threat to humans, or are humans a greater threat to Gila monsters? Use text evidence to support your opinion.

Explain Relationships Between Ideas

In informational texts, writers state important ideas and support those ideas with details. Readers identify and explain relationships between ideas to better understand the text.

1. **MyTURN** Go to the Close Read notes in "Tracking Monsters" and underline the parts that show central ideas in the text.

2. **Text Evidence** Use the parts you underlined to complete the graphic organizer and explain relationships between the ideas.

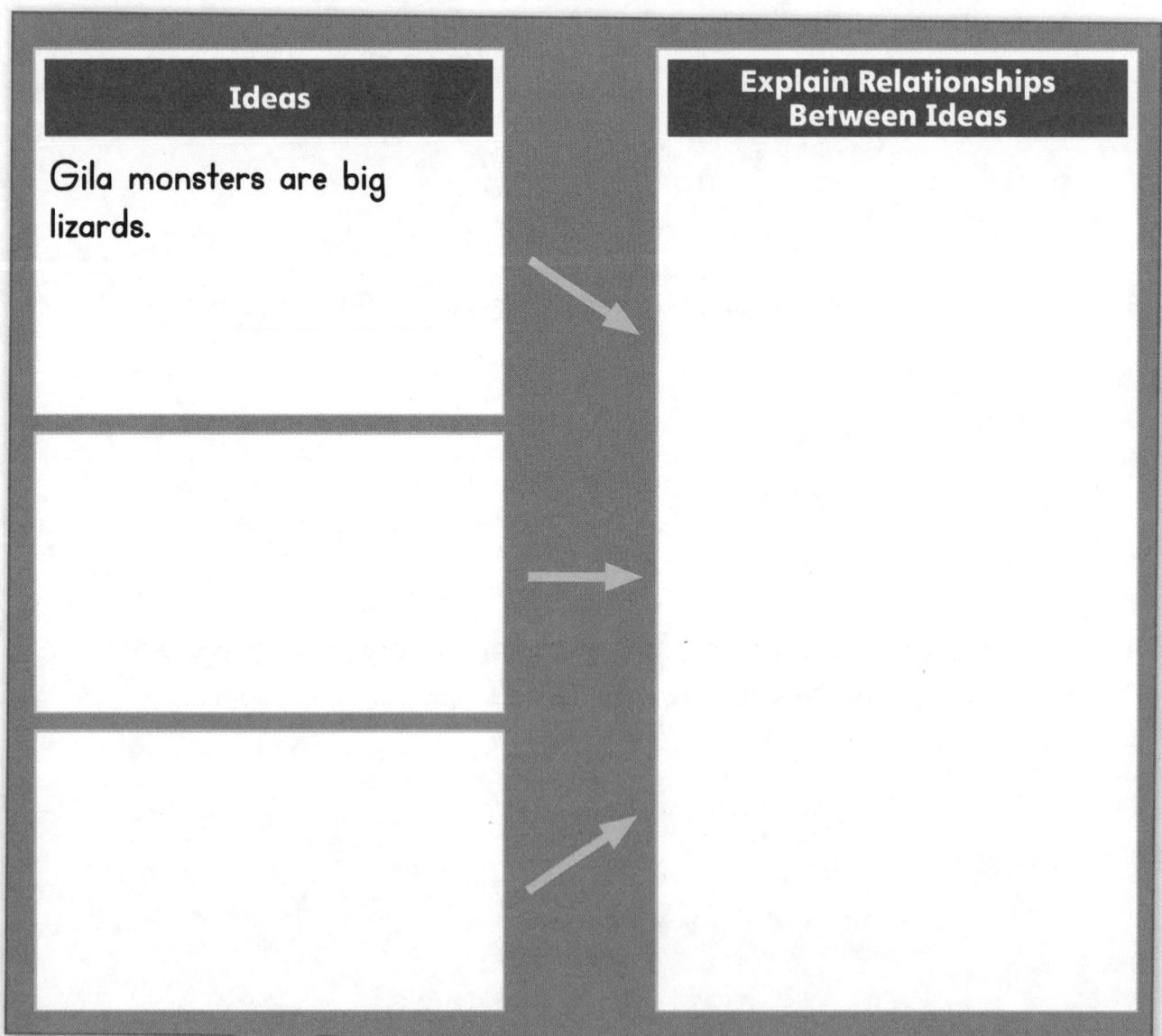

Ideas	Explain Relationships Between Ideas
Gila monsters are big lizards.	

Confirm or Correct Predictions

Before reading, preview parts of the text to **make predictions,** or guesses, about what it will be about. Use the structure, or organization of ideas, to help you predict. While reading, **confirm,** or check, your predictions using text evidence. Correct your predictions based on information you learn.

1. My TURN Go back to the Close Read notes, look at the text's structure, and highlight details that help you confirm a prediction you made before reading. If necessary, correct the prediction.
2. **Text Evidence** Use your predictions and highlighted text to complete the graphic organizer.

Prediction

Evaluate Your Prediction

My prediction is: CORRECT PARTIALLY CORRECT INCORRECT

I know this because

Reflect and Share

Write to Sources Consider the texts you read this week. What scientific studies did you learn about? What makes these studies important? Use these questions to help you write an opinion about why it is important to share knowledge with others.

Use Text Evidence In opinion writing, you need to gather text evidence to support your opinion, or claim, and to develop your supporting reasons. Evidence should relate directly to your claim.

On a separate sheet of paper, write a claim about why scientific studies are necessary. Next, choose two texts. Identify evidence from each to support your claim. Use these questions to evaluate text evidence:

- Does this quotation clearly support your claim?
- Will this quotation help make your claim more persuasive to readers?
- Are there better quotations to make your claim even more convincing? If yes, review your text annotations and notes.

Replace evidence as needed. Finally, write a short paragraph on your own paper to express and support your opinion.

Weekly Question

What can we learn from studying animals in their natural habitat?

Academic Vocabulary

Learning Goal

I can develop knowledge about language to make connections between reading and writing.

An **analogy**, which is a type of **figurative language**, compares two unlike things that have something in common. Through analogies, readers learn relationships and connections between words.

My TURN For each analogy,

1. **Identify** the relationship between words in the analogy.
2. **Write** the missing word on the line.
3. **Explain** the comparison in the analogy.

Knowledge is to **expert** as wedding cake is to ______________.

Focus is to camera as ______________ is to airplane.

Visible is to eye-catching as ______________ is to thunderstorm.

Overlook is to **detect** as thrive is to ______________.

Prefixes *il-*, *in-*, *im-*, *ir-*

The **prefixes *il-*, *in-*, *im-*,** and ***ir-*** tell information about relationships between things. All four prefixes mean "not."

The word *illegal* in the last paragraph of the "WARNING! Armed and Armored" text feature in "Tracking Monsters" means "not legal" or "against the law." If you know the definition of a base word, you can figure out the meaning of a new word formed by adding a prefix that means "not."

MY TURN Review the prefixes in the box. Add the correct prefix for each base word. Read the new words.

il-	***in-***	***im-***	***ir-***

______ perfect	______ responsible	______ complete
______ regular	______ visible	______ polite
______ capable	______ possible	______ formal

High-Frequency Words

High-frequency words are words that you will see in texts over and over again. They often do not follow regular word study patterns. Read these high-frequency words: *record, value, rhythm, science, shoulder, company*. Try to identify them in your independent reading.

Read Like a Writer

The message is the author's main point or a lesson the author wants to teach in the text. Authors can convey their message through the text and text features.

Model! Read the text from "Tracking Monsters."

> While Gila monsters look tough, they aren't aggressive and don't go after people. If you see one, it's likely to be shuffling away from you.

1. **Identify** Mary Kay Carson uses details to describe Gila monsters.
2. **Question** How do the details support the author's message?
3. **Conclude** The details support the author's message that Gila monsters are not aggressive.

Read the text.

> One of the goals of the Gila Monster Project is learning what these large, venomous lizards need to thrive, so they can be protected in the future.

My TURN Follow the steps to analyze the passage. Explain the author's message.

1. **Identify** Mary Kay Carson uses details to ______________________________

______________________________.

2. **Question** How do the details support the author's message?
3. **Conclude** The details support the author's message, or main idea, that

______________________________.

Write for a Reader

This is my message! This is important!

Authors use elements of craft, such as repetition, to emphasize information in the text. Authors also include facts and relevant details to underscore the message, or lesson.

My TURN Consider how Mary Kay Carson develops her message in "Tracking Monsters." Determine which elements, such as repetition of important facts and details, help you understand her message. Now identify how you can use craft to develop and emphasize a message in your own writing.

1. When writing an informational text, what elements would you use to best communicate your message?

2. Write an informational text on a topic of your choice. Use one element of craft, such as a text feature or repetition, to express your own author's message, or lesson.

Spell Words with Prefixes *il-*, *in-*, *im-*, *ir-*

Prefixes add meaning to base words. In most cases, the spelling of the base word does not change. Instead, the prefix is simply added to the beginning of the word.

My TURN Read the words and find the related word pairs. Spell the words of each related word pair and write them side by side.

SPELLING WORDS

logical	adequate	accurate	rational
inoffensive	offensive	impassable	illegal
irrational	irreplaceable	inadequate	passable
probable	inaccurate	mobile	replaceable
legal	illogical	improbable	immobile

logical	illogical

Perfect Verb Tenses

The past tense tells what has happened or already been (*marched*). The present tense tells what is happening now (*march*). The future tense tells what is going to happen or will be (*will march*).

Perfect tenses use a helping verb to specify the relationship between actions in time.

- The **past perfect** tense shows an action that began and ended in the past.
  Last week, we had marched in the parade.
- The **present perfect** tense shows an action that began in the past and ended in the present.
  Now we have marched from Main Street to City Hall.
- The **future perfect** tense shows an action that will start and end in the future.
  By the end of the year, I will have marched in four parades.

My TURN Edit this draft by changing each verb to past perfect tense.

Researchers check data after they arrive at the laboratory. Last month, one of the machines failed to measure the migration patterns. The manager asked the university for better equipment. The state-of-the-art device arrived last week.

Use Precise Language and Domain-Specific Vocabulary

Learning Goal

I can use elements of informational writing to write an informational article.

The goal of an informational article is to give information about a topic. A writer can achieve this goal by choosing precise words and phrases so the reader understands exactly what the writer means.

Precise language and word choice replace general nouns with specific descriptions and replace vague verbs with action verbs.

> The tallest building in the world is in the Middle East.
>
> The tallest skyscraper in the world, the Burj Khalifa, towers over Dubai, United Arab Emirates.

Domain-specific language is vocabulary that applies to a particular study, or domain. These words may need to be defined for readers.

> The Burj Khalifa is so tall that the Council on Tall Buildings has classified it as a megatall building.
>
> The Burj Khalifa is so tall that the Council on Tall Buildings has classified it as a megatall building, a structure that surpasses 1,968 ft (600 m).

My TURN Replace each underlined word or words with a precise word. Use domain-specific vocabulary when appropriate.

1. We saw <u>big</u> frogs at our pond. ______________________

2. When we <u>looked closely at</u> the water, we saw <u>little frog babies with tails</u>.

   ____

3. Jude wanted to catch a frog, but Mrs. Reyes said that would <u>bother</u> the <u>way the whole pond works</u>. ______________________

My TURN Use precise language and domain-specific vocabulary to explain the topic of your informational article.

Use Correct Verb Tense

Writers use **verb tense** to show various times, sequences of events, states, and conditions. The perfect tense uses a form of *have* with the past participle.

Tense	Shows	Example
Present Perfect	Action that began in the past and is completed in the present	I *have* finished the painting. She *has* graduated from art school.
Past Perfect	Action that began in the past and was completed in the past	I *had* decided to be an artist when I was young.
Future Perfect	Action that will be completed at some point in the future	I *will have* finished the project by Saturday.

Writers usually avoid shifts in tense within a sentence.

Salvador chooses red paint and had brushed it on his canvas.

Incorrect: *Chooses* and *had brushed* are different tenses.

Salvador chooses red paint and brushes it on his canvas.

Correct: *Chooses* and *brushes* are both present tense.

Sometimes, however, there is a good reason for a shift in tense.

After she goes to the art supply store, I will have what I need to finish the painting.

Correct: *Goes* and *will have* are different tenses, but they show a relationship between present and future action.

My TURN Form the correct perfect tense of each verb.

1. In less than three months from now, Julie ________ (compete) in five marathons.

2. She ________ (train) hard every day to get in shape.

3. She ________ (decide) to become a competitive runner after watching the Chicago Marathon last year.

Edit for Adverbs

An **adverb** tells how, when, or where something happens. It can describe a verb, an adjective, or another adverb.

Lauren sings **quietly** to herself.

Quietly describes how Lauren sings.

A **conjunctive adverb** shows a relationship between ideas within a sentence. It can introduce an independent clause, connect two independent clauses, or link sentences with similar ideas. Common conjunctive adverbs include *however, eventually, meanwhile, nevertheless, then*, and *finally*.

Sam went to the store; **meanwhile**, I vacuumed the house.

In sentences with two independent clauses, the conjunctive adverb is preceded by a semicolon and followed by a comma.

By the time we finished our chores, **however**, I thought we were going to be late. **Nevertheless**, we managed to get the house ready just in time for the party.

In other sentences, commas set off conjunctive adverbs.

My TURN Edit the paragraph to correct punctuation with conjunctive adverbs.

Alexander Hamilton, the founding father shown on the $10 bill, grew up in poverty. He worked hard to get an education subsequently he became George Washington's secretary during the Revolutionary War. Later he served as a delegate to the Constitutional Convention. Then Washington asked him to serve as Secretary of the Treasury consequently Hamilton became the father of our nation's financial system.

My TURN Edit a draft of your informational article to correct punctuation with conjunctive adverbs.

Edit Simple and Compound Sentences

A complete simple sentence has one independent clause, or at least one subject and one verb. A sentence without a subject or a verb is called a fragment. Writers edit to avoid fragments. A complete compound sentence has two independent clauses that are connected with a comma and a coordinating conjunction, such as *and*, *but*, or *or*. Joining independent clauses without a comma and coordinating conjunction creates a run-on sentence. Writers can also correct run-on sentences by adding end punctuation to separate the independent clauses into two simple sentences.

Sentence	Subject	Verb	Sentence Type
The horse whinnied with excitement.	horse	whinnied	simple
Daisy was eager to run, so she reared up on her back legs.	Daisy she	was reared	compound

The subject and verb of a sentence must work together, or **agree**.

The **mare fears** fire.

Mare is singular, and *fears* is a singular verb.

My TURN Edit the paragraph for subject-verb agreement. Correct the fragment and the run-on sentence.

Painting with watercolors are challenging. You add water depending on how light or intense you wants the color to be. More water mean the color will be weaker more of the paper show through. Less water and more paint creates bolder colors. Easier to see.

My TURN Edit your informational article for subject-verb agreement and to be sure simple and compound sentences are complete and correct.

Edit for Prepositions and Prepositional Phrases

A **preposition** creates a relationship between a noun and a verb, adjective, or other noun.

Some common prepositions are *above, across, at, before, below, between, by, during, from, in, near, of, off, out, over, to, under, until, up,* and *with.*

Many prepositions are adverbs by themselves. They become prepositions when they are used in **prepositional phrases.** A prepositional phrase ends with a noun or pronoun called the **object of the preposition.**

Sentence	Prepositional Phrase	Preposition	Object of the Preposition
Mom and I stood in line to buy tickets.	in line	in	line

Prepositional phrases can cause confusion in sentences. A verb must agree with a sentence's subject, not the object of the prepositional phrase.

My aunt's collection of old movies is famous.

The verb *is* agrees with *collection,* the singular subject of the sentence.

MY TURN Edit the paragraph for subject-verb agreement with prepositional phrases.

The hairs on the polar bear is water-repellant. These hairs and the deposits of fat on the polar bear helps keep him warm. The warmest water of the Arctic Ocean still only reach extremely cold temperatures.

MY TURN Edit a draft of your informational article for subject-verb agreement. Watch for prepositional phrases. Discuss your edits in Writing Club.

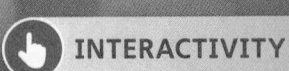

INTERACTIVITY

SAVING
Natural Habitats

How do animals interact with their habitats? Watch and read about how threatened animals have been returned to places where they once lived.

WATCH

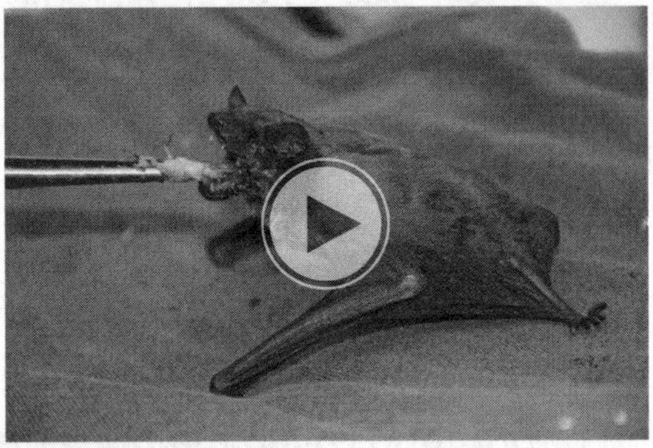

EUROPEAN BISON The European bison was nearly extinct, but conservation groups like Rewilding Europe are reintroducing the animals. Today more than 2,000 bison live in plains and forests of the Netherlands.

OREGON SPOTTED FROG
The frogs' Pacific Northwest wetland home is threatened, but the Northwest Amphibian Recovery Project has helped return over 1,000 Oregon spotted frogs to their habitat.

BLACK RHINO Black rhinos have been victims of horn poaching, in which hunters remove and sell an animal's horns. Successful anti-poaching efforts have allowed black rhinos to make a comeback in southern Africa.

RED DEER Illegal hunting has decreased deer populations in Europe. However, a rewilding group recently released 36 red deer in the Rhodope Mountains. The team expects to see the population increase in the future.

WEEK 5

Weekly Question

What are some different ways people can observe and protect wildlife?

TURN and TALK Summarize what you learned from watching the video. Discuss what you know about how animals survive in natural habitats. Take notes on your thoughts about the video, photos, and captions. Discuss characteristics unique to each type of media, and explain how each helped you understand the topic better than text alone.

Learning Goal

I can learn more about the theme *Observations* by analyzing argumentative texts.

Argumentative Text

Learn to recognize the characteristics and structures of argumentative text. The purpose of argumentative text is to persuade the reader that the argument is valid. It includes

- A **claim**, or opinion statement
- Supporting **reasons**
- **Facts, examples, quotations,** and other **evidence**
- A logical **text structure**

You can tell a text is argumentative if it states a claim and supports it with reasons and evidence.

TURN and TALK Compare and contrast informational text and argumentative text. How are they similar? How are they different? Use the anchor chart to help you. Write your thoughts and discuss them with a partner.

My NOTES

Argumentative Text Anchor Chart

Purpose: To persuade, or convince, the reader to think or act a certain way

Claim: an opinion about the topic

Reasons: support the claim

Transitions: clarify how reasons and evidence support the claim

Supporting Evidence: supports the claim and reasons

- Facts
- Details
- Examples
- Quotations

Meet the Author

David Bowles's love of reading comes from his grandmother, Marie Garza. She shared many folktales from the Rio Grande Valley, in southern Texas, where Bowles grew up. She also taught him about wildlife in the region. Bowles became a writer because he wanted to preserve and share the culture, history, and ecology of his homeland.

Let Wild Animals Be Wild

Preview Vocabulary

As you read *Let Wild Animals Be Wild*, pay attention to these vocabulary words. Note how the words relate to the ideas and relationships discussed in the text.

sanctuaries	**diminished**
thrive	**unfettered**

Read

You will read two **argumentative texts** in this unit. Follow these strategies as you read the texts for the first time.

First Read

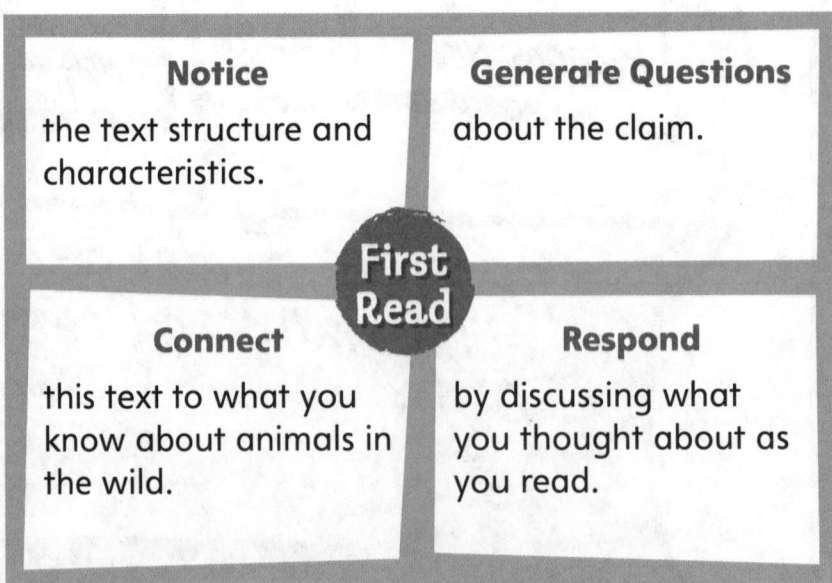

Notice the text structure and characteristics.

Generate Questions about the claim.

Connect this text to what you know about animals in the wild.

Respond by discussing what you thought about as you read.

Genre Argumentative Text

Let Wild Animals BE WILD

BY DAVID BOWLES

AUDIO

ANNOTATE

CLOSE READ

Analyze Argumentative Texts

Underline the author's claim in paragraph 1. Then underline reasons that support the author's claim and identify his intended audience.

sanctuaries human-made places of safety and protection

Vocabulary in Context

Context clues can help you understand the meaning of an unfamiliar word by telling what the word is as well as what it is not.

Underline context clues that help you determine the meaning of the word *rehabilitating*.

1 Many people feel a responsibility to protect and care for Earth's living creatures. People take action in many ways that either directly or indirectly benefit wildlife. One of the direct ways that we protect wildlife is by raising endangered wild animals in captivity, to ensure their survival. Another way that we directly protect wildlife is by treating injured wild animals and rehabilitating them in captivity. The goal of both actions should be to release animals back into the wild where they belong.

2 For endangered or injured animals, the benefits of living under human protection are clear. Animals in zoos and sanctuaries have plenty of food and water. They're safe from predators. They aren't threatened by hunting, environmental pollution, and habitat destruction. For endangered species, every death in the wild means another step toward extinction. If even a few members of an endangered species are successfully raised in captivity, hope for the species stays alive.

3 But keeping animals alive in captivity is not the final purpose of conservation. Real success comes when animals are plentiful and strong enough to return to their natural habitat. Only then can an ecosystem be in balance. An ecosystem is all the animals and plants that live in a certain area.

4 Here's one such success story. The California condor is one of the largest flying birds in the world. It was once found in many parts of the United States. But during the past two centuries, the species diminished. Settlers shot and poisoned the condors and took their eggs. Hunting condors was outlawed more than 100 years ago. However, their numbers continued to fall because of pollution, pesticide use, and other threats. Finally, by the 1970s, scientists discovered that only a few dozen wild condors were left. In the early 1980s, the U.S. government started a program to keep the condor from going extinct. Scientists began to collect wild condor eggs and hatch them in zoos. They also captured some condors. They kept these condors in zoos so they could lay eggs and raise their young in safety.

5 By 1987, there were no more condors left in the wild. However, there were 27 California condors in captivity. All along, the plan was to raise and then release condors back into the wild. No one was sure it would work. But it did. By the end of 2015, the total population of California condors was up to 435. That included 268 condors living in their natural habitat, once again soaring through the skies.

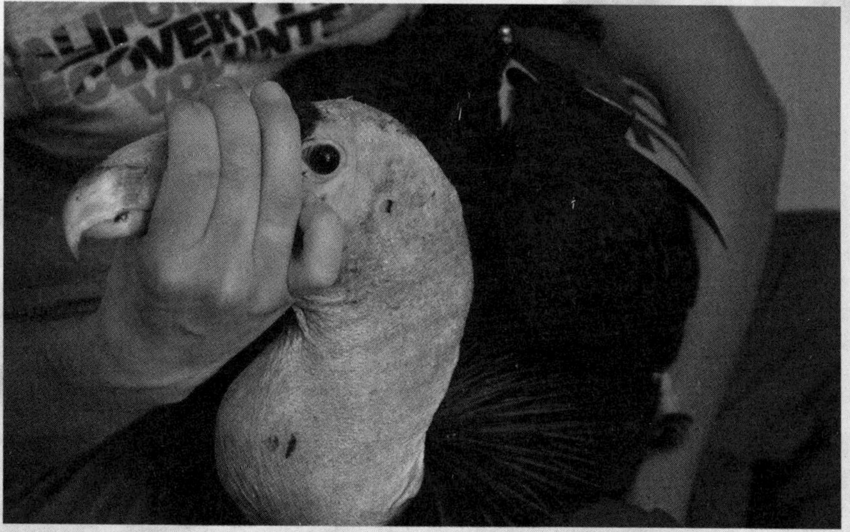

CLOSE READ

Analyze Argumentative Texts

How does the author use facts to support his claim? Underline a sentence that lets the reader know the author is presenting evidence.

diminished shrank, became smaller or fewer

CLOSE READ

Analyze Argumentative Texts

Underline a reason the author uses to support the claim.

thrive do well, be successful, grow

unfettered not limited, not restricted

6 Returning wild animals to the wild is good for both animals and people. Let's start with the animals. Imagine a bird that was forever kept from flying free. Or what if a wild cat could never prowl the savannah? Wild animals such as these may be safe and protected under human care, but they can truly thrive only in the wild, where their natural instincts and behaviors are unfettered.

7 All of nature benefits when an endangered species is restored to its habitat. Many studies have shown the enormous effect even one species has on an ecosystem. This is particularly true of what are known as "keystone" species.

8 A keystone species is an animal or plant that plays an essential role in an ecosystem. If that species becomes extinct, or even threatened, the ecosystem is threatened. That's because other living things depend on that species for their own survival.

9 Beavers are a keystone species in the United States and Europe. Beavers use logs and sticks to build dams in rivers and streams. Their dams and the pools that form behind them become habitats for many other animals. For example, ducks, otters, and dragonflies may live there. When beavers became extinct in Scotland and other parts of Europe due to hunting, other animal populations suffered as well. In 2009, beavers were reintroduced to wild areas of Scotland, where they were monitored through 2014. Biologists declared the program an "outstanding success." The first several generations of beavers thrived and had a positive impact on the environment.

10 Animals can benefit in another way when they are released to the wild. Scientists have begun to put tracking devices on animals raised in captivity and on injured animals rehabilitated in captivity before returning both groups to their habitats. The devices allow scientists to follow the animals' movements and to study their behaviors. Information gathered helps us better understand and protect species.

CLOSE READ

Synthesize Information

Highlight information that relates to a claim made in *Don't Release Animals Back to the Wild.*

CLOSE READ

Analyze Argumentative Texts

How does the author use facts in this argument? Underline text evidence that supports your response.

11 The Siberian tiger, found mainly in the far east of Russia, is one of many threatened species that has benefited from tracking. Starting in the 1990s, members of the Siberian Tiger Project, based at the University of Idaho, began to catch Siberian tigers. They fitted the big cats with radio collars. Then they released the tigers. Scientists have been monitoring the tigers for decades, gathering valuable data. Wildlife workers use the information to help them effectively treat and release injured tigers. Scientists also hope to reintroduce Siberian tigers into areas where they have disappeared, such as northern Korea. Ongoing monitoring will ensure the tigers have the resources they need to thrive.

12 Releasing captive animals into the wild also makes financial sense. Many people will travel almost anywhere to see animals. Therefore, reintroducing animals to a wilderness area brings in tourists. And tourists spend money. For example, wolves were reintroduced to Yellowstone National Park starting in 1995. A 2006 study by the University of Montana estimated that wolf-related tourists—people who visit Yellowstone primarily to see wolves—brought in tens of millions of dollars each year. That money helps Yellowstone. It also helps surrounding businesses, such as motels and restaurants.

CLOSE READ

Synthesize Information

Highlight details that support the author's claim.

13 Some people argue against releasing animals back into the wild. For one thing, they say animals raised or rehabilitated in captivity can't survive on their own. However, scientists are learning more and more about what wild animals need to live independently. Wildlife biologists and other specialists carefully prepare animals for life in the wild before releasing them. In the end, of course, the animals have to fend for themselves. But that's nature's way.

14 Other people say that reintroducing predators to the wild is bad for humans. (They might attack us! They might attack livestock!) But animals that live in a balanced ecosystem, with adequate food and space, rarely hurt people or livestock. The U.S. Department of Agriculture reported that of all cattle that died in 2010, only about 5 percent were killed by predators. An ecosystem needs all animals, predator and prey alike, to stay in balance.

15 Humans have the power to save and protect species. We also have the responsibility to let wild animals be wild and live according to their instincts. Releasing animals back into nature, whenever possible, is the best course of action for them, for us, and for Earth.

Meet the Author

René Saldaña Jr. loves two things: writing and teaching. He teaches college students at Texas Tech University and writes a lot of books for children and young adults. His favorite part about writing is meeting his readers face-to-face.

Don't Release Animals Back to the Wild

Preview Vocabulary

As you read *Don't Release Animals Back to the Wild*, pay attention to this vocabulary word.

cooperate

Read and Compare

As you read the second of the two argumentative texts, follow these strategies to compare and contrast each argument's claim.

First Read

Notice the counterclaim that the author includes in the text.

Generate Questions about facts and opinions.

Connect this text with information you learned from *Let Wild Animals Be Wild*.

Respond by discussing the similarities and differences between texts with a partner.

Genre Argumentative Text

Don't Release Animals Back to the WILD

BY RENÉ SALDAÑA JR.

Synthesize Information

How is this text similar to and different from *Let Wild Animals Be Wild?* Highlight text evidence that supports your answer.

cooperate work together, participate in shared activity

1 Sometimes wildlife needs a helping hand. Biologists and conservationists often rescue orphaned, injured, or endangered animals. It's the only way to ensure their survival. Helping animals may require keeping them in captivity for weeks, months, or even years. Endangered species, in particular, may need to stay in captivity for extended periods. That way, they can begin to rebuild their population. Then what? One argument is that wild animals always should be released back to the wild. However, scientific research raises serious questions about the benefits of doing so. For several reasons, it makes more sense to keep these animals in captivity.

2 For one thing, many animals that have been kept in captivity simply can't survive in the wild. This is especially true of animals that were born in captivity or raised in captivity from an early age.

3 All animals are born with certain instincts, or natural abilities. These instincts help them to survive. But animals also learn important survival skills after they're born from their parents or other members of their species. These may include how to hunt for food, recognize enemies, and cooperate with others. When orphaned or injured animals are raised in captivity, they miss out on this learning process. Therefore, when these animals are released into the wild, they are poorly equipped to survive.

4 Scientists at the Animal Behavior Research Group at the University of Exeter, England, examined the survival rates of animals released in the wild. The scientists studied 45 cases that involved 17 different species. The species included wolves, bears, foxes, African wild dogs, and otters.

5 The first group was made up of animals born in captivity and released into the wild. The second group was made up of animals caught in the wild and moved to a new area. The scientists found that the animals born in captivity had a much lower survival rate in the wild. These animals were more likely to starve to death. That's because they lacked hunting skills. The captive-born animals were also were less likely to find mates and start families. That means their species as a whole was less likely to thrive.

6 The captive-born animals also were less likely to avoid dangerous situations. "Captive-born animals have less natural fear of other large carnivores," said researcher Kristen Jule. She noted that "animals that are more bold, particularly toward humans, are more likely to die." African hunting dogs raised in captivity, for example, were frequently attacked by lions. Many African hunting dogs were also hunted or trapped by humans after their release into the wild.

CLOSE READ

Analyze Argumentative Texts

Underline reasons the author gives to support the main claim.

CLOSE READ

Synthesize Information

Highlight facts and details the author provides to support the claim. Synthesize these facts with those presented in *Let Wild Animals Be Wild* to develop a new understanding of the role of zoos and aquariums.

7 Animals that are captured rather than born in captivity also face peril when they're released back into the wild. One example is Keiko, the orca that starred in the movie *Free Willy*. Keiko was captured from the North Atlantic Ocean, near Iceland. At the time, he was about three years old. After *Free Willy,* people around the world pushed to have Keiko released to the wild. The campaign succeeded. First, Keiko was returned to Iceland. There, he lived in a huge pen in the ocean. Scientists helped Keiko regain his health after years living in poor conditions. They took him out on "ocean walks" so he could get used to the open ocean. They even introduced him to wild orcas. Finally, in July 2002, he was released into the wild. But Keiko was unable to integrate into, or join, a wild orca group. Scientists believe this is key to orcas' health in the wild. Keiko died alone in December 2003.

8 Here's a second reason it makes sense to keep captive wild animals in captivity, rather than release them to the wild. Many modern zoos and other facilities offer everything these animals need to live long, healthy, and happy lives. And in many cases, nature does not.

9 Some people object to keeping animals in zoos. They compare zoo life to life in prison. But their

objections may be based on outdated ideas. The bare, concrete spaces and small cages of the past have given way to far more natural enclosures.

10 Many zoo designers now focus on behavioral enrichment. That means giving animals choices about where to go and what to do. In well-designed zoos, animals can roam large spaces that feature dirt, trees and other plants, and water. Moats or ditches have replaced cages and wire fences. Animals can climb, burrow, or simply stretch out and nap. They can do what comes naturally. Zoo personnel also provide toys and activities to prevent boredom. Animals have private space, too. They aren't always in view of visitors.

11 In some important ways, zoos and sanctuaries improve on nature. In captivity, animals can always eat well. Their food intake doesn't depend on their hunting skills. It doesn't vary according to the season or other environmental factors. Captive animals don't need to compete for scarce resources. They need not fear predators, hunters, or speeding cars. They won't lose their habitat to human development. Regular vet visits keep them healthy. And if animals reproduce in captivity, their babies will be born into, and raised in, a safe environment.

12 This is particularly important for animals whose species are dwindling in the wild—or entire species that no longer exist in the wild. The International Union for Conservation of Nature (IUCN) lists 33 species as extinct in the wild. Thirty-one of these species remain alive and well in zoos, aquariums, and other facilities. In many cases, these animals can't survive in the wild due to habitat destruction, poaching, or other factors. In captivity, they get the care they need to thrive.

CLOSE READ

Vocabulary in Context

Skilled readers use context clues to determine the meaning of unknown words.

Underline context clues that support your definition of the word *enclosures*.

Synthesize Information

Highlight information that is similar to what you read in *Let Wild Animals Be Wild*.

CLOSE READ

Analyze Argumentative Texts

How does the author use reasons and facts to support the text's claim? Underline examples to support your answer.

13 Individual endangered animals also may be rescued, taken to zoos or sanctuaries, nursed back to health, and kept in safe surroundings. For example, the Jungle Place in Quintana Roo, Mexico, provides food, shelter, medical care, and attention to rescued spider monkeys. The monkeys were victims of illegal pet trade, poaching, and habitat loss. There's no longer any safe wild environment for them in Mexico. Sanctuaries such as the Jungle Place keep these monkeys safe.

14 There's a third reason to keep rescued wild animals in captivity rather than releasing them back into the wild. Both scientists and the general public can learn a great deal from captive animals.

15 Carefully observing captive animals allows scientists to make discoveries about species' health and behavior that they can't make in the wild. What scientists learn about captive animals can benefit other members of the species that remain in the wild.

16 Seeing wild animals in captivity also helps people appreciate wildlife and wildlife-protection efforts. People are more likely to contribute to conservation organizations after seeing a member of an endangered species up close. That's unlikely to happen in the wild. Zoos, sanctuaries, and similar places also offer signs, guides, lectures, and other information to educate people about the animals living there.

17 In October 2014, the Monterey Bay Aquarium, in California, rescued an orphaned sea otter. She was part of a population of threatened Southern California otters. The pup was thought to be less than a week old. She was far too young to be without her mother.

18 Staff cared for the pup for a month. Then they moved her to the Shedd Aquarium in Chicago, Illinois, and named her Luna. They knew they couldn't release Luna to the sea. Pups learn most of their survival skills from their mothers. Luna missed out on this learning stage. She wouldn't last long in the wild.

19 Luna soon became a huge attraction for the public and the media. Tim Binder oversees the aquarium's animal care and its rescue program. He refers to Luna as an "ambassador" for her species and her ecosystem. Binder says Luna "reminds us that what we do on land has repercussions on the ocean environment and the animals that live there, inspiring us to make a difference." By studying Luna, scientists at Shedd have learned important information about sea otters and how to care for them. For example, they now know the exact calorie intake and activity levels an otter needs to grow to full size. Scientists can use such information to help sea otters in the wild.

20 In some cases, captive wild animals can, and should, be released to the wild. For example, if a sick or injured animal can be treated quickly, it can probably be released with little risk. However, for many captive animals, release is not worth the risk. Captivity offers safety, health, and well-being. It may even save entire species. For animals in peril, those benefits far outweigh freedom.

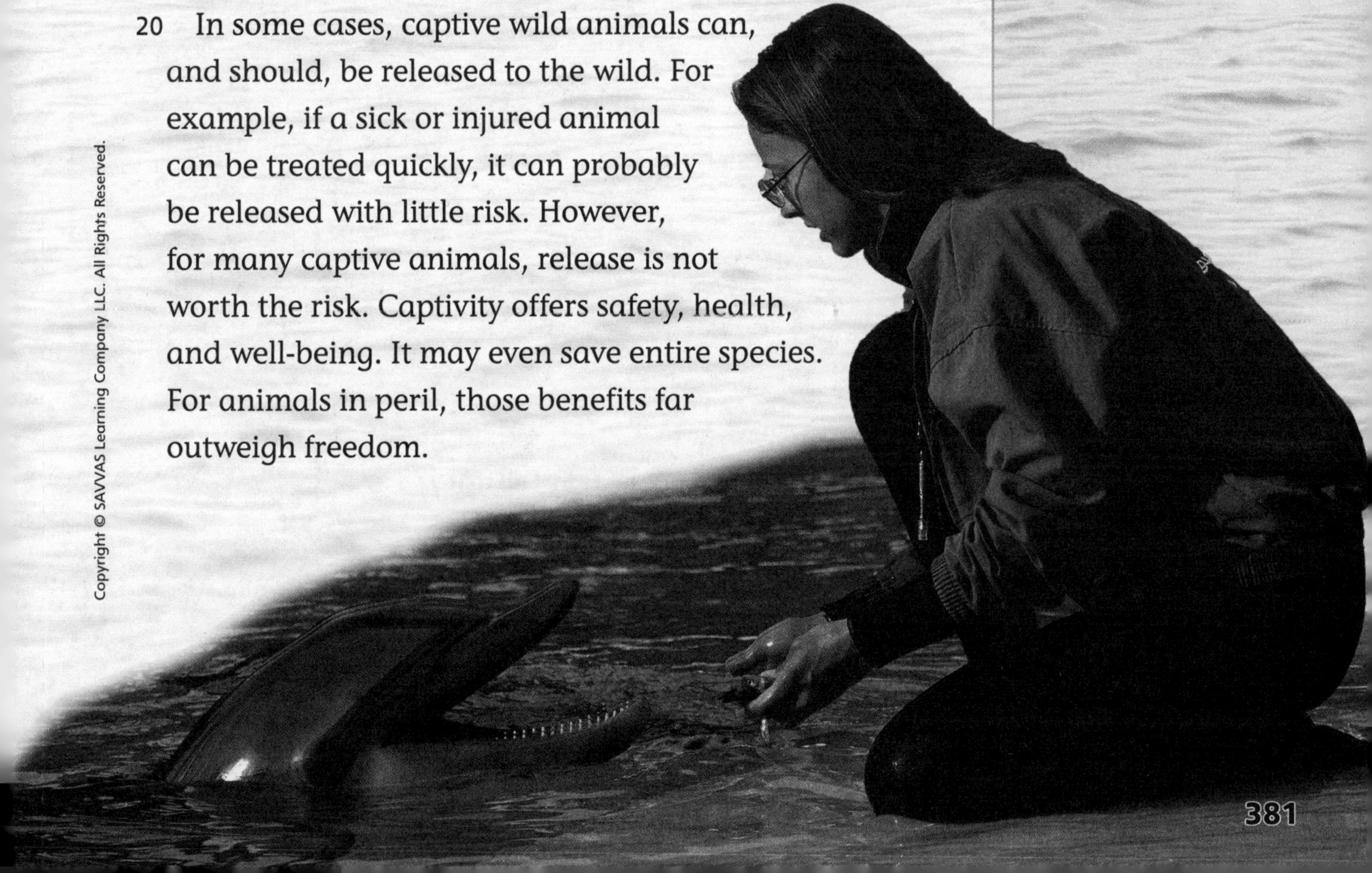

CLOSE READ

Analyze Argumentative Texts

Underline a restatement of the text's main claim.

Develop Vocabulary

In argumentative texts, authors use precise words to state and support their opinions and to connect ideas.

My TURN Make connections between vocabulary words by answering the questions. Use the vocabulary words in your responses.

1. How did **sanctuaries** help the **diminished** population of condors?

2. Why do some people think that wild animals do not **thrive** in a **sanctuary**?

3. How do animals' **unfettered** instincts help them **thrive** in the wild?

4. Do animals learn to **cooperate** with others in a **sanctuary**?

Check for Understanding

MY TURN Look back at the texts to answer the questions.

1. How do you know that *Let Wild Animals Be Wild* and *Don't Release Animals Back to the Wild* are argumentative texts? Give three examples.

2. Choose one of the two texts, and assess how effective the author's argument is.

3. How does each text use animal sanctuaries to support its claim? Use text evidence in your comparison.

4. Based on what you read, analyze claims about animal conservation from both texts.

Analyze Argumentative Texts

Authors write **argumentative texts** to persuade an audience or reader of their claim, or main opinion. The author supports the claim with reasons and then supports each reason with evidence, including facts, details, quotations, statistics, or examples.

1. **My TURN** Go to the Close Read notes in *Let Wild Animals Be Wild* and *Don't Release Animals Back to the Wild*. Underline the parts that help you understand and analyze the arguments in each text.

2. **Text Evidence** Use the parts you underlined to complete the chart for the text of your choice.

Title:	**Claim:**

Intended Audience:

Reason	**Facts and Other Supporting Evidence**

Analyze how the reasons and evidence support the author's claim.

Synthesize Information

Readers **synthesize information,** or create new understanding based on information from multiple sources. Synthesizing information helps readers deepen their understanding of a topic. Readers can synthesize information to discover how authors can make an argumentative text effective.

1. **My TURN** Go back to the Close Read notes and highlight details that support each author's claim.

2. **Text Evidence** Use your highlighted text to complete the graphic organizer with details that support the claim in each text. Synthesize this information to make and support your own claim about animal conservation.

Details and Supporting Evidence

Let Wild Animals Be Wild	Don't Release Animals Back to the Wild
"An ecosystem needs all animals, predator and prey alike, to stay in balance."	They need not fear predators, hunters, or speeding cars."

Synthesize Information to Make a Claim

Reflect and Share

Talk About It *Let Wild Animals Be Wild* argues for animal conservation. *Don't Release Animals Back to the Wild* presents a different claim about how wildlife should be protected. What other arguments and opinions about the environment have you read this week? Discuss specific ideas in the texts to support your own opinion about animal conservation.

Present an Opinion When giving an opinion, organize and present your ideas clearly.

- Write a short summary of how the authors of the texts you have chosen used reasons to support the points they made.
- Explain why these reasons made you agree or disagree with their points. Include your own observations to support your opinion.
- Speak clearly, at a natural rate and volume.

Use these sentence frames to guide your responses:

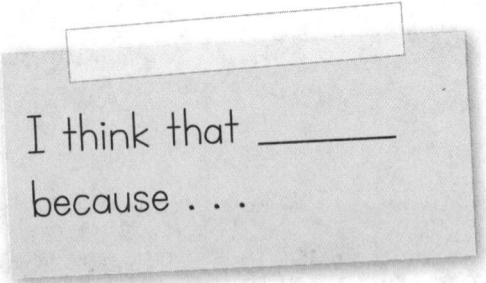

I think that ______ because . . .

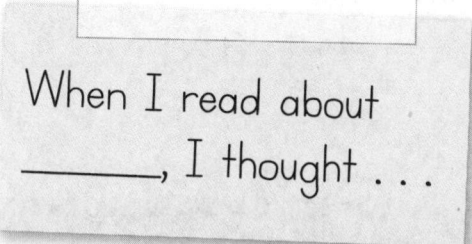

When I read about ______, I thought . . .

Weekly Question

What are some different ways people can observe and protect wildlife?

Academic Vocabulary

Learning Goal

I can develop knowledge about language to make connections between reading and writing.

Parts of speech are categories of words, which include nouns, verbs, adjectives, and adverbs.

Words can often be used as more than one part of speech. Often, when changing a word to a different part of speech, the spelling of the word changes as well.

My TURN For each sentence,

1. **Read** the underlined academic vocabulary word in the sample sentence.
2. **Identify** the word's part of speech.
3. **Write** your own sentence using the base word as a different part of speech. Include the part of speech after your answer. If necessary, check a print or online dictionary.

Sentence	Part of Speech	My Sentence
The expert used his years of experience to estimate the sculpture's value.	noun	The master carpenter expertly built and stained a bench. (adverb)
Jin focused on his math homework instead of reading.		
There was a visible shadow across the painting.		

Base Words and Endings

A **base word** is the most basic form of a word. Add an **ending** to a base word to change the word's meaning or part of speech. For example, adding *-tion* to the verb *cooperate* creates the noun *cooperation.*

The word *government* in paragraph 4 of *Let Wild Animals Be Wild* means "an organization that governs." The noun *government* is formed by adding the ending *-ment* to the verb *govern*.

My TURN Read each base word. Complete the chart by adding an ending to each base word and telling how it changes the part of speech. Check your endings and words in a print or online dictionary.

Base Word	Base Word with Ending	Change in Meaning
require		
captive		
recognize		
active		
conservation		

Read Like a Writer

Authors sometimes use point of view to determine how to present information to readers. In argumentative texts, some writers use first-person pronouns—*I*, *we*, *us*, *mine*, and *ours*—to strengthen their opinions.

Model! Read the text from *Let Wild Animals Be Wild.*

> Humans have the power to save and protect species. We also have the responsibility to let wild animals be wild and live according to their instincts.

first-person

1. **Identify** David Bowles uses the first-person pronoun *we* in his conclusion.
2. **Question** Why does he use *we* at the end of his argument?
3. **Conclude** David Bowles uses first-person point of view so that readers feel included in his argument: Wild animals belong in the wild.

Read the text.

> I believe that we should protect endangered species from dangers they would face in the wild. It is our responsibility to keep wild animals safe.

My TURN Follow the steps to analyze the author's point of view.

1. **Identify** The author uses ______________________.
2. **Question** Why does the author use this point of view?
3. **Conclude** The author uses ______________________ so that readers ______________________ ______________________.

Write for a Reader

Use first-person point of view to strengthen your opinion.

Some writers use literary devices in argumentative texts to emphasize their claims and help persuade readers. Using first-person point of view is one way to do this.

My TURN Think about how the use of first person at the beginning and end of *Let Wild Animals Be Wild* appealed to your emotions, beliefs, and sense of reason. Now identify how you can use first-person point of view as a tool to help emphasize points and persuade your own readers.

1. If you were trying to persuade a reader about your opinion on animals in captivity or in the wild, how would you use first-person point of view?

2. Write an argument about animal conservation using information from the text and some of your own research. Include facts to support your opinion, and use first-person point of view for emphasis and effect.

Spell Base Words with Endings

A **base word** is the most basic form of a word. When you add an **ending** to a base word to change the word's meaning or part of speech, you may have to change the spelling.

Spelling changes can include dropping *e*, changing *y* to *i*, and doubling final consonants.

My TURN Read the words. Spell each base word and write it in the first column. Then spell the base word with the ending and write it in the second column so the words match up.

SPELLING WORDS

equipped	conveying	revise	revising
program	theories	rely	industry
relies	permit	involvement	conveys
permitting	involve	equip	programming
benefit	benefited	theory	industries

program	programming

Active Voice

In the **active voice**, the subject of a sentence performs the action in the sentence. In the passive voice, the subject of the sentence receives the action. Writers replace passive voice with active voice to make their writing clear, concise, and direct.

Scientists caught the **animals**.
subject performing action

The animals were caught by **scientists.**
subject acted upon

Lions frequently attacked **African hunting dogs**.
subject performing action

African hunting dogs were frequently attacked by **lions**.
subject acted upon

My TURN Edit this draft by changing all of the passive voice to active voice. Rewrite the revised paragraph.

> The World Wide Fund for Nature (WWF) was founded in 1961 by British naturalists. Animals and their habitats are protected by the organization. Today, money is provided by the WWF to fund environmental proposals all over the world.

Edit for Punctuation Marks

Learning Goal

I can use elements of informational writing to write an informational article.

Commas create small breaks within a sentence and can be used in a variety of ways.

Separate items in a series	We saw a camel, a kangaroo, and an elephant at the zoo.
Form a compound sentence, using *for, and, nor, but, or, yet, so*	The trainers threw fish into the pool, so the sea lions dove into the water.

Quotation marks are used for dialogue, direct quotations, and some titles.

Set off dialogue with commas and end punctuation	Sarah said, "I want to see the red pandas." "Where is the exhibit?" she asked.
Indicate a direct quote	The brochure said, "Red pandas are not closely related to giant panda bears."
Cite titles of articles, short stories, or poems	The brochure was titled "Learning About Red Pandas."

MyTURN Edit the paragraph for correct use of commas and quotation marks.

Where is Dan? I asked. We are going to be late for the movie and I really don't want to miss the previews!

Well, what do you expect? Mom said. He stayed up late reading again.

I held up a short story called The Case of the Missing Backpack.

He loves mysteries thrillers and detective stories I said.

MyTURN Edit a draft of your article for commas and quotation marks.

Edit for Capitalization

Capitalizing does not only apply to the first word of a sentence and to proper nouns, such as names, places, and titles. Capitalization is also used for **abbreviations** of addresses and personal titles.

	Sample	Abbreviation	Example
Addresses	South	S.	391 S. Broadway
	Colorado	CO	Denver, CO
Titles	General	Gen.	Gen. Nguyen
	Junior	Jr.	Samuel Lee Jr.

Initials in place of personal names should be capitalized: J. R. Warren.

Organizations and **acronyms** also require capitalization. For example, NASA stands for National Air and Space Administration.

My TURN Edit the paragraph to have correct capitalization.

Our trip took us through Texas. We visited the L.b.J. Presidential Library, where we learned a lot about pres. Lyndon Johnson's time in the White House. Did you know that nasa named the space center in Houston for him? You can write to the library for more information:

2313 Red River st.

Austin, Tx 78705

My TURN Edit a draft of your informational article to have correct capitalization of abbreviations, initials, acronyms, and organizations.

Publish and Celebrate

A writer publishes his or her work after revising and editing it. Some writers choose to publish by printing and handing out copies to readers. Others publish by posting the writing to a blog or other digital platform.

My TURN Answer the questions. Write legibly, or clearly, in cursive writing to describe your writing experience. Make sure that your writing can be easily read by others.

My favorite topic to write an informational article about was

____

____

____

____.

I would like to keep writing informational articles because

____

____

____

____.

My favorite illustration to include in an informational article was

____

____

____.

The next time I write an informational article, I will

____

____

____.

Prepare for Assessment

My TURN Follow a plan as you prepare to write an informational article in response to a prompt.

1. **Relax.**
   Take a deep breath.

2. **Make sure you understand the prompt.**
   Read the prompt. Underline what kind of writing you will do. Highlight the topic you will be writing about.

   Prompt: Write an informational article about the life of a plant or animal that you have learned about through observation.

3. **Brainstorm.**
   List three topics you could write about. Highlight your favorite.

4. **Plan your informational article.**
   Answer the questions your readers will ask: *who, what, where, when, why,* and *how.*

5. **Write your draft. Remember to include an introduction and a conclusion.**
   Use your own paper to write your article.

6. **After you finish, revise and edit your article.**
   Read your article again to yourself. Review it for subject-verb agreement and proper punctuation.

Assessment

MyTURN Before you write an informational article for your assessment, rate how well you understand the skills you have learned in this unit. Go back and review any skills you mark "No."

IDEAS AND ORGANIZATION	Yes!	No
I can brainstorm an engaging idea.	☐	☐
I can set a purpose for writing.	☐	☐
I can structure an informational article.	☐	☐
I can write a lead paragraph.	☐	☐
I can write an introduction and a conclusion.	☐	☐
I can group related information.	☐	☐

CRAFT		
I can select facts and concrete details.	☐	☐
I can include definitions, quotations, and examples.	☐	☐
I can select meaningful visuals and multimedia.	☐	☐
I can use transitions to show logical order.	☐	☐
I can format text to call attention to important information.	☐	☐

CONVENTIONS		
I can use precise language and define domain-specific vocabulary.	☐	☐
I can include conjunctive adverbs and prepositional phrases.	☐	☐
I can edit for verb tense.	☐	☐
I can edit for subject-verb agreement.	☐	☐
I can edit for punctuation and capitalization.	☐	☐

UNIT THEME
Observations

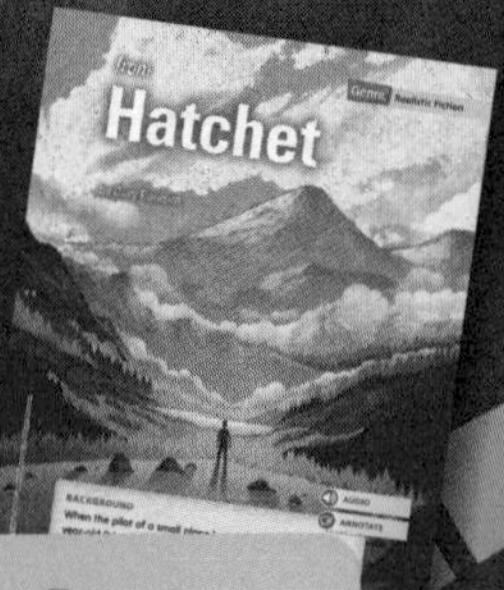

WEEK 3 from **Hatchet**

TURN and TALK

In a Word With a partner, look back at each text to choose and record a word that best shows the unit theme, *Observations*. Then use those words to help answer the Essential Question.

BOOK CLUB

WEEK 2 **A Place for Frogs**

BOOK CLUB

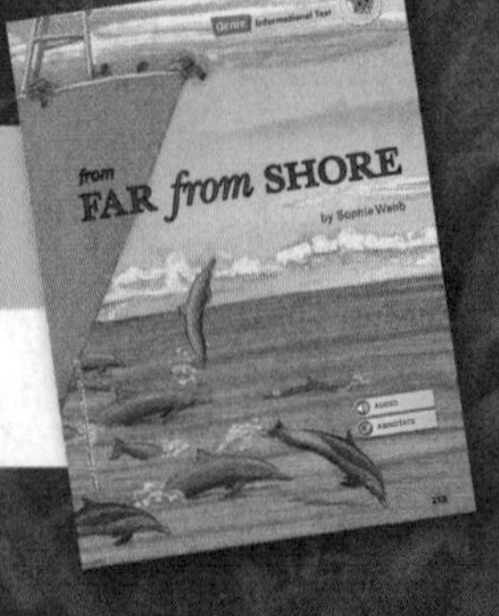

WEEK 1 from **Far from Shore**

WEEK 6

BOOK CLUB

WEEK 4

"Tracking Monsters" from **Park Scientists**

BOOK CLUB

WEEK 5

Let Wild Animals Be Wild and **Don't Release Animals Back to the Wild**

Essential Question

MyTURN

In your notebook, answer the Essential Question: How do we learn through our observations?

BOOK CLUB

Project

WEEK 6

Now it is time to apply what you learned about *Observations* in your **WEEK 6 PROJECT: Staying Alive!**

Staying Alive!

Activity

Create a survival guide for visitors to a natural area, such as a national park.
Include information on how to use clues found in nature to track animals, determine if bad weather is coming, find your way if you are lost, and carry out other activities that help protect you in a natural area.

RESEARCH

Research Articles

With your partner, read "Sights and Sounds in a Forest Preserve" to generate questions you have about surviving in the wilderness. Make a research plan for writing your survival guide.

1. **Sights and Sounds in a Forest Preserve**
2. **Do You See What I See?**
3. **Naturally Inspired**

Generate Questions

COLLABORATE Read "Sights and Sounds in a Forest Preserve" and then generate three questions you have about the article. Compare your questions with a partner. Answer any you can before sharing them with the class.

1. ______________________________

2. ______________________________

3. ______________________________

Use Academic Words

COLLABORATE In this unit, you learned many words related to the theme of *Observations*. Work with your partner to add more academic words to each category. If appropriate, use this vocabulary when you write your survival guide.

Academic Vocabulary	Word Forms	Synonyms	Antonyms
expert	expertly expertness expertise	authority professional specialist	amateur student beginner
focus	focused focusing focuses	apply concentrate direct	disregard ignore neglect
visible	visibly visibility visibilities	detectable noticeable obvious	hidden invisible inconspicuous
relate	related relating relatable	associate connect identify	detach disconnect separate
detect	detected detecting detectable	discover find observe	conceal hide overlook

Information, Please!

Informational writing focuses on facts, not opinions.

People write informational texts to provide information on a topic to a specific audience. For your survival guide for visitors to a natural area, you will need to

- provide an introduction with a main idea
- include facts that support your main idea
- organize your writing in a logical way
- provide a conclusion that restates your main idea

RESEARCH

COLLABORATE With your partner, read "Do You See What I See?" Then answer the questions about the article.

1. What is the author's main idea?

2. What facts does the author include to support the main idea?

3. How does the author structure, or organize, the article?

Plan Your Research

COLLABORATE Before you begin researching your survival guide, work with your partner to develop a research plan. Use the activity to write a main idea and plan how you will look for facts and details.

Definition	Examples
MAIN IDEAS A main idea is the main point an author makes in an informational text. A main idea • defines a goal, • is specific, and • is supported by details, such as facts and examples. Read the two examples in the right column. On another sheet of paper, write a main idea for your survival guide.	Pick the best main idea for an informational survival guide. ☐ In my opinion, people must take the proper precautions to stay safe in the water. ☐ Taking the proper precautions will keep you and your children safe in the water.
SUPPORTING DETAILS Support your main idea with details, such as • facts • statistics • direct quotations • examples	**Fact:** Learning basic water safety skills can save your life. **Statistic:** Sixty-four percent of children who go swimming cannot perform the five basic water safety skills. **Quote:** According to the CDC, "CPR performed by bystanders has been shown to save lives." **Example:** Safety precautions include learning how to swim.

With your partner, list options for finding details for your survival guide.

Evaluating Sources

A **search engine** is an online tool used to gather and identify relevant information. When researching, choose a search engine, enter keywords, and get search results. You must evaluate those results to determine if the sources are **credible**, or accurate and trustworthy.

EXAMPLE Jonas is going to the neighborhood pool with friends. He wants to know how to be safe while swimming. Jonas enters the keywords *Swimming Safety* to search for information online. How can he tell which Web sites are credible?

The part of the URL before the slash is the domain extension. A ".gov" URL is run by the government. To make sure Web site information is accurate, always try to locate the author of the article, and determine if he or she is an expert. Many government Web sites include research from leading scientists.

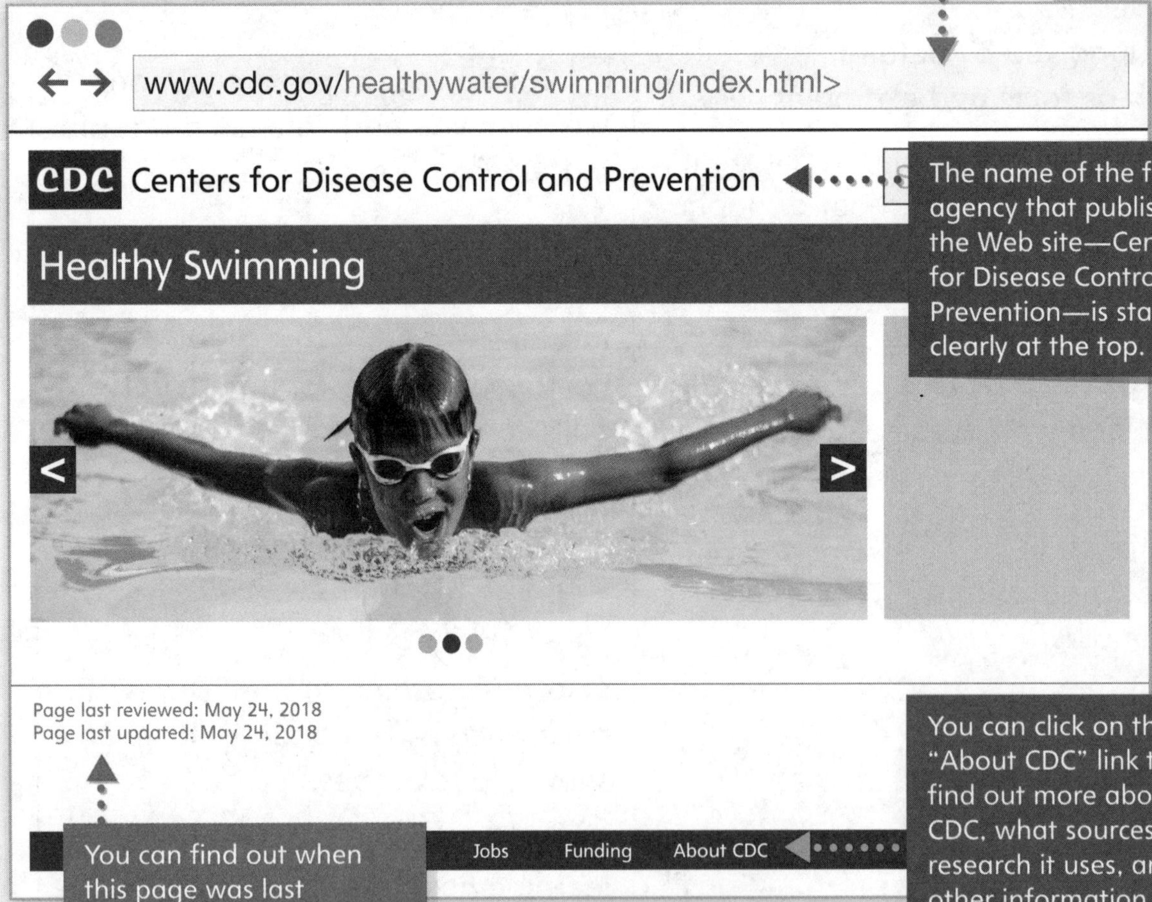

The name of the federal agency that publishes the Web site—Centers for Disease Control and Prevention—is stated clearly at the top.

You can find out when this page was last reviewed and updated. This tells you how current the information is.

You can click on the "About CDC" link to find out more about the CDC, what sources and research it uses, and other information that can help you decide if the Web site is credible.

COLLABORATE With your partner, go online to research your survival guide. Evaluate the credibility of each Web site that you visit. In your notebook, take notes on relevant information you gathered. On the lines, explain why you did or did not decide to use each Web site. For example, "The purpose of this Web site is to sell camping equipment, so I'm not sure I can trust its recommendations on the equipment needed to be safe."

Web site:

Author's expertise or source:

Why this Web site is or is not credible:

Web site:

Author's expertise or source:

Why this Web site is or is not credible:

Discuss the credibility of the Web sites you visited. Are you confident that you chose credible Web sites? If needed, do another search.

Word to the Wise

People write informational texts to inform an audience about a topic. An informative guide, such as one about survival skills in natural areas, provides a central idea about its topic. The guide then supports the main idea with facts.

Before you begin writing, decide on the audience for your survival guide. The audience you choose will determine the way in which you write your guide. Will it appeal to

- students?
- adults?
- families with children?
- senior citizens?
- people experienced in exploring natural areas?
- people new to exploring natural areas?

COLLABORATE Read the Student Model. Work with your partner to recognize the characteristics of informational writing.

Then decide how best to deliver your survival guide, whether in print, online, or as a multimedia presentation.

Now You Try It!

Discuss the checklist with your partner. Work together to follow the steps to create your survival guide.

Make sure your informational survival guide

- [ ] has an introduction and conclusion with a clear main idea.
- [ ] supports the main idea with facts from your sources.
- [ ] uses a text structure that makes sense for the topic.
- [ ] uses transitions to link ideas.
- [ ] uses graphics and text features to clarify ideas.

Student Model

Water Safety

If you are planning a day of swimming at a pool, lake, or beach, you probably are thinking mainly about the fun you will have. However, it is also important to keep water safety in mind. Taking the proper precautions will keep you and your children safe in the water.

Highlight a transition that links ideas.

Underline the main idea.

Highlight a detail that reveals the intended audience.

The Red Cross reports that sixty-four percent of children who participate in water activities cannot perform the five basic water safety skills. The five basic skills are jumping into water over your head, returning to the surface to float or tread water for one minute, turning in a full circle to find an exit, swimming 25 yards to the exit, and exiting the water.

Underline a fact that supports the main idea.

Without teaching basic water safety and taking other important precautions, you could be putting your children's lives in danger. Read each section for more information:

- Swimming Lessons
- CPR and First Aid
- Dangers of Air-Filled Toys
- Life Jackets
- Pool Fences
- Adult Supervision

No one wants to think about his or her children being injured. However, an ounce of prevention is worth a pound of cure. You and your children will be safer if you follow the precautions discussed here.

Underline the main idea.

Primary and Secondary Sources

Primary sources are written or made by people who have knowledge of an event because they were there. **Secondary sources** are written by people who only have secondhand knowledge of an event or topic. Information in secondary sources comes from primary sources or other secondary sources. A source, whether primary or secondary, is **credible** if the facts are accurate and the author can be trusted.

Primary sources include

- diaries, journals, and letters
- firsthand accounts
- photographs and recordings
- interviews and speeches
- government documents

Secondary sources include

- secondhand accounts
- encyclopedia articles
- biographies and histories
- textbooks

RESEARCH

COLLABORATE Read "Naturally Inspired." Discuss why the article is a secondary source. Find a primary source about the topic. Compare and contrast the types of facts that are included in both sources.

Fact from "Naturally Inspired"	
Fact from Primary Source	

COLLABORATE Read the excerpts from the two documents. Then answer the questions.

Water Wings Unsafe for Children

This section of the guide will teach aspiring lifeguards about safe and unsafe flotation devices. That way lifeguards can educate parents. The only safe flotation devices are life jackets, according to the Centers for Disease Control and Prevention (CDC). Water wings, "floaties," and pool "noodles" are not safe, because they often deflate, slip off children, or slide out of children's grasp.

Dear Diary, 4/30/2018

Today I went to the pool. It was a million degrees outside! It was so hot that I decided to take off my life jacket. I can swim, so it doesn't matter if I wear one or not. My older brother told me that. He also told me there's a dragon that lives in the deep end. Of course I don't believe him, but I stayed in the shallow water just to be safe.

1. Is the first document a primary source or a secondary source? How do you know if it is credible?

2. Is the second document a primary source or a secondary source? How do you know if it is credible?

Write a Business E-mail

People use print and online sources when doing research. Sometimes, they also contact experts to conduct an interview, ask questions, or request relevant materials. Today, with so much technology at our fingertips, people often contact experts via a business e-mail rather than a letter. The two are similar; however, business e-mails are usually shorter and have a subject line.

This e-mail shows the proper format for a business e-mail.

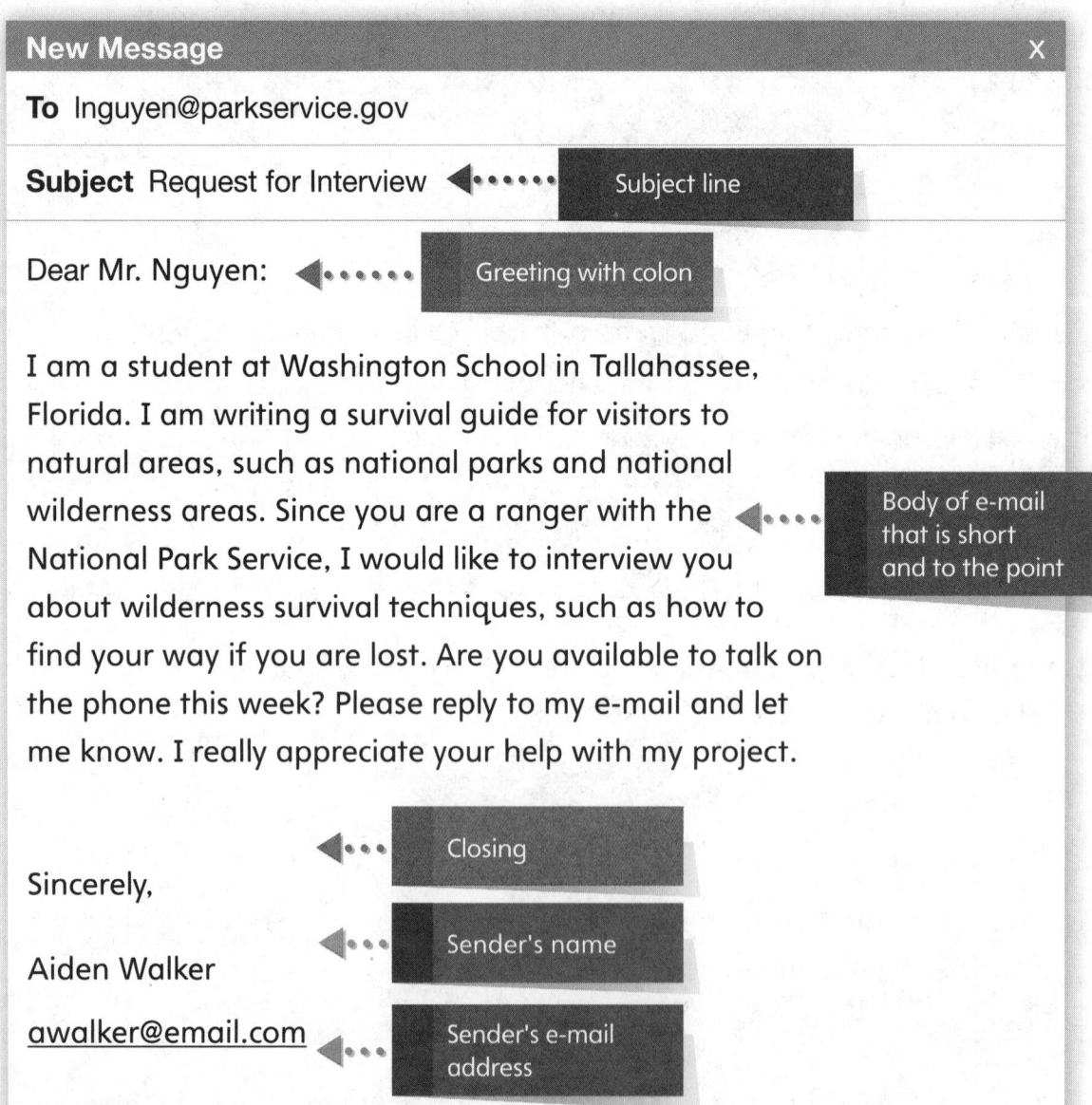

New Message X

To lnguyen@parkservice.gov

Subject Request for Interview ← Subject line

Dear Mr. Nguyen: ← Greeting with colon

I am a student at Washington School in Tallahassee, Florida. I am writing a survival guide for visitors to natural areas, such as national parks and national wilderness areas. Since you are a ranger with the National Park Service, I would like to interview you about wilderness survival techniques, such as how to find your way if you are lost. Are you available to talk on the phone this week? Please reply to my e-mail and let me know. I really appreciate your help with my project. ← Body of e-mail that is short and to the point

Sincerely, ← Closing

Aiden Walker ← Sender's name

awalker@email.com ← Sender's e-mail address

COLLABORATE With your partner, go online to find the name and e-mail address of a National Park Service ranger. Then use the outline to compose a business e-mail to the ranger. When you are finished, send the e-mail. Use the ranger's response to help you write your informational survival guide.

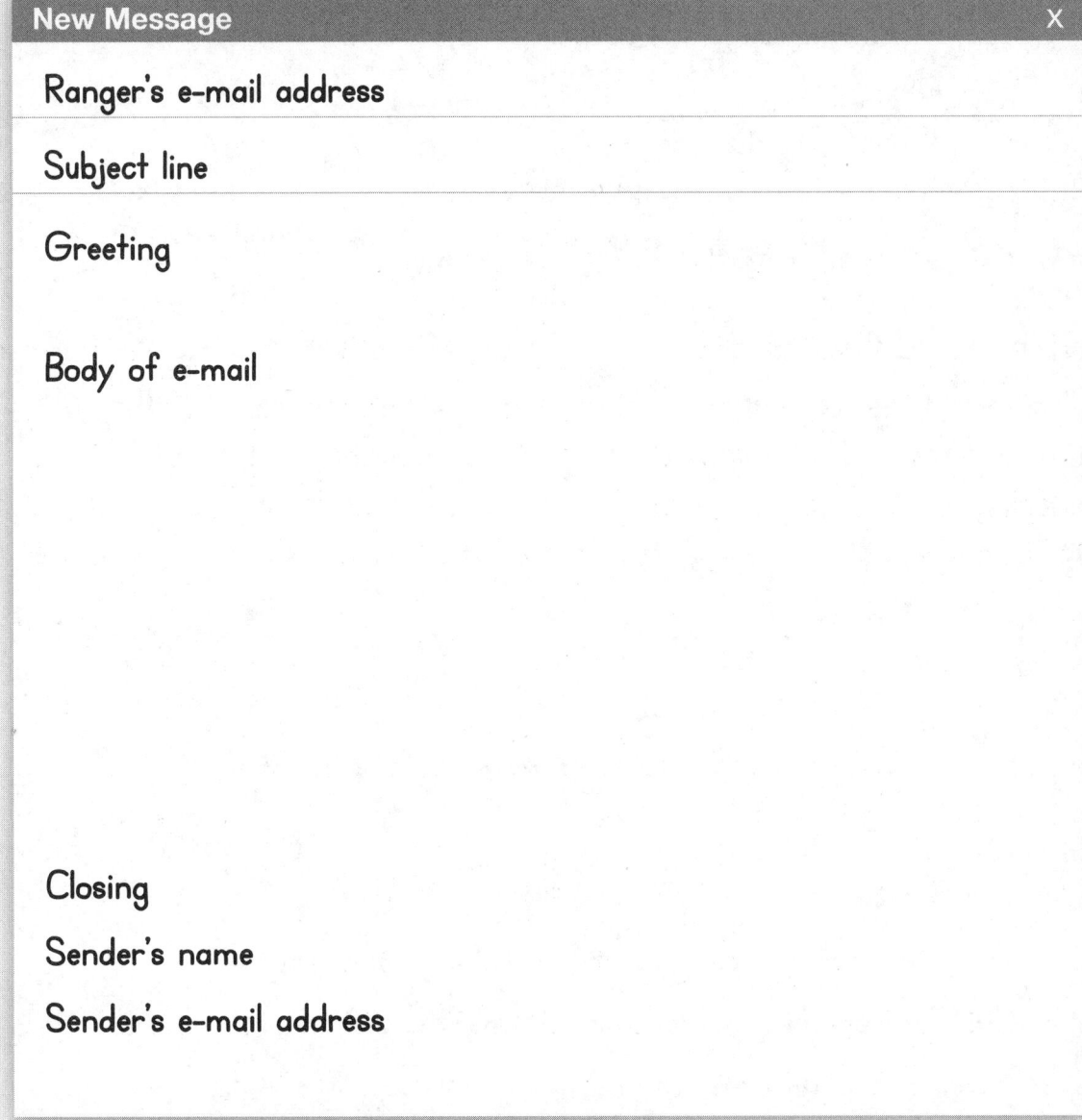

New Message X

Ranger's e-mail address

Subject line

Greeting

Body of e-mail

Closing

Sender's name

Sender's e-mail address

Revise

Vocabulary Reread your informational survival guide with your partner. Have you included

- ☐ relevant academic vocabulary from the unit?
- ☐ accurate domain-specific vocabulary related to the topic?
- ☐ transitions that show relationships and help readers move from one idea to the next?

Revise Word Choice

The writers of the survival guide about water safety realized that they did not include many academic or domain-specific vocabulary words. They replaced general or imprecise words with precise academic and domain-specific words to make their guide more accurate and informative.

focus on
However, it is also important to ~~keep~~ ^ water safety ~~in mind~~.

The
^~~There are~~ five basic water safety skills. ^
are jumping into water over your head, returning to the surface to float or tread water for one minute, turning in a full circle to find an exit, swimming 25 yards to the exit, and exiting the water.

Edit

Conventions Read your survival guide again. Have you used correct conventions?

- [ ] spelling
- [ ] punctuation
- [ ] correct simple and compound sentences
- [ ] subject-verb agreement
- [ ] active voice

Peer Review

COLLABORATE Exchange survival guides with another group. As you read, try to recognize characteristics of the informational survival guide. Look for the main idea, the facts that support the main idea, the intended audience, and the text structure. Then identify which supporting fact was the most informative and helpful. Tell the authors why you think that supporting fact would be the most useful in a survival situation in a natural area.

Time to Celebrate!

COLLABORATE Present your survival guide to another group. Choose the best way of presenting the information to your audience. For example, decide if you want to publish a print, digital, or multimedia survival guide. Then demonstrate one of the survival techniques—such as reading a compass—that you wrote about in your guide.

As you present, remember to make eye contact and enunciate, or speak clearly at a natural rate and volume. Then listen to any questions from the group. How did group members respond to your survival guide? Write some of their reactions.

Reflect on Your Project

My TURN Reflect on your informational survival guide. Which parts do you think are the strongest? How might you improve your informational writing in your next project? Write your thoughts here.

Strengths

Areas of Improvement

Reflect on Your Goals

SCALE	1	2	3	4	5
	NOT AT ALL WELL	NOT VERY WELL	SOMEWHAT WELL	VERY WELL	EXTREMELY WELL

Look back at your unit goals.
Use a different color to rate yourself again.

Reflect on Your Reading

Which three texts that you read independently during this unit best informed you about how people can use their observations of nature to aid the survival of many species (including humans)?

Reflect on Your Writing

Which type of text structure did you choose for your informational article? Explain why you chose that type and describe any challenges you had using it.

How to Use a Glossary

This glossary can help you understand the meaning, origin, pronunciation, and syllabication of some of the words in this book. The entries in this glossary are in alphabetical order. The guide words at the top of each page show the first and last words on the page. If you cannot find a word, check a print or digital dictionary. To use a digital resource, type the word you are looking for in the search box at the top of the page.

The entry word in bold type is divided into syllables.

The pronunciation is in parentheses. It also shows which syllables are stressed.

The part-of-speech label shows the function of an entry word.

ad•mit•ted (ad mit′id), *v.* granted access to a place. from the Latin word *admittere*, meaning "to send in"

The definition shows what the word means.

The word origin tells what language the word came from.

My TURN

Find and write the meaning of the word *inspired*. Say the word aloud.

____

Write the syllabication of the word. _______________

Write the origin of the word. _______________

____

How did the origin help you understand the meaning of the word?

____

____

TURN and TALK Discuss how you can find the meaning of a word that is not in this glossary.

Aa

ad•ven•ture (ad ven′chər), *N.* an exciting experience

as•tro•bi•o•lo•gists (as′trō bī ol′ə jists), *N.* scientists who study life in the universe

Bb

bur•rows (bėr′ōz), *N.* holes or tunnels dug by animals as a place to live. from the Middle English word *borough*, meaning "fortress"

Cc

chlo•ro•phyll (klôr′ə fil), *N.* a green substance found in plants that allows them to make food. from the Greek words *chlōros*, meaning "green," and *phyllon*, meaning "leaf"

cit•i•zens (sit′ə zənz), *N.* people who belong to a particular place

col•o•ny (kol′ə nē), *N.* a group of animals living in one place. from the Latin word *colonus*, meaning "settler"

come•back (kum bak), *N.* a return to a healthy state

Pronunciation Guide

Use the pronunciation guide to help you pronounce the words correctly.

a in *hat*
ā in *age*
â in *care*
ä in *far*
e in *let*
ē in *equal*
ėr in *term*
i in *it*
ī in *ice*
o in *hot*
ō in *open*
ȯ in *all*
ô in *order*
oi in *oil*
ou in *out*
u in *cup*
u̇ in *put*
ü in *rule*
ch in *child*
ng in *long*
sh in *she*
th in *thin*
in *then*
zh in *measure*
ə = a in *about*
ə = e in *taken*
ə = i in *pencil*
ə = o in *lemon*
ə = u in *circus*

com•po•si•tions (kom′pə zish′ənz), *N.* works of art, such as paintings or songs

co•op•er•ate (kō op′ə rāt′), *V.* work together; participate in shared activity

course (kôrs), *N.* the direction of travel

cur•i•ous (kyu̇r′ē əs), *ADJ.* having an interest to learn about something. from the Latin word *curiosus*, meaning "inquisitive"

Dd

de•tect (di tekt′), *V.* to discover the truth, or fact of, something. from the Latin word *detectum*, meaning "uncovered"

di•mi•nished (də mi′nishd), *V.* shrank; became smaller or fewer

Ee

e•co•sys•tem (ē′kō sis′təm), *N.* a community of living things and the environment it inhabits

ex•hib•it (eg zib′it), *N.* a group of artworks or other objects arranged for public viewing. from the Latin word *exhibitum*, meaning "held out"

ex•pert (ek′spėrt), *N.* one who shows special skill or knowledge gained from training

ex•press (ek spres′), *V.* show or tell thoughts and feelings to others. from the Latin word *expressum*, meaning "pressed out"

Ff

fath•oms (faᴛʜ′əmz), *N.* units of length that measure the depth of water. from the Old English word *faethm*, meaning "width of outstretched arms"

fly•ing bridge (flī′ing brij), *N.* the highest place on a ship from which it can be steered

fo•cus (fō′kəs), *V.* direct attention to something. from the Latin word *focus*, meaning "hearth"

frag•men•ted (frag′mən′tid), *ADJ.* broken into pieces. from the Latin word *frangere*, meaning "to break"

fun•gus (fung′gəs), *N.* an organism that gets nutrition from decaying matter. from the Latin word *fungus*, meaning "mushroom"

Gg

gin•ger•ly (jin′jər lē), *ADJ.* cautiously; with great care

girth (gėrth), *N.* distance around something; circumference

grat•i•fied (grat′ə fīd), *ADJ.* felt great satisfaction. from the Latin words *gratus*, meaning "pleasing," and *facere*, meaning "to make or do"

Ii

i•con•ic (ī kon′ik), *ADJ.* famous, popular, and representative of a place or time. from the Greek word *eikōn*, meaning "image"

ig•nite (ig nīt′), *V.* catch fire. from the Latin word *ignitum*, meaning "fired"

im•i•ta•ted (im′ə tā tid), *V.* copied; tried to do the same things others did. from the Latin word *imitatum*, meaning "copy"

im•mi•gra•tion (im′ə grā′shən), *N.* the act of moving to a new country to live there

in•sight (in′sīt′), *N.* clear or complete understanding of a situation

in•spired (in spīrd′), *V.* caused something to be created. from the Latin *in-*, meaning "in," and *spirare*, meaning "to breathe"

in•ter•sect•ing (in′tər sekt′ing), *ADJ.* crossing or overlapping. from the Latin word *intersectum*, meaning "divided"

Jj

jaunts (jônts), *N.* short, enjoyable journeys

Ll

leagues (lēgz), *N.* units of distance. from the Latin word *ligare*, meaning "to bind"

Mm

ma•rine (mə rēn/), *ADJ.* of or relating to the ocean. from the Latin word *marinus*, meaning "of the sea"

mi•crobes (mī/krōbz), *N.* the smallest living things. from the Greek words *mikros*, meaning "small," and *bios*, meaning "life"

mi•grat•ing (mī/grāt ing), *ADJ.* moving from one habitat to another with the seasons. from the Latin word *migratum*, meaning "moved"

Nn

na•tive (nā/tiv), *ADJ.* belonging naturally to a specific place

nau•ti•cal (nô/tə kəl), *ADJ.* related to ships or navigation. from the Greek word *naus*, meaning "ship"

noc•tur•nal (nok tėr/nl), *ADJ.* awake and active at night. from the Latin word *noctem*, meaning "night"

Oo

op•por•tu•ni•ty (op/ər tü/nə tē), *N.* an agreeable situation or chance

Pp

pains•tak•ing (pānz/tā/king), *ADJ.* done with great care and attention

pas•sage (pas/ij), *N.* an entry or doorway

peer•ing (pi/ring), *V.* looking closely at something that is hard to see

proc•ess•ing (pros/es ing), *N.* a series of steps in a legal action

Rr

ra•di•a•tion (rā/dē ā/shən), *N.* dangerous energy rays that cannot be seen

re•late (ri lāt/), *V.* to tell; to show a relationship between two things. from the Latin *re-*, meaning "back," and *latum*, meaning "brought"

re•store (ri stôr′), *v.* return to original condition. from the Latin word *restaurare*, meaning "repair, rebuild"

rov•ers (rō′vərz), *N.* vehicles used to explore a planet's surface. from the Middle English word *roven*, meaning "to shoot arrows at targets while moving"

Ss

sanc•tu•ar•ies (sangk′chü er′ēz), *N.* human-made places of safety and protection

sen•sors (sen′sərz), *N.* devices that detect changes in light, moisture, or other physical conditions

sput•tered (spu′tird), *v.* gave out popping sounds

Tt

thrive (thrīv), *v.* do well, be successful, grow

tide (tīd), *N.* the rise and fall of the ocean. from the Middle English word *tīd*, meaning "time"

trans•mit•ter (trans mi′tər), *N.* equipment that makes and sends electromagnetic waves that carry messages. from the Latin *trans-*, meaning "across," and *mittere*, meaning "to send"

tra•versed (trə vėrsd′), *v.* traveled through; moved across. from the Latin word *transversare*, meaning "to move across"

Uu

un•fet•tered (un fe′tərd), *ADJ.* not limited, not restricted

Vv

vi•a (vī′ə), *PREP.* by way of; by means of; through. from the Latin word *via*, meaning "way"

vis•i•ble (viz′ə bəl), *ADJ.* easily seen

Ww

wan•dered (won′dərd), *v.* walked slowly or aimlessly

Text

Boyds Mills Press
From Pedro's Journal by Pam Conrad. Copyright © 1991 by Pam Conrad. Published by Boyds Mills Press. Used by permission.

Charlesbridge Publishing
Life on Earth And Beyond. Text copyright © 2008 by Pamela S. Turner. Used with permission by Charlesbridge Publishing, Inc. 85 Main Street, Watertown, MA 02472 (617) 926-0329. All rights reserved.

Cricket Media
The Path to Paper Son by Grant Din, Cobblestone magazine, February 2016, Volume 37, Number 2, p. 21. Used with permission from Cricket Media.
Louie Share Kim, Paper Son by Barbara D. Krasner, Cobblestone magazine, February 2016, Volume 37, Number 2, pp. 2-5. Used with permission from Cricket Media.

Flannery Literary Agency
Hatchet by Gary Paulsen, © Gary Paulsen.

Kristine O'Connell George
Learning the World by Kristine O'Connell George. Used with permission of author who controls all rights.

James Hildreth
Latitude Longitude Dreams by Drew Lamm & James Hildreth, Thanks to Drew for this fun collaboration.

Houghton Mifflin Harcourt Publishing Company
FAR FROM SHORE: Chronicles of an Open Ocean Voyage by Sophie Webb. Copyright© 2011 by Sophie Webb. Reprinted by permission of Houghton Mifflin Harcourt Publishing Company All rights reserved.
From Park Scientists: Gila Monsters, Geysers, and Grizzly Bears in America's Own Backyard by Mary Kay Carson, with photographs by Tom Uhlman. Text copyright © 2014 by Mary Kay Carson. Photographs copyright © 2014 by Tom Uhlman. Reprinted by permission of Houghton Mifflin Harcourt Publishing Company. All rights reserved.

Drew Lamm
Latitude Longitude Dreams by Drew Lamm & James Hildreth, Reprinted by permission.

Peachtree Publishers, Ltd.
First published in the United States under the title A Place for Frogs by Melissa Stewart, illustrated by Higgins Bond, Text©2009, 2016 by Melissa Stewart. Illustrations © 2009, 2016 by Higgins Bond. Published by arrangement with Peachtree Publishers.

Simon & Schuster, Inc.
From HATCHET by Gary Paulsen. Copyright© 1987 by Gary Paulsen. Reprinted with the permission of Athenaeum Books for Young Readers, an imprint of Simon & Schuster Children's Publishing Division. All rights reserved.

Marilyn Singer
Early Explorers From Marilyn Singer's Footprints on the Roof: Poems about the Earth, New York: Knopf Books, 2002.

Karen O'Donnell Taylor
A Map and a Dream poem by Karen O'Donnell Taylor. Used by permission of the author who retains all rights.

Photographs

Photo locators denoted as follows Top (T), Center (C), Bottom (B), Left (L), Right (R), Background (Bkgd)

8 (BL) Everett - Art/Shutterstock, (Bkgd) I Love Photo/Shutterstock; **9** (T) Everett Historical/ Shutterstock, (TL) Denis Belitsky/Shutterstock, (B) M-imagephotography/iStock/Getty Images Plus/Getty Images, (BL) Dlinca/iStock/Getty Images Plus/Getty Images; **14** (CL) PA Archive/PA Images/Alamy Stock Photo, (BR) Vlad G/Shutterstock, (Bkgd) Bekulnis/ Shutterstock; **15** (TL) Wayne Hsieh78/Shutterstock; **19** Everett Historical/Shutterstock; **20** Library of Congress Prints and Photographs Division [LC-DIG-det-4a13264]; **21** Andreasnikolas/Shutterstock; **22** (TL) Used with permission from Cricket Media., (TC) Library of Congress Prints and Photographs Division Washington [LC-DIG-ds-03059], (TR) Hywit Dimyadi/ Shutterstock, (CL) Used with permission from Cricket Media.; **24** (Bkgd) Used with permission from Cricket Media., (C) Melissa King/Shutterstock; 27 (T),(B) Used with permission from Cricket Media.; **28** Radoslaw Lecyk/Shutterstock; **29** (C) Used with permission from Cricket Media., (Bkgd) Banana Republic images/ Shutterstock, (TC) Pakhnyushchy/Shutterstock; **46** (Bkgd) James Cohen/Shutterstock; **46** (TR) Fisherss/ Shutterstock, (CL) Tifonimages/Shutterstock, (BR) Gary Yim/Shutterstock; **47** (TL) Stephen Girimont/ Shutterstock, (BL) MarcelClemens/Shutterstock; **50** Used with permission from Charlesbridge Publishing.; **51** Denis Belitsky/Shutterstock; **52** (B) NASA; **53** Pablofdezr/Shutterstock; **54** (T) Christopher McKay/ NASA; **58** (BR) Centers of Disease Contro/RGB Ventures/SuperStock/Alamy Stock Photo; **59** (T) NG Images/Alamy Stock Photo; **60** Christopher McKay/ NASA; **61** (B) Detlev van Ravenswaay/Picture Press/ Getty Images; **62** (B) JPL/NASA; **64** Patrick Zachmann/ Magnum Photos; **66** (TL) Dr. Jacek Wierzchos, (TR) Cornell/JPL/NASA; **67** (B) satellite of the Americas/ NASA; **88** (T) Pam Conrad author of Pedro's Journal. Copyright © 1991 by Pam Conrad. Published by Boyds Mill Press. Used by permission.; **89** Valentin Agapov/Shutterstock; **124** (TC) Anna Chusova/ Shutterstock, (C) Lina Truman/Shutterstock, (BR) Paper_Owl/Shutterstock, (BL) Meilun/Shutterstock; **124** Drical/Shutterstock; **125** (TR) Pogorelova Olga/Shutterstock, (TL) Natcha29/Shutterstock, (BR)Victor Brave/Shutterstock, (BL) M. Stasy/ Shutterstock; **128** Used with permission of author.; **129** M-imagephotography/iStock/Getty Images;

131 Imtmphoto/Shutterstock; **133** Uschools/iStock/Getty Images Plus/Getty Images; **135** DiversityStudio/Shutterstock; **137** Wavebreakmedia/Shutterstock; **154** (T) Historic Collection/Alamy Stock Photo, (C) Print Collector/Hulton Fine Art Collection/Getty Images, (B) Universal History Archive/Universal Images Group/Getty Images; **154** Africa Studio/Shutterstock; **155** Universal History Archive/Universal Images Group/Getty Images;**159** Dlinca/iStock/Getty Images Plus/Getty Images; **160** (C) Bettmann/Getty Images, (T) Bphillips/iStock/Getty Images Plus/Getty Images; **161** The Artchives/Alamy Stock Photo, © 2017 Banco de México Diego Rivera Frida Kahlo Museums Trust, Mexico, D.F./Artists Rights Society (ARS), New York; **162** Archivart/Alamy Stock Photo; © 2017 Banco de México Diego Rivera Frida Kahlo Museums Trust, Mexico, D.F./Artists Rights Society (ARS), New York; **164** Admin_design/Shutterstock; **165** CSU Archives/Everett Collection/Alamy Stock Photo; © 2017 Georgia O'Keeffe Museum/Artists Rights Society (ARS), New York; **167** FineArt/Alamy Stock Photo, © 2017 Georgia O'Keeffe Museum/Artists Rights Society (ARS), New York; **168** Peter Horree/Alamy Stock Photo; **170** The Print Collector/Alamy Stock Photo; **171** (CR) Solarisys/Shutterstock; **172** (BL) Martin Valigursky/Shutterstock; **173** Peter Horree/Alamy Stock Photo; **191** CWB/Shutterstock; **196** (TR) The Ohio Collection/Alamy Stock Photo; **198** (Bkgd) Serban Bogdan/Shutterstock; **199** (BR) Illpos/Shutterstock, (BC) Joyfuldesigns/Shutterstock; **200** (Bkgd) Globe Turner, LLC/Getty Images; **205** (B) FatCamera/E+/Getty Images; **208** (BL) Cubephoto/Shutterstock, (Bkgd) ESB Professional/Shutterstock; **214** (TL) Vlad61/Shutterstock, (TR) Seaphotoart/Shutterstock, (B) AF Archive/Alamy Stock Photo; (Bkgd) Rich Carey/Shutterstock; **215** (TL) Yakov Oskanov/Shutterstock, (B) Dmitri Ma/Shutterstock; **252** (T) Ritesh Chaudhary/Shutterstock, (B) Ammit Jack/Shutterstock; **253** Gudkov Andrey/Shutterstock; **256** Used with permission from Peachtree Publishers, Ltd.; **289** Ekaterina V. Borisova/Shutterstock; **290** Anteromite/Shutterstock; **294** Al Grillo/AP images; **328** (BR) Everett Historical/Shutterstock, (Bkgd) James Chen/Shutterstock; **329** (TL) John A. Anderson/Shutterstock, (C) Nicole Baly/Shutterstock, (CL) Brandon Baker/Shutterstock, (BL) Albert Czyzewski/Shutterstock; **332** Used with permission from Mary Kay Carson.; **333** Matthijs Kuijpers/123RF; **338** (Bkgd) K.Narloch-Liberra/Shutterstock; **362** (T) Belizar/Shutterstock, (B) Johan Swanepoel/123RF, (C) Szczepan Klejbuk/Shutterstock, (Bkgd) Arturas Kerdokas/123RF; **367** (TL) Andriy Blokhin/Shutterstock, Kruraphoto/Shutterstock, (TR) Valentyna Chukhlyebova/Shutterstock, (TC) Bumihills/Shutterstock, (C) Npeter/Shutterstock, (CL) Christian Musat/Shutterstock, (CR) Miroslav Chytil/Shutterstock, (BR) Worlds wildlife wonders/Shutterstock; **368** Martin Schneiter/123RF; **369** USFWS Photo/Alamy Stock Photo; **370** (B) Robert McGouey/Wildlife/Alamy Stock Photo, (Bkgd) Dennis MacDonald/Age Fotostock/Alamy Stock Photo; **372** (Bkgd) Mikhail Serdiukov/EyeEm/Getty Images; **373** Yuri Smityuk/ITAR-TASS Photo Agency/Alamy Stock Photo; **375** (TL) Greg Dale/National Geographic/Getty Images, (TR) Belizar73/iStock/Getty Images, (C) ZJAN/Shedd Aquarium/Newscom, (CL) Andrey_Kuzmin/Shutterstock, (CBL) Kris Wiktor/Shutterstock, (BL) Ohm2499/Shutterstock, (BC) Patrick Kientz/Biosphoto/Alamy Stock Photo, (BR) Paulette Sinclair/Alamy Stock Photo; **376** Pakhnyushchy/Shutterstock; **377** Holly Kuchera/Shutterstock; **378** (BC) Rafael Ben-Ari/Alamy Stock Photo, (Bkgd) Mr.Rapisan Swangphon/123RF; **380** Pavel Vakhrushev/Shutterstock; **381** Stewart Cohen/Stockbyte/Getty Images; **398** All_about_people/Shutterstock; **400** Radius Images/Alamy Stock Photo; **404** Rdanailova/Shutterstock; **406** Ozerov Alexander/Shutterstock; **408** Furoking300/Shutterstock; **410** Stan Wakefield/Foap/Getty Images; **415** Monkey Business Images/Shutterstock.

Illustrations

17, 255 Valentina Belloni; **49, 331** Ilana Exelby; **87, 127, 217, 365** Olga & Aleksey Ivanov; **129** TM Detwiler; **131** Jo Tronic; **133** Kevin Rechin; **135** Nathalie Beauvios; **137** Sarah McMenemy; **157** Valeria Cis; **160, 169, 171, 196, 372,** 380 Karen Minot; **293** Ken Bowser; **295–311** Brave Union; **367, 375** Jeff Mangiat.

NOTES

NOTES

NOTES

NOTES

NOTES